International studies in the history of sport
series editor J. A. Mangan

A bit of a flutter

A bit of a flutter

**Popular gambling and English society,
c. 1823–1961**

Mark Clapson

MANCHESTER UNIVERSITY PRESS

Manchester and New York

Distributed exclusively in the USA and Canada by St. Martin's Press

Published by Manchester University Press
Oxford Road, Manchester M13 9PL, UK
and Room 400, 175 Fifth Avenue, New York, NY 10010, USA

Distributed exclusively in the USA and Canada
by St. Martin's Press, Inc., 175 Fifth Avenue, New York, NY 10010, USA

British Library Cataloguing-in-Publication Data
A catalogue record for this book is available from the British Library

Library of Congress Cataloging in Publication Data
Clapson, Mark.
    A bit of a flutter : popular gambling and English society, *c.*
1823–1961 / Mark Clapson.
        p. cm. —— (International studies in the history of sport)
    Includes bibliographical references and index.
    ISBN 0–7190–3436–1
    1. Gambling—England—History—19th century.   2. Gambling—
England—History—20th century.   I. Title.   II. Series.
    HV8722.G86E43   1992
    394'.3—dc20   91–29779

ISBN 0 7190 3436 1 *hardback*

Photoset in Linotron Palatino
by Northern Phototypesetting Company Limited, Bolton
Printed in Great Britain
by Billings Ltd, Worcester

Contents

Acknowledgements

I would like to thank Tony Mason for his comments on and criticisms of earlier drafts of the thesis, upon which this book is based. I am also grateful to Ian Bridgeman, Anne Bullman, Carl Chinn, Clive Emsley, Steve Fielding, James Kilmartin, James Obelkevich and John Walton. I am especially grateful to Caroline, who has been the most encouraging of all.

Historians are heavily dependent on those who own or run archives. May I thank the staff of the Bolton, Liverpool and Manchester local history libraries, the BBC Data Archive in Reading, the British Library, the Football Association, the Jewish Museum in Manchester, the Manchester Tape Studies Collection at Manchester Polytechnic, the Trustees of the Mass Observation archive at the University of Sussex, the Newspaper Library at Colindale, and the Police archives in Maidstone, Manchester, Peterborough and Worcester.

Finally, I would like to thank those people who replied to my request for information in the local and national press. Whether or not I have used their testimonies below, I am especially indebted to all of them.

Series Editor's foreword

Francis Bacon may have asserted that the looker-on sees more than the gamester, but Mark Clapson clearly doubts it.

This social history of popular gambling from the abolition of state lotteries in the 1820s to the Betting and Gaming Act of the 1960s traces the evolution of gambling in Lancashire from an informal, loosely arranged pre-industrial activity to the later formal, commercial industrial activity.

Lancashire is well chosen. It was a centre of the industrial revolution, a seedbed of nineteenth-century social and economic change and a prominent location of proletarian gambling.

In the nineteenth and twentieth centuries moralisers, frequently from a relatively safe middle-class haven, have consistently viewed popular gambling as a 'shabby mass culture' made up of millions of simple-minded losers, but Clapson argues that for the most part the gambling urban masses of North-Western England exercised careful self-restraint. Their gambling was 'regular and moderate'. Furthermore theirs was eventually a punter's culture that combined subscription to traditional irrationality (belief in luck) with modern rationality (the study of form in the sporting press) and one that was further characterised by self-help, self-assertion and active choice. It was not, claims Clapson, an irresponsible, passive working-class consumerism that needed to be monitored and controlled by its social 'betters' in its own interest, but 'a moderate, economistic and expressive form of recreation'.

This restrained betting on horse-racing, pigeon-racing, greyhound-racing, bowls and soccer raised the level of enjoyment of these activities by heightening the tension of recreational competition. It was for this reason that gambling and sport went together 'like a horse and carriage'.

A series of Betting Acts were passed between 1880 and 1930 in an attempt to bring the masses to their senses and to curb their apparent foolish impetuosity. Not for the last time did the law reveal itself to be an ass and the working-class of Lancashire did not bother to wage war upon it. They simply defied and ignored it. And the 'Poor Man's Stock Exchange' blithely survives. The same soon may not be true, at least in its present form, of the Stock Exchange of the rich man; a curious reversal of moral opprobrium.

J. A. Mangan

Abbreviations

ACA	Amusement Caterer's Association
BGTCS	British Greyhound Greyhound Tracks Control Society
BOHP	Bolton Oral History Project
BPA	Bookmaker's Protection Association
CIU	Clubs and Institutes Union
FA	Football Association
GRA	Greyhound Racing Association
HC Debs	House of Commons Debates
HL Debs	House of Lords Debates
IHS	Irish Hospital Sweepstake
JSC	Joint Select Committee, Parliament
LBO	Licensed Betting Office
MO	Mass Observation
NAGL	National Anti-Gambling League
NBPA	National Bookmaker's Protection Association
NCC	National Coursing Club
NGRC	National Greyhound Racing Club
NGRS	National Greyhound Racing Society
NHC	National Hunt Committee
NSL	National Sporting League
PEP	Political and Economic Planning
PGTCO	Provincial Greyhound Tracks Central Office
PP	Parliamentary Papers
Qre	Questionnaire
RBA	Racecourse Bookmakers Association
RBCB	Racecourse Betting Control Board
RC	Royal Commission, Parliament
SC	Select Committee, Parliament
TGS	Turf Guardian Society
TPS	Turf Protection Society

Chapter 1
Setting the scene

I

Dr Johnson rarely pulled his punches. In his *Dictionary of the English Language* (1755) he gave no noun for 'gamble', but 'Gambler' was 'a cant word' for gamester, a 'knave whose practice it is to invite the unwary to game and cheat them'.[1] Canting language was the slang of the poor. As a twentieth-century edition of the *Oxford English Dictionary* notes, the verb did not make its appearance in the language until the second half of the eighteenth century, before which 'gambler' was a slang term for a fraudulent gamester, a sharper, or one who played for excessive stakes.[2] 'To game', the more established and commonly used sporting verb, was expressed by Johnson as 'to play wantonly and extravagantly for money'. 'Gaming' was the term for roulette and for rouge et noir, baccarat, chemin de fer and other card games played by the wealthy in clubs and salons whose social cachet and high entrance fees kept out the hoi polloi. Amongst the poor it referred to gambling schools based on coins and cards. In Johnson's time the verbs 'to bet' and 'to wager' meant the same thing and were less disreputable than the newer verb 'to gamble'. 'To wager' – a derivation of the German word 'waegen', meaning to venture – was 'to lay; to pledge as a bet; to pledge upon some casualty or performance.' 'Gambling' then was a newer pejorative term for gaming and wagering. In England, it was associated with the lower-class, with cheating and with indulgence.

People who bet are called 'punters', a more familiar word than 'better'. It seems to have entered the language in the later nineteenth century, from a number of sources. It originally meant an auction bidder, but came to mean 'an outsider betting on horses in a small way'. Both 'punt', occasionally also used for 'poona' (costermonger's slang for 'one pound') and *ponter*, the French verb 'to bet', were the origins of 'punter'.[3]

II

Histories of gambling in England are few and far between, and what exists falls mostly into the camps of popular journalism, fond antiquarianism or alarmist tract. The latter usually provide a potted history of gambling which rests on the perception, whatever the year it was written, that gambling is becoming ever more popular and its attendant dangers ever more widespread and unmanageable.[4] Journalistic and antiquarian histories of betting and gambling, whilst often entertaining and informative, tend to concentrate on the infamous rogues and scandals of low life. There is little or no attempt to relate changes in the organisation and extent of betting and gambling to broader economic and cultural developments.

The serious historical study of betting and gambling and its relationship to society is a relatively recent one which developed out of the concerns of the social history of leisure. These concerns may be broadly summarised as the impact of commercialisation on older 'traditional' pre-industrial recreations, and the relationship of different social classes and groups to this massive and continuing transition. Historians have sought to ascertain how far commercialisation changed the nature of pre-industrial recreations; at what level these earlier forms survived; the different uses of leisure between classes, and why certain sections of the middle class sought to convert both the indulgent gentry above them and the indigent masses below to a more rational, that is restrained and cerebral, way of passing time not spent at work.[5] Outside of the physical arenas of sport, the commonplace activities of drink, sex and gambling constituted an 'unholy trinity'[6] in the eyes of the professional and religious promoters of rational recreation. These popular activities threatened the virtues of hard work, thrift and self-denial, as propounded by Victorian moralists, most notably Samuel Smiles in his popular treatise *Self Help* (1859). Too much alcoholic consumption led to drunken violence and to the neglect of personal and family health. Too much sex, especially in public, posed a threat to propriety and spread nasty diseases. And too much gambling was indicative of a something-for-nothing attitude which usually resulted in ruin for the punters and their families.

A number of historians have examined the changes in the nature of sport and popular amusements from the eighteenth to the twentieth centuries.[7] The roles of drink and of love and sex in people's lives have been the subject of some sensitive and insightful enquiries.[8] Yet the

2

social history of betting and gambling in England remains sporadic. It is confined to a number of scholarly articles,[9] to chapters in books or theses which are concerned primarily with the history of sport,[10] with local histories of the working class[11] and with interpretations of working-class culture and its relationship to other classes.[12]

In the 1970s, both Ross McKibbin's and James Mott's work established a social history of gambling. McKibbin primarily examined illegal off-course ready-money betting on horses and argued that the growth of commercialised betting from the 1880s, a time of relative working-class prosperity, reflected its importance as a means of intellectual and rational expression amongst working-class punters. Wagering was an opportunity for those who possessed little money and a limited formal education to study the form of a horse or greyhound in past races, to predict its likeliness of winning, and to back up their considered opinion with a small investment which carried a measure of hope. Motts' longer time span, roughly from the 1820s to the inter-war years, looked at the democratisation of many forms of betting from the ending of the state lotteries to the growth of the football pools from the 1920s. Mott interpreted organised betting with bookmakers, betting on whippet and pigeon races and more spontaneous coin and card gaming as subcultural recreations whose communality and excitement were impervious to the anti-gambling campaign of the religious and professional middle class. The commercialisation of betting and the continuing adaptation of informal wagering on animal sports were important 'bottom upwards' determinants of betting forms in the twentieth century. This book owes much to Mott's and McKibbin's work.

More recently, David Dixon's excellent study of the gambling laws 'from prohibition to regulation' that is, from the height of the moral and legal campaign against gambling in the Edwardian era to the period since the introduction of Licensed Betting Offices in 1961, examines the role of the National Anti-Gambling League's (NAGL) agitation for the 1906 Street Betting Act, the subsequent failure of this legislation and the growing realisation of police and government that the laws were unworkable because they were unfair and unpopular. His work examines the 'social legal and political reactions to betting' between the 1880s and the 1980s. It is not 'an attempt to provide a history of popular betting, which would be a very valuable but different exercise'.[13]

This book discusses the nature and growth of popular betting and gambling from the abolition of the state lotteries in the 1820s to the 1960 Betting and Gaming Act. The focus is largely but not exclusively on

Lancashire, and within this county it falls mainly on Manchester, Liverpool and Bolton, important centres of the industrial revolution from the 1780s. Manchester, a city of 600,000 by 1914, and the smaller town of Bolton (population 180,000 in 1914) just north of it, were major manufacturing centres based largely on textiles and to a lesser extent machine engineering. Liverpool, with a population of 700,000 by 1914, was a mercantile city with a large and impoverished casual labour force.[14] The reason for studying Lancashire is that it was one of the heartlands of the industrial revolution. Social and economic changes in the nineteenth century anticipated many developments which were to come later to other parts of Britain. It enables us 'to capture the essentials of the common experience of leisure in urban and metropolitan England'[15] during the period under study.

Yet Lancashire has special claims to fame in a history of popular gambling. In horse racing, the Grand National steeplechase has been held at Aintree in Liverpool since 1839, and along with the Manchester Races, was among the first commercialised race meetings to be established in the Victorian years. Football coupon betting was mostly a Lancashire phenomenon at first and the largest pools firms have been established there, in Liverpool, since the 1920s. The most famous hare coursing meeting in England, the Waterloo Cup, has been held in Lancashire since 1836, and whippet racing without live bait appears to have been especially prominent there from the 1880s to the 1920s. It was perhaps no accident that Manchester first played host to the electric hare in 1926. This speedy but insentient creature, propelled around the track by an electric running rail, signified more than just a departure of the sport from the use of live quarry. It also ushered in American-style stadia and a 'night out' at the dogs which peaked in popularity during the 1930s and 1940s.

Amongst others, social investigators in the twentieth century were aware of this prominence of gambling in working-class Lancashire. The Pilgrim Trust highlighted the prominence of betting and gambling within working-class recreation on Merseyside between the wars, and Mass Observation (MO), who went to Bolton ('Worktown') in the late 1930s to carry out their detailed surveys of working-class life, have provided historians with a great deal of lively material on betting.[16] In the post-war years sociologists at the University of Liverpool, such as John Barron Mays and Madelaine Kerr, continued the tradition of observing the lives of the local working class, and they saw more than a little betting and gambling.

It comes as no surprise then, to find that the anti-gambling campaign was particularly strong in the north-west during the Victorian, Edwardian and inter-war years. The NAGL, formed in 1889–90, had one of its three offices in Manchester (the other two were in York and London). The Anglican and Nonconformist Protestant churches were a strong local presence and provided many of the pamphleteers, preachers and press articles against betting and gambling throughout the period under study. For example, Canon Green of Salford was the staunchest and most prodigious campaigner against the problem in the first forty years of the twentieth century.[17]

There is thus a good deal of contemporary evidence on betting and gaming and the opposition to it in Lancashire. Yet more national primary sources exist which also enable us to understand the social experience of and official attitudes towards gambling elsewhere. Social surveys for other parts of Britain, ranging from Henry Mayhew's *London Labour and the London Poor* in the 1850s to Ferdynand Zweig's investigations into affluence and poverty after the second world war, have provided many interesting glimpses of the role of betting and gaming in the social and economic life of its practitioners. They also tell us much about the perceptions of social investigators themselves.

The parliamentary debates which preceded prohibitive or permissive pieces of gambling legislation provide detailed if sometimes discursive intelligence on contemporary betting. As well as revealing much about the individual preferences of politicians, the point of view of different constituency interest groups was often articulated by MPs in the Commons. In the Upper House a number of their Lordships had a lineal association with the equally unelected ruling elites of horse racing, the Jockey Club and the National Hunt Committee. Sporting gentlemen were also members of the greyhound racing fraternity and, from the 1920s, sat with businessmen and bookmakers on the boards of the newly formed dog racing companies. A number of peers, however, provided support for anti-gambling legislation.

The most important official materials in the period under discussion are the parliamentary enquiries into betting and gambling. The writer includes the Select Committee on Premium Bonds of 1917–18 in this category. The enquiries of 1808, 1844, 1901, 1902, 1923, 1932–3, 1949–51, and the little Select Committee into Lotteries and Indecent Advertisements in 1908, contain the statements of various pro- and anti-gambling interests, most notably the Jockey Club and the National Hunt Committee in horse racing, of anti-gambling spokesmen, of magistrates and high-ranking policemen, and of Home Office and Government departments concerned with the volume and legality of betting and gambling. Those from the Select Committee of 1923 collected evidence from all the above, and also from bookmakers, and from the 1932–3 enquiry the Football Association and Football League with regard to coupon betting, the greyhound racing companies and their detractors, other businessmen in the world of gambling and voluntary workers with the young. Yet in the period under study not one ready-money punter was called upon to put the client's point of view. As McKibbin has argued, much of the evidence of those witnesses representing an economic interest or moral viewpoint is often 'tendentious and inaccurate' but if used with care it 'can be very fruitful'. [18]

This observation applies with equal accuracy to oral testimony and autobiographies. Much of what is said or written down about the past is often coloured by a rosy nostalgia or a tendency of interviewees to relate present-day concerns and attitudes to past events. Yet the historian is ultimately responsible for how the data is used, and an otherwise carefully researched piece can buckle dangerously close to anecdotalism by carelessly deploying a gobbet or two of the spoken word without a proper contextualisation of the speakers and their experiences. However, oral testimony and autobiography have provided valuable information where manuscript or published sources are lacking. For this reason, the writer undertook a modest oral project, carried out in the spring of 1985, containing fourteen tape-recorded testimonies and over sixty written remembrances of betting and gaming in the form of letters and simple, general questionnaires. The nature of information in the letters was, beyond the call for information on street betting and gaming, determined by the respondents themselves. They wrote what they remembered as significant or amusing. The interviews were based on questions about the organisation of street betting and the role of the bookmaker and his runners within it. Questions on gaming attempted to find out any differences in such amusements from town to town or region to region, and to learn about the role they played in the day-to-day recreation of the punters. This is not intended to be a representative cohort of gamblers and ex-bookmakers, as patterns of organised ready-money betting, and, especially, the plethora of gaming activities, varied in innumerable formations from place to place. Hence, existing archives of oral testimonies and, especially, the sizeable and growing number of autobiographies, drawn from all walks of life, have also been mined to give an idea of the diversity of gambling forms in different parts of

England.[19] Autobiographies are almost as useful as a specific oral project on gambling because some of the most revealing anecdotes and reminiscences were unsolicited by historians, and given by the writer as significant episodes or developments in their life or that of their community. The writers explore the making of their own life through a subjective chronology of important experiences and episodes. However, when using oral and autobiographical evidence it is necessary to bear in mind Luisa Passerini's view, that it is a bigger methodological limitation to interpret a particular interviewee or autobiographer as representative of one whole group or stratum than to admit to the limitations of generalising from the experiences of one or two individuals.[20] Such links, from the individual to the local, from the local to the national, have to be made of course, but it is dangerous to assume that the testimonies of one or two respondents give us a true picture of the entire social reality.

For this reason, oral testimony has whenever possible been set alongside contemporary Mass Observation materials. The raw materials of the Mass Observation archive have contributed much to the descriptions of betting throughout the book. Before Mass Observation became a market research organisation in the late 1940s, its instigators, Tom Harrisson and Charles Madge, and the various observers who have left us their manuscripts of life in Bolton (Worktown), provided a sensitive, if sometimes romanticised, picture of life in an industrial town.

Another major contemporary source is that of newspapers, journals and periodicals of all persuasions, be they national, local, serious, tabloid, sporting, political, trade-based, religious, satirical, sociological or economic. The local press, not surprisingly, provides a great deal of detailed information on betting and gaming cases in various areas, and, like the national press, was often a forum where pro- or anti-betting interests fought their corner in letters or articles. Few writers, even in the more staid periodicals and magazines, could resist humorous or fearful exclamations when writing about gambling. And well-meaning observers in journals of social analysis often brought a moral slant to their work which rendered otherwise insightful pieces gloomy and pessimistic.[21]

Statistical or economic estimates of betting and gaming cannot really be viewed as objective until after 1945. Before then, with the exception of a few articles in *The Economist* or in statistical journals, the exaggerated guesses of anti-gambling interests held sway over these more dispassionate estimates. Similarly, the police and judicial statistics need careful use. As McKibbin notes, they are a better reflection of the extent of police activity than of the extent of the subject under study.[22] Changes in compilation criteria also affect the reliability of the statistics. However, national judicial statistics have been used to assess the arrest rates over time and from area to area, and the *Annual Reports of the Chief Constables of Bolton, Liverpool and Manchester* have provided some useful insights into police perceptions of gambling.

Novels or short stories about gambling tell us as much about the author's concerns as gambling itself. Different writers had particular bees in their bonnets and employed gambling as a literary device to get their meanings over to the reader. In *Esther Waters* (1894), for example, George Moore's portrayal of the tension in a woman's love for two men, one a member of the anti-gambling Plymouth Brethren and the other a publican-bookmaker, illustrated his concern for the dangers of heavy betting and the flamboyant world of horse racing. In *Daniel Deronda* (1876) George Eliot uses a game of casino roulette as a literary device intended to establish the social artifice and financial vulnerabilities in the life of a wealthy merchant's daughter. *Brighton Rock* (1938), Graham Greene's novel about protection rackets and racetrack violence, was also a criticism of the Catholic Church for creating a sexually repressed gangster who took out his frustrations on minor bookmakers.

In the same way that no historian can develop his or her arguments in isolation from the work of others, nor can the discipline of history itself ignore other schools of academic enquiry. Large and growing bodies of sociological studies, concerned with the relation of gambling to society, and, less importantly for this work, psychological considerations of the individual and gambling, must be acknowledged.

Psychological studies are valuable in their own right but are largely irrelevant to a history of popular gambling in England. The problem for historians is how to retrospectively test a view that relates gambling to neuroses quietly and unconsciously simmering away since childhood, which are apparently suddenly unleashed in an uncontrollable and sustained urge to place money on events with uncertain outcomes. The classic core text of this approach, Sigmund Freud's *Dostoyevsky and Parricide*,[23] interpreted the Russian author's gambling addiction as a symptom of transmuted masturbatory tendencies and of the secret wish to kill his father. These urges were guiltily suppressed at the time of the mother's unspoken refusal to initiate her son painlessly into the joys of sex. But the 'passion for gambling related to masturbation conflicts' hypothesis has been described as 'a somewhat wild assertion based on a small number of case studies'.[24] Furthermore, as John Cohen (a behavioural psychologist) has written, in criticism of a Freudian psychoanalysis of gambling, anyone who gambles and uses scatological terms in their vocabulary is open to the charge of being a neurotic who bets as 'an unsuccessful defence against an underlying anal-fixation'.[25] This, apparently, also results from an unsatisfactory sexual development in which to go through the excitement of the win or loss of the gamble is to experience vicarious orgasm or a disappointing climax. Without a sizeable number of contemporary testimonies from anally fixated or oedipal punters[26] a psycho-history of gambling is impossible.

The second major problem for a psycho-history of popular gambling is that psychoanalyses are usually concerned with compulsive or pathological gamblers. How can the regular but controlled or occasional betting of the vast majority of punters, for example the ten million people who were filling in a football pools coupon by the 1940s, and who showed no visible signs of psychosis, be explained? Moreover, in the 1950s many women liked a flutter every week on the pools and went in for bets on the big horse race meetings, yet most psychoanalyses say little on the issue of female gambling. A social history must avoid such lacunae.

The sociology of betting and gambling relates gambling either to the social structure as a whole or to particular social groups. American work has been prolific in both respects. In relation to gambling and capitalist society the contributions of Herbert Bloch and E. C. Devereaux have viewed gambling as a structural – functional response to American capitalism, an activity which enabled people from all social strata to speculate for gain. Religious critics attacked gambling as an unethical representation of the spirit of enterprise and money-making. It was thus a convenient scapegoat for the contradictions and shortcomings of a Protestant America based upon business activity and the diligence and effort required for its success.[27] Many American sociological studies are phenomenological and ethnographic; that is, they accept things as they are and assess their significance in the social and economic life of distinct ethnic groups or classes. A number of such approaches have provided some useful insights and comparisons between English and American experience.[28]

The major British sociological study of the relationship of gambling to society in general is D. M. Downes et al.'s *Gambling, Work and Leisure: A Study Across Three Areas* (1976). It is limited by a rigid application of discreet hypothetical models which render it a suggestive rather than conclusive book in its attempt to explain why different classes gamble as they do. Yet their statistical work was more fruitful. They found, in the mid 1970s at least, that men gambled more than women, that younger men tended to bet more frequently than their elders, and that the regularly employed working class betted more regularly and in consistently higher sums than the poor.[29] These are useful findings and, given the unscientific basis and the scaremongering of most statistics before the post-war years, they confirm earlier post-war findings, such as Kensley and Ginsburg's *Betting in Britain* of 1951, which in turn help to support broad, careful *post hoc* arguments about the level of gambling amongst different social groups.

For a social history of gambling, these approaches and sources have to be harnessed to an over-arching synthesis which explains why, and in what ways, the forms of popular gambling in Britain developed between the early to mid nineteenth and mid twentieth centuries. The major contention of this book is that during the nineteenth century, as betting and gaming evolved from an informal pre-industrial sporting and betting culture into a mass commercialised gambling market based upon bookmakers and the sporting press, a sporting discourse from the culture of 'the Fancy' and the free-born English punter was absorbed into this growing market. The punters, despite the claims of irrationality and wastefulness made against them, participated in this culture of betting and gambling with an outlook based on a complex system of beliefs and
• betting strategies which was almost always underpinned by self-restraint.

Chapter 2 describes the social, economic and moral issues which arose in the development of mass commercialised betting and bookmaking between the eclipse of state lotteries in the 1820s and the 1906 Street Betting Act. Gambling may be as old as money, but the development and establishment of a capitalist social system whose wealth depended upon speculation and investment raised important ethical questions about what D. H. Lawrence called 'filthy lucker'.[30] Something-for-nothing was filthy lucre.

Chapter 3 examines the social organisation of off-course betting between the 1906 Street Betting Act, the social and economic significance of street betting, and the reasons for and immediate effects of legalisation in 1961.

Chapter 4 explores the non-commercialised side of gaming, that is, the use of coins, cards and local sports as media for friendly or informal wagering in which people betted with each other, not through a bookmaker. The sports discussed here are pigeon racing and bowling in Lancashire from the 1890s, when they were becoming increasingly popular sports amongst the urban working class.

Chapter 5 argues that horse racing and betting were bread and butter . to each other. The extension of the national racing calendar from the Victorian years, the cultural weight of what was seen as a traditional sport, and the role of the sport as the pivot of mass betting, came together to render horse racing the heart of the national sporting and betting culture which has embraced all classes and social groups who had no antipathy to gambling.

Chapter 6 looks at the development of whippet racing from hare coursing in the later nineteenth century to the commercial venues of the greyhound tracks introduced from 1926. Like horse racing, coursing and dog racing had long been a sport associated with betting and the patronage of the local gentry but greyhound racing never achieved the social acceptability of the turf.

The idea of fixed-odds coupons or of football competitions for prizes had been kicked-off by the sporting press and bookmakers in the 1880s and 1890s. The development of football coupon betting from the 1890s to the rise of Littlewoods and other large 'pools' firms between the wars and up to 1960 is examined in chapter 7.

Chapter 8 looks at lotteries and the premium bonds. It is argued that . changes in governmental attitudes to lotteries, and the introduction of the premium bonds in 1956, further signified a wider liberalisation in British society which ended a century of unworkable and class-biased legislation.

Finally, chapter 9 concludes by discussing what gambling reveals about the social evolution of the English working class during the period under study. It questions the view held by a number of historians and · sociologists, that leisure since the industrial revolution has become abstracted from reality, or divorced from wider economic and political · considerations in people's minds.

Notes

1 Samuel (Dr) Johnson, *A Dictionary of the English Language*, 1983 edition (first published in 1755). There are no page numbers.
2 *Oxford English Dictionary*, 1961 edition, p. 35.
3 Eric Partridge (ed.), *The Penguin Dictionary of Historical Slang*, 1988, p. 734.
4 John Ashton, *A History of Gambling in England*, 1898. Canon Peter Green, *Betting and Gambling*, 1927 especially Chapter 2, 'Social Evils Due to Gam-

bling'. E. Benson Perkins, *Gambling in English Life*, 1950. Perkins was Chairman of the Churches Committee on Gambling in the 1940s. For an insightful journalistic treatment of gambling see Alan Wykes, *Gambling*, 1964. Popular histories of horse racing and its associated betting include Michael Wynn Jones, *The Derby*, 1979. See also any books from the John Freeman Fairfax Blakeborough library.

5 For example, Peter Bailey, *Leisure and Class In Victorian England: Rational Recreation and the Contest for Control, 1830–1885*, 1978. Hugh Cunningham, *Leisure in the Industrial Revolution, c.1780–1840*, 1980.

6 This is Wray Vamplew's term. See *Pay Up and Play the Game*, 1988, p. 47.

7 James Walvin, *Leisure and Society, 1830–1950*, 1978; Vamplew, *op. cit.*

8 A. E. Dingle, *The Campaign for Prohibition in Victorian England*, 1980. Brian Harrison, *Drink and the Victorians*, 1971. On sex see John Gillis, *For Better or Worse*, 1986.

9 Ross McKibbin, 'Working-Class Gambling in Britain, 1880–1939', *Past and Present*, No. 82, 1979. James Mott, 'Popular Gambling from the Collapse of the State Lotteries to the Rise of the Football Pools', Paper given at the Society for the Study of Labour History Conference on Working-Class Leisure, 1975. See also James Mott, 'Miners, Weavers and Pigeon Racing', in M. Smith et al., *Leisure and Society in Britain*, 1973.

10 On the historical relationship of gambling to sport in modern Britain see Tony Mason, *Sport in Britain*, 1988, pp. 59–68. On betting and horse racing see Wray Vamplew, *The Turf: A Social and Economic History of Horse Racing*, 1976; On football coupon betting see Tony Mason, *Association Football and English Society, 1863–1915*, Brighton, 1981, pp. 187–95.

11 Carl Chinn, 'Social Aspects of Sparkbrook, Birmingham, in the Twentieth Century', unpublished Ph.D thesis, University of Birmingham, 1987; Chapter 8, 'Cultural Dissension: Gambling', pp. 140–53. Jerry White, *The Worst Street in North London, Campbell Bunk, Islington*, 1985.

12 G. S. Jones, 'Working-Class Culture and Working-Class Politics in London, 1870–1914: Notes on the Re-Making of a Working-Class', in *Languages of Class*, 1983. Standisch Meacham, *A Life Apart: The English Working Class, 1890–1914*, 1977.

13 David Dixon, *From Prohibition to Regulation: Bookmaking, Anti-Gambling and the Law*, Oxford, 1991, p. 10. See also his 'The Street Betting Act of 1906 as an Attack on Working-Class Culture', in A. Tomlinson (ed.), *Leisure and Social Control*, Brighton, 1981. 'Class Law: The Street Betting Act of 1906', *International Journal of the Sociology of Law*, 8, 1980; *The State and Gambling: Developments in the Legal Control of Gambling in England, 1867–1923*, Hull, 1981; *Illegal Gambling and Histories of Policing in Britain*, Hull, 1984.

14 John K. Walton, *Lancashire: A Social History*, 1987, pp. 218–19.

15 Bailey, *op. cit.*, p. 7.

16 The Pilgrim Trust, *Men Without Work*, 1938. Mass Observation (MO), *First Year's Work*, 1939. MO, *The Pub and the People*, 1941. The writer has also used the Mass Observation archive, kept at the University of Sussex library.

17 C. E. B. Russell and E. T. Champagnac, 'Gambling and Aids to Gambling', *Economic Review*, Vol. X, 1900; *Manchester Boys: Sketches of Manchester Lads at Work and Play*, 1905; *Social Problems of the North*, 1913.

18 McKibbin, *op. cit.*, p. 147.

19 The autobiographies are given throughout the text. Acknowledgement must be made to John Burnett, David Mayall and David Vincent's invaluable source

references, *The Autobiography of the Working Class*, volumes 1 and 2. Apart from the writer's own endeavours, the collections of oral data used were Carl Chinn's oral project for his book on bookmakers, James Power and others' *Bolton Oral History Project*, at Bolton Local History Library, Bill Williams, Audrey Linkman, Dermott Healy and others' *Manchester Tape Studies Collection* at Manchester Polytechnic, Bill Williams and others' *Manchester Jewish Museum Tape Collection* at Cheetham Hill, Elizabeth Roberts' *North West Oral History Project* at Lancaster University, and a couple of individual testimonies mentioned in the text.

20 Luisa Passerini, *Fascism in Popular Memory*, Cambridge, 1987, p. 10.
21 Charles Dimont, 'Going to the Dogs', *New Statesman and Nation*, 30 November 1946, pp. 395–6.
22 McKibbin, *op. cit.*, p. 151.
23 Sigmund Freud, *The Complete Psychological Works of Sigmund Freud*, edited by John Strachey, Vol. 21, 1974, pp. 190–4.
24 Paul Kline, *Fact and Fantasy in Freudian Theory*, 1972, p. 264. On Eysencks' criticism of Freud see H. Eysenck, *The Uses and Abuses of Psychology*, 1953, *passim*.
25 Quote from John Halliday and Peter Fuller, *The Psychology of Gambling*, 1974, in John Cohen, 'Oedipus at Odds On', The *Times Literary Supplement*, 18 October, 1974, p. 1151.
26 Jack Dowie discusses Stefan Zweig, in 'Gambling and the Gamblers', Open University U201, *Risk*, Volume 2, 1980, p. 42.
27 H. A. Bloch, 'The Sociology of Gambling', *American Journal of Sociology*, Vol. 57, No. 3, 1951. E. C. Devereaux, 'Gambling', in the *International Encyclopedia of the Social Sciences*, Vol. 6, 1968, pp. 53–61.
28 Robert Perrucci, 'The Neighbourhood "Bookmaker": Entrepreneur and Mobility Model', in P. Meadows (ed.), *Urbanism, Urbanisation and Change: Comparative Perspectives*, 1969. R. D. Herman, *Gamblers and Gambling*, Lexington, 1976. Ned Polsky, *Hustlers, Beats and Others*, 1971. W. Foot Whyte, *Street Corner Society: The Social Structure of an Italian Slum*, 1981 (first published 1943). I. K. Zola, 'Observations on Gambling in a Lower Class Setting', *Social Problems*, Vol. 10, No. 4, 1963, pp. 353–61.
29 D. M. Downes et al., *Gambling, Work and Leisure: A Study Across Three Areas*, 1976, pp. 89–95.
30 D. H. Lawrence, 'The Rocking Horse Winner', in *Love Among the Haystacks*, 1986, p. 83 (first published 1926).

Chapter 2

Gambling, culture and economy
in England, *c*.1823–*c*.1906

This chapter describes the development of popular betting and gambling from the abolition of the lotteries in the 1820s to the perceived epidemic of gambling in late Victorian and Edwardian England, which culminated in the Street Betting Act of 1906. It looks primarily at the growth and commercialisation of off-course betting in the face of the legislative and moral campaign against it.

I

State lotteries existed in Britain from 1569 to 1826.[1] A lottery can be defined as a game of pure chance. It includes raffles, that is, tickets sold with prize numbers on them which are later drawn, and sweepstakes, where tickets are bought containing a name of one of many horses in a race, which the purchaser hopes will win.[2] State lotteries resembled a sort of national raffle, which had the same basic function throughout the 260-plus years of their existence.[3] They were set up to finance public works schemes. A project to build a bridge across the Thames, the British Museum and the campaign against Napoleon all received financial assistance from state lotteries. Lotteries were a useful source of income for the Exchequer. The tickets, issued by Licensed Lottery Office Keepers, but also occasionally farmed out to stockbrokers to sell on behalf of government, were aimed at the wealthy property-owning classes. A lottery ticket cost sixteen pounds during the French wars. But the lotteries generated a great deal of interest amongst the lower orders, a development which greatly worried the Whig governments from the 1780s. In defiance of the intention of government, people pooled their pennies to purchase collective shares in a lottery ticket. An Act in 1802 tried to stop the growing number of purchases of 'illegal insurances' and 'little goes' amongst the poor.

The Whig government established a Select Committee on Lotteries in

1808 to ascertain 'how far the Evils attending Lotteries have been remedied by the Laws passed respecting the same'.[4] The witnesses to the commission comprised Lottery Office keepers, local magistrates, officers of police in London, and lawyers. Of particular concern was the network of 'middle men', the enterprising publicans, gin shop owners, milkmen and others who served milk to servants 'and took their money for insurances'. 'Morocco Men', named after the leather covers of their ledger books, set themselves up as agents for the distribution of tickets and took insurances from house-to-house and in 'the shops of common barbers' in London and the major cities in England.[5] As well as servants, mechanics, 'inferior tradesmen' and 'people from workhouses' were amongst those buying shares of tickets.[6] The middle man went to the legitimate Office Keeper with 'one or more numbers of Lottery Tickets' and paid over a premium to insure against those numbers coming up blank on the days of the draw.[7]

It was clear that where the lower classes were prevented from participation in a form of gambling intended for the rich, they evolved their own schemes. This disregard for the law led to a realisation that the state itself was in large part to blame for the growth of speculative insurances amongst the poor. The second report of the Select Committee argued that if government was to extract revenue from the 'pecuniary resource' of a lottery, 'a spirit of adventure must be excited amongst the community' which militated against a spirit of hard work and encouraged sharp and criminal practice:

> by the effects of the Lotteries, even under its present restrictions, idleness, dissipation and poverty are increased, the most sacred and confidential trusts are betrayed, domestic comfort is destroyed, madness often created, crimes, subjecting the perpetrators of them to the punishment of death, are committed, and even suicide itself is produced.[8]

In the same terms as Adam Smith the committee felt that 'lotteries destroyed those habits of continued industry' for 'delusive dreams of sudden and enormous wealth' which led only to ruin. These social costs could 'only be done away with by the suppression of the cause from which they are derived'.[9]

The financial demands of the French wars were probably the key reason for the continuance of the lotteries after 1808. But from 1821, Lord Liverpool's government, supported in large part by the reformists known as 'liberal Tories', decided to abolish the lotteries. As Beales points out, it is often difficult to know what were the differences between old-style Whiggery and the new Toryism. The major parliamentary spokesmen of the latter creed were Wilberforce, Canning, Sir Samuel Whitbread, the ex-chairman of the Lottery Committee of 1808, and Sir Samuel Romilly. They possessed a paternalistic willingness 'to take up certain proposals of reform' but also promoted the principles of laissez faire and the Smithite notion of a self-regulating economy.[10] Whitbread, Wilberforce and Romilly campaigned against the lotteries as 'a monopolistic device of a mercantilist regime (disappearing) along with Speenhamland and wage regulation'.[11] The lottery, whose revenue was decreasing anyway, was accordingly abolished in 1823. The last draw took place in 1826.

However, publicans and others of an entrepreneurial outlook amongst the working class continued to offer small lotteries, in the form of sweepstakes, to their customers and locals. This is further discussed in chapter 8. But the point is, the number of small sweeps got up in pubs, clubs and workplaces illustrated that as the campaign against gambling was getting off the ground, the lineage of clandestine and collective betting easily adapted to meet the new circumstances of prohibition.

II

Gambling, as a pecuniary accompaniment to sporting and recreational activities, had been endemic in the leisure culture of eighteenth century England. It was an essential feature of both plebian and patrician, lower-class and noble, recreation. The combat sports of pugilism – more commonly known as 'prize fighting' – wrestling, the cruel sports of cock fighting, dog fighting and bull and bear baiting, athletic sports – most commonly pedestrianism, that is, foot racing – and horse racing were all important events in the popular holiday calendar, and were heavily associated with wagering.[12]

Amongst the lower class, the pub was central to sports and betting. In 1851, *Chambers Edinburgh Journal* noted for foot-racing, most competitors: 'where money passes are poor men, who literally walk or run for their bread; the match is generally concocted by a tavern keeper who plans it so as to make it a matter of business'.[13] The same was true for prize fighting, or the 'Prize Ring' as it was commonly known. The contemporary sporting press was full of little calls to combat like this one:

> William Green, better known by the name of Butcher Bill, is anxious to have another shy with the Ferryman, his late antagonist, for from £5 to £10 a side.

The money is ready at the Crown Inn, Bolton, whenever the Ferryman thinks proper to accept the offer.[14]

Yet prize fighting still lent itself to the patronage of wealthy gentleman who often assumed the role of matchmaker, trainer and gambler.[15] William Hazlitt, for example, the radical essayist and journalist, provided a vivid contemporary description of a prize fight in Hungerford, Berkshire, in 1821, and both the poor and genteel followers of it.[16] Over twenty years later, in the famous fight between 'Bendigo' and Ben Gaunt, both 'roughs' and 'swells' travelled to Buckinghamshire to cheer on the boxers and bet amongst themselves on the anticipated result.[17]

It was in the desire to satisfy the genteel interest in such sports and in field sports such as hunting, shooting and fishing that papers such as *Bell's Life in London* and the *Sporting Times* had their origins. *Bell's Life*, for example, was begun in 1822 under the proprietorship of the sporting journalist Pierce Egan. It was dedicated to the pursuit of 'the Fancy' and was full of news and sometimes scandal to do with 'The Ring'. In 1830 it was preoccupied with the affair of 'Ned Neal and Young Dutch Sam' and the 'unmanly and ungenerous imputations' which the supporters of each pugilist were hurling at each other. The acrimony was such that even *Bell's Life*, whose sales depended on its largely aristocratic readership, felt it could be excused for 'advising those gentlemen who have been in the habit of indulging in secret slander (that they) cannot expect countenance among the honest circles of the family of John Bull'.[18] This was the disreputable side of the fancy.

But what was the fancy, and who followed it? Hazlitt revered 'the FANCY' (which he insisted in writing in capital letters) and the prize ring. To him, it was indicative of something vital and brave, strengths which the elitist and rational detractors lacked: 'Ye who despise the FANCY, do something to shew as much pluck, or as much self-possession as this, before you assume a superiority which you have never given a single proof of by any one action in the whole course of your lives!'[19]

Attempting to define the fancy is not easy, yet it seems to mean more than just simple choice. For the better, it would appear to be an inclination towards an object, animal or sports person which gave expression to his or her aesthetic longings. Doctor Johnson, for example, gave eight definitions of 'fancy', including: 'An opinion bred rather by the imagination than the reason', an 'inclination liking, or fondness' and 'something that pleases or entertains'.[20] Choice was not necessarily grounded in logic or reason, as this could detract from the intuitive basis of the attraction. Mott argues that as the nineteenth century wore on the disreputable tenor of the fancy as the 'ton of low life' declined, giving way not just to the picking of winners in horse racing, but also to the liking for pigeons, flowers, and other hobbies associated with the working class.[21] Thus in his survey of London in the 1890s, Charles Booth observed the colourful 'fancy market' of Sclater Street in the East End, with its haranguing bookmakers and tipsters, while 'all around were the buyers and sellers of dogs, pigeons and other pets'.[22] The popular phrase 'to fancy' a horse, the inclination that set many people to betting, probably filtered into common parlance after the decline of the prize ring from the 1840s and during the growth and commercialisation of horse racing and horse race betting.

III

Throughout the eighteenth century 'the sport of Kings' had been increasingly associated with the gentry rather than royalty, 'the Kings themselves not playing a major part in its government'.[23] The Jockey Club, founded in 1751 to control the sport, was composed almost entirely of aristocratic and military gentlemen, a class domination which has remained largely intact until the present day.[24] For those who, like Anthony Trollope, venerated horse racing as a sport, rather than as a vehicle for betting, the Jockey Club was entrusted to ward off the excesses and excrescences that went with the capitalisation of horse racing and the spread of mass bookmaking.[25]

Thus disrepute was seen to proceed from, rather than to preface, mass betting. Benjamin Disraeli, viewed the spread of bookmaking and betting amongst the lower classes as the pollution of a once noble activity. In *Sybil* (1845), his literary paean to a new England revitalised under the political rule of a strong Tory aristocracy, he counterposed Hump Chippendale, the hunch-backed 'keeper of a second rate gaming house', with Captain Spruce, a 'debonair personage', who took bets for the wealthy at Newmarket and in the salons of Pall Mall. Whereas Spruce was a man of 'gentle failings', Hump Chippendale was a 'democratic leg, who loved to fleece a noble, and thought that all men were born equal; a consoling creed that was a hedge for his hump'.[26] Disraeli's caricature was based on a fear that lower-class bookmaking was expanding and spoiling what was once a noble hobby.

Most landed witnesses to the Select Committee of 1844 had a vested interest in arguing along such lines. They had been embarrassed by a series of turf-betting frauds in the previous year, the culmination of the so-called 'demoralisation of the Turf'.[27] In the face of the criticism from the reformed House of Commons they felt the need to distinguish between their own legitimate gambling and that of the poorer classes. Admiral Rous, the leading Steward of the Jockey Club, argued that 'the poor should be protected; but I would let a rich man ruin himself if he pleases'.[28] Such paternalism was in keeping with the spirit of the subsequent legislation.

Yet the distinction between the less reputable gambling of the lower class and that of the rich found only limited sympathy with the House. It is not really surprising that the gambling of rich and poor came under attack from an ascendant reforming middle class at this time. For critics of gambling the demoralisation of the turf and the association of betting with cruel and violent sports were typically associated with a selfish and unimproving leisure activity. The ideology of the reforming middle class has been described as resting upon the Protestant work ethic, that is, upon the individual and social virtues of the prudential and the self-improving. These were values which were necessary for the accumulation of capital, essential as a route to social mobility in the face of hereditary power and wealth. As Harold Perkin argues, for the reforming middle class 'aristocracy and working class were united in their drunkenness, profaneness, sexual indulgence, gambling and love of cruel sports'.[29] In relation to drink, Brian Harrison has shown that the temperance campaign was more effective amongst the middle class, claiming that an elite was 'insulated from temptation' by the 1870s whilst an intemperate working class drank on regardless.[30] But how was the elite to be insulated from the temptation of gambling? The answer was to remove the legal facilities for the recovery of gambling debts.

The Act of 1845 'to Amend the Law Concerning Games and Wagers' was a direct product of the two parliamentary enquiries into gambling that had reported the previous year. It gave expression to the intention that 'henceforth the law shall take no cognizance of wagers' and that all contracts or agreements made in a wagering spirit were to be outside the affairs of a court of law.[31] In contrast to the prohibitive tenets of the subsequent Act of 1853, the legislation of 1845 was a clear statement of the economics and morality of laissez faire:

> nobody now disputes the opinion of Adam Smith that government ought not to pretend to watch over the economy of private people, and to restrain their expense by Sumptuary Laws; but if they look well after their own expenses

they may safely trust the people with theirs.[32]

Morally, the Act was designed to remove the Victorian state from the dirty business of settling gambling debts. In simple terms, if someone was foolish enough to gamble they alone should suffer the consequences. Gambling, with its reliance upon risk, and with the return of capital based upon contingency only, subverted the meritocratic principles of the Puritan work ethic, in which capital was earned by hard work, talent and deferred gratification. It thus undermined the principles underpinning the social progress of the middle class. The acquisition of property was only legitimate if, as anti-gambling campaigners later argued, it was based upon deferred gratification and the application of effort and skill. The language of the Report of the 1844 *Select Committee on Gaming* illustrates this, with terms like 'prudence' 'providence' and their oppositional categories well to the fore. As Devereaux points out, the 'quasi utilitarian' character of gambling appears 'to make a mockery of the legitimate economy' as it distributes rewards purely on the basis of chance rather than effort and merit.[33] Hence a number of witnesses to the Select Committee distinguished between legitimate speculation on the Stock Exchange and that which was, in essence, merely gambling. 'Time bargains', for example, were not 'bona fide' because no stock was transferred between speculator and stockbroker. The speculator merely bought, held and sold stock while its price went up in order to make money.[34]

This problem of gambling in stocks was by no means new to the early Victorian period, although the debate about gambling focused attention upon it. 'Stock jobbing' had been the cause of the infamous South Sea Bubble fiasco in 1720, entailing the excessive wholesaling of securities on the Stock Exchange. Here, remuneration – or profit – was determined by the difference between the price at which the jobber bought and sold stocks. This activity often led to the excessive and unscrupulous buying-up of stocks in order to secure maximum and often exclusive income from the selling price. Yet over-inflated prices led to the 'bubble' bursting, and hundreds of speculators were ruined. Hence 'An Act to prevent the infamous Practice of Stock Jobbing' was passed. This was designed to prevent a repetition of such events but, over a century later, the Act was 'habitually, and even daily, broken'.[35]

Deals of this sort were derided as 'gambling' for two reasons. Firstly, the unprincipled buying and selling of stocks was fraught with economic and social dangers: what if the bottom fell out of the market? This was not calculated investment but unexpurgated risk, and whole fortunes could be lost, bringing ruin on families. Secondly, there was no socio-economic advantage in such transactions except to the pockets of the broker and his client. It was not a socially beneficial investment, not a utilitarian use of capital. It was widely believed that a campaign against gambling and the principle of gambling would remove the most venal speculations from the Stock Exchange, or would 'purify capital'.[36] As a legal commentator argued to the Select Committee, 'a great deal of the gambling in the Stock Exchange would cease if the Act which prevents persons being obliged to pay their losses occasioned by speculation were repealed'.[37] In other words, if the state were to remove the legal rights which enabled the succesful party to push for debt recovery from the loser, the incentive to bet might be reduced. This was the substance and intention of the 1845 Act. It was an attempt to foster a more rational and principled form of speculation than gambling. Yet gambling was sewn inextricably into the fabric of the Stock Exchange. This problem was seen as particularly acute in Lancashire where the growth of the local economy was based in large part on the fortunes of the textile industry. The Liverpool satirical journal the *Porcupine*, parodying *Punch*, enacted a 'raid' on a fictitious betting house run by the notable local sportsman Lord Derby, comparing landed gambling with the 'betting, booking – gambling of all descriptions arranged and prepared in the most open and flatigious manner' at the Liverpool Business Exchange where 'our merchant princes' were caught betting.[38]

This was the problem of speculation on 'futures', another system of investment by options which did not require delivery of the goods. This meant that financiers and merchants could place their money heavily on one commodity by purchasing large amounts to force its price up, and then cream off the profit in the form of interest paid on shares by the wholesale selling of their share options. They then re-invested in likely goods elsewhere. It was an artificial investment which flung capital this way and that, a market manipulation in which the wealthier operators were out to make a fast buck. As an American economist noted, many smaller businesses lost out on investment opportunities and many were broken by the rapid fluctuations in prices which artificially inflated or depressed the market.

> the essence of the system, which is the great evil of it, is this – that those who engage in it, while nominally trading in commodities, in ninety nine cases out of a hundred are simply betting upon future prices. If they did this in the ordinary gambling 'hells' it might not matter to those who are interested in the

commodities concerned; but the mischief is that this betting is carried on in the name of business in the ordinary markets, and that it completely controls the price quotations issued. This is the case in all the great markets of the United States and in Liverpool, and these markets to a great extent rule the prices of cotton and grain in the whole world.[39]

The *Porcupine* frequently 'had occasion to denounce the prevalence of gambling in the cotton market in Liverpool' and attacked the 'culpable laxity of the rules' governing transactions on the 'Change.[40] As Huizinga notes, the words 'playing' or 'gambling' on the Stock Exchange illustrate the hazy borderline between play and seriousness, between reckless speculation as a form of betting and proper investment. 'In both cases the operative factor is the hope of gain.'[41]

So, it may be concluded that in its intention to persuade the ruling class to desist from gambling, and in seeking to remove gambling from the process of capital accumulation, the Act of 1845 failed miserably. Firstly, throughout the period under study anti-gamblers were at pains to distinguish between 'the destructive spirit of gambling' in commerce and proper commerce. E. B. Perkins, for example, a prominent antagonist of gambling from the 1920s to the 1950s, felt that the Manchester Cotton Exchange and the London Stock Exchange should take steps to get rid of their most unprincipled 'stock-jobbers'.[42] Secondly, the aristocratic patronage and control of horse racing and other sports continued well into the twentieth century, and remained associated with upper-class wagering, as is shown in chapters 5 and 6. As the Attorney General, addressing parliament before the passage of the 1853 Betting Houses Act argued, 'The difficulty in legislating upon this subject' was to refrain from 'interfering with that description of Betting which had so long existed at Tattersalls and elsewhere'.[43] With the rise of street betting and bookmaking, the high days of the great gaming salons of the wealthy described by Disraeli and Thackeray's *Vanity Fair* were drawing to an end, but this did not spell the end of aristocratic participation in popular gambling.

Governmental concern soon shifted away from the gentry to the 'common gaming houses' springing up in the larger towns and cities. The 1853 Betting Houses Act was specifically intended to eradicate the 'new form of betting' in which the owner of a betting house 'held a bag against all comers'. This was, at its most fundamental, the distinction between the older 'traditional' sidestake wagering, and ready-money betting with a bookmaker, the basis of mass betting. The Act of 1853 made it an offence to resort to any place or person for the purposes of betting and bookmaking.[44]

Who were the clients of the new betting shops? The Manchester Police •
returns for the 1840s and 1850s show that they were mostly working
class, and drawn in no small part from the local textile mills. For
example, of the seventy-three persons taken into custody for betting and
gaming in 1847, twenty-five were 'weavers, piecers &c.', and there were
six spinners, twelve hawkers, eleven labourers, five with 'no trade', two
shoemakers, one smith, one roper, one fustian cutter, one butcher, one
from porters and packers, one publican and one from glass cutters and
blowers. Out of sixty-two people taken into custody in 1856, twenty-five
were 'weavers, piecers &c.' and twelve were hawkers, a catch-all term
for street sellers. Of the sixty-two, four were women: one from 'weavers.
piecers &c.', two hawkers, and one with no trade.[45]

It is also interesting to note from these statistics that gambling was
nowhere near as much of a public order problem for the police as drink
offences. Throughout the whole of the period under study, betting and
gambling offences in the police statistics rarely increased beyond a
quarter of those misdemeanours committed under the broad categories
of drunk and disorderly or drunk and incapable.

The Attorney General, introducing the Betting Houses Bill to parliament, stated that:

> The mischief arising from the existence of these betting shops was perfectly
> notorious. Servants, apprentices, and workmen, induced by the temptation
> of receiving a large sum for a small one, took their few shillings to these places
> and the first effect of their losing was to tempt them to go on spending their
> money, in the hope of retrieving their losses, and for this purpose it not
> infrequently happened that they were drawn into robbing their masters and
> employers.[46]

Many of the 'attendant vices' of popular gambling, which would later
become abiding concerns in the anti-gambling literature of the twentieth
century, most notably the temptation of a large sum for a small one, the
corruption of the young, the relationship of gambling to the criminal
subculture of the towns and cities were pointed out to the House of
Commons by the Attorney General.

The 1853 Act gave expression to the desire to stop the ascendancy of
bookmakers and betting houses, yet it was both too late, and too flawed,
to be succesful. The cultural weight of a betting and 'sporting' culture
and its commercial transformation was developing on too large a scale
and at too great a momentum to be contained. In the event, it made the

activity illegal, and in so doing was responsible for the thin diaphanous veil which rested over ready-money betting until 1960.

IV

Vamplew is only partly right when he says that 'the general effect of the 1853 Act was to shift the locus of working-class betting from the public house to the street'.[47] That cash betting shops were flourishing in Manchester during the 1860s is evident from the pages of the local press. The liberal journal the *Free Lance* explained to its middle-class readership the disguise, locality, and clientele of 'list houses', so-called due to the lists of racing results and starting-price odds, that is, those winnings offered in return for the successful stake.

> They may be known by the swarm of clerks, operatives, stable-men, soldiers and even women that pass in and out in an unceasing stream. As far as outward signs are concerned . . . betting might be the last thing in life they knew of or cared about. 'John Smith, cigar maker' or 'James Robinson-chops and steaks always ready' are the lying legends inscribed on their doors and windows, though an enquiry with a view to chops or cigars would meet with no very satisfactory answer. Generally the 'house' is a hutch about as big as a bathroom, with a wooden partition dividing the bookmaker from his customers. On the outside of the partition hang the cards of the different races, with the odds 'marked in plain figures' as the drapers say.[48]

In Liverpool, less than three years after the passage of the 1853 Act, the journalist Hugh Shimmin found a list house in the back of a public house in Liverpool frequented by all sorts of low-lifers.[49]

This visible failure of the anti-gambling legislation led to more of the same. In 1874 a further Act was passed to prevent street betting. The Act also prohibited the sending of advertisements through the post which induced people to bet.[50] This caused many bookmakers to set up offices on the Continent which they advertised in the sporting press and to which cash stakes might be sent without fear of interference from the authorities. The problems of the national legislation were compounded by local bylaws against obstruction, passed in haste from the 1870s as a means of shoring up the gaps in the national legislation, and in part as a response to criticisms of the visibility of betting in the streets from the local press. These laws varied in scope and sentence from borough to borough. Taken as a whole, the laws over gambling were 'lacking in principle, confused and inconsistent'. The powers of the police were 'inadequate to check the practice'.[51]

For those who opposed gambling, then, there was an urgent need for the legislation to be made more strongly effective. The local press in Liverpool and Manchester stressed this during the 1860s and 1870s, calling upon the police authorities to halt 'the betting nuisance' or 'the betting pest'. In a series of four articles in 1877, detailing the existence of gambling in Liverpool despite the 1874 Betting Houses Act, the *Porcupine* accused the police of 'authorising' the wilful lack of intervention against 'the daily crowds' of betters and bookmakers.[52] Yet the police were damned if they didn't, and damned if they did. As the *Porcupine* lamented, a spate of arrests against bookmakers running subterranean clubs in defiance of the 1853 and 1874 Acts, merely caused bookmakers to come out on to the streets in greater numbers, defying the law in order to attract customers. The *Porcupine* also attacked the failure of the Watch Committee to co-ordinate with the police in a sustained effort against bookmakers.[53] In 1884, the *Liverpool Review* also pilloried the police for failing to take action against 'the permitted, it might also be said the authorised' betting clubs and bookmakers in the area of Williamson Square and Tarleton Street. The *Review*'s correspondent 'Paul Pry' described one club run by a 'ci devant hairdresser' who spoke in American parlance about 'bossing the shop' where those whom Pry called 'hungry sporting loafers' came to bet on horses, play cards, and take drinks.[54]

In Manchester, however, police action against betting clubs was more successful, at least in the short term. Following a 'great raid on betting clubs' by Detective Jerome Caminada and 170 constables, over 200 people were arrested, and over two thousand pounds was seized. The majority of those who appeared in court were bookmakers, accompanied by publicans and the waiters and barmen of the clubs.[55]

Some clubs, however, which had not been intended for gambling, soon fell foul to it. Charles Booth lamented the failure of religious and political social clubs in East London to 'create a great fellowship of men drawn from its own neighbourhood', and in so doing he blamed the early victory of the working class taste for beer and betting over the designs of the Clubs and Institutes Union (CIU), a recently established organisation designed to foster a spirit of rational recreation, of providence and sobriety, in the use of free time. Drinking and betting were soon common in CIU and other clubs, and viewed by Booth as the two most prominent evils, 'ruining so many of the great social and political working men's clubs, and causing them to be regarded as curses to the community'.[56] Yet for Booth, such clubs, and the bookmakers who touted for trade in them, were not to be confused with the 'bookmakers of good repute' who went to the respectable clubs of London.[57]

Who were these bookmakers, and when did bookmaking begin? To take the latter question first, the idea of making a book of tickets or receipts in order to bet with more than one person probably began in the gaming salons of the wealthy, most notably 'White's famous betting book' which was started in the mid eighteenth century.[58] This concept was adapted by the Morocco Men mentioned above and, most pertinently, by the earliest on-course bookmakers, the 'legs', an early vocational title for bookmakers which developed from the pejorative 'blackleg'. Samuel Johnson attached a servile connotation to the noun 'leg' as involving 'an act of obeisance', someone who bent the knee to authority. Two of his definitions of 'black' were 'cloudy of countenance' and 'horrible, wicked, atrocious'.[59] Another intriguing definition was provided by the sporting journalist, John Bee, in his *Dictionary of Sportsman's Slang*:

> Legs i.e., blacklegs. The monosyllable is, however, most elegant, as it leaves something to be guessed at. They are well-dressed, sometimes well-educated, sharpers at gambling-houses or race-courses, &c.; but legs appear at private parties, frequently assuming much of the surface of gentility.[60]

An historian of bookmaking suggests that the disreputable origins of the term 'leg' may have stemmed from the actions of regular turf sharpers who ran away when they could not pay.[61] Either way, the birth of the bookmaking profession was associated with a measure of dishonour.

The same historian attributes the earliest form of bookmaking to one William ('The Leviathan') Davies. Davies was 'the undisputed leader of the Ring' from the 1840s who extended the concept of paid on-course bets to off-course list houses where 'he would lay the odds from half a sovereign to half a plum (fifty pence to £50,000) etc'. He argues it was 'the Leviathan's modus operandi (which) opened the racing game for all to play'.[62] This view is based upon the apocryphal and anecdotal evidence of *Bell's Life*, or the *Illustrated London News* and other high-life periodicals of the early Victorian years, and tends towards the great man interpretation of history rather than the identification of social processes and economic change such as the transmission of racing results and odds by the electric telegraph, and the expansion of the sporting press, discussed below. As Sidney himself points out, 'list houses', set up by gambling entrepreneurs some thirty years or so before bookmakers like Davies and John Gully came on the scene, had 'inaugurated' off-course betting.

Concomitant with the rise of common gaming houses were legal credit bookmakers' establishments. Two of the first and largest were Valentine and Wrights' and Topping and Topping of London, both established in the 1860s. In the north west, credit firms such as Shepherd and Son were established in Blackpool in 1876, William Vincent of Manchester in 1886, Arthur Magnus of Manchester was established in the 1870s and Tom Gibbons, also of Manchester, in about 1886. These firms announced to their customers, through advertisements in the sporting press and by circulars, that 'the settlement of bets would be governed by the SP returns published in the *Sporting Life*'.[63] This clientele was composed of largely middle-class punters who could afford to keep a cheque account with a bookmaker. Moreover, credit commission agents or turf accountants advertising in Liverpool or Manchester trade directories from the 1920s addressed themselves to 'householders'. It is reasonable to suggest, especially as gambling debts could not be legally recovered, that a sizeable regular wage and an address in a respectable suburban or artisan district would have been required for a bookmaker to extend trust and credit. As Itskovitz points out, however, there is very little information on middle-class betting. Yet while he is undoubtedly correct to say that far fewer 'ethnographic excursions into middle class life'[64] exist than working-class autobiographies, those that do exist provide revealing glimpses of the credit punter. For example Dyke Wilkinson, a comfortably off jewellery manufacturer of Birmingham in the mid 1840s, who eventually became a bookmaker, used to bet on and off course with a credit commission agent.[65]

The growing working-class betting market was supplied by working-class bookmakers. John Benson, discussing the informal economy of 'penny capitalism' in the nineteenth century argues that 'most bookmakers probably began their careers by organising sweepstakes on the big races like the Oaks or the Derby, going on perhaps to run a regular "book" during their lunch hour.'[66] Despite the lack of contemporary evidence for this, subsequent oral testimony and autobiography for the twentieth century support this view. Moreover, the salient aspects of penny capitalism, most particularly the control by the petty entrepreneur 'over the use to which his capital and labour was put' was especially applicable to bookmakers. The aspiring layer of odds needed enough venture capital and a likely site from which to compete. Finally, it is reasonable to speculate that the growing number of working-class bookmakers during the later nineteenth century, as between the wars, was in part an economic response to unemployment during a time of relative prosperity for those in regular industrial employment. The market – the punters – was underpinned by falling costs of living and higher wages during this time.[67] As in the 1920s and 1930s, the informal economy expanded as the national economy contracted,[68] and the making of books, or working full or part time as a bookie's agent, was a means of making a living.

Despite the alleged prominence of the Leviathans or Captain Spruces in the mid nineteenth century, the Hump Chippendales were of increasing historical significance from that time. Their class position rather than their profession was the major cause of complaint in some journals. The *Free Lance* appropriated the terms 'commission agent' and 'bookmaker' for 'the trustworthy layer of odds' in comparison to the poor counterpart in a list house.[69] The invective directed at the poorer bookmakers castigated them metaphorically as both parasite and predator, as 'lice on the national head' or 'the spider catching the fly' or (in Liverpool) 'the Betting Harpies of Williamson Square'.[70] For Charles Booth, the low-class bookmaker was an unprincipled opportunist in the street economy of the poor. He was one of the 'worst class of corner men who hang round the doors of public houses', who destroyed rather than created wealth.[71] Moreover, the final insult for some anti-gambling campaigners was that many of those bookmakers who were caught and successfully prosecuted could usually afford to pay their fines. As John Hawke, the Secretary of the National Anti-Gambling League (NAGL) told the Select Committee in 1901, one Blackpool bookmaker gave change from his fine, asking the magistrate to put it in the poor box'.[72]

These life of these alleged villains was made considerably easier from the 1870s, as the sporting press expanded and its tenor and coverage changed. As James Greenwood had complained in 1869, horse-racing had replaced cruel sports and prize fighting as the main interest of the sporting press, 'not for its own sake but for the convenient peg it affords to have a bet on'.[73] This betting content was boosted by the adaptation of the telegraph to sporting and betting news during the 1860s and 1870s, thrown into sharp relief by the shift to the transmission of racing news from general news by the Exchange Telegraph Company in 1872.[74] The telegraph and the printed page transmitted the information which was vital to ready-money betting away from the course. Both the results of the races and the odds determined by bookmakers in Tattersall's Rings, the exclusive betting enclosures at the courses, were now printed in all national and local newspapers. There was now a national average to the odds collated from the starting-price odds which largely replaced the individual offerings of off-course bookmakers. This made it easier for the bookmaker to convince the punter that the odds were fair. As the report in 1902 of the Select Committee of the House of Lords argued, rejecting the proposal from the NAGL to abolish sporting intelligence in newspapers, 'the chief results of such prohibition would be to facilitate and encourage dishonesty among bookmakers'.[75]

The two major sporting papers were the *Sporting Chronicle* and the *Sporting Life*. The *Sporting Chronicle*, begun by Edward Hulton and his businessman partner, Bleakley, in Manchester in 1871 was the first of what became a flood of sporting papers and tipping and coupon competition sheets in the later Victorian and Edwardian years. Its readership was estimated at 30,000 daily in 1883. In 1885 Hulton purchased the *Sporting Life*, the successor of *Bell's Life in London*, thus establishing Manchester as the provincial capital of the sporting press. The *Life*'s circulation was estimated at 150,000.[76] The contents of both publications were based upon betting and racing information for all course, track and field events associated with gambling, but they also propagated the art of the tipsters, those who claimed to know the winners of future races. 'Augur' was the tipster of The *Sporting Life* and 'Kettledrum (Edward Hulton's pseudonym) of the *Sporting Chronicle*. As Mason shows, many sporting journalists had graduated from the print room, or had family or nepotistic connections within the sporting press circle.[77]

The two forces, for and against gambling, were now fully lined up against each other. In favour were the bookmakers and more potently, the sporting press, discussed further below. On the anti-gambling side was the National Anti-Gambling League, formed in 1890 from a coalition of Nonconformist Protestant churches. It had its three English offices in London, Manchester and York, and that it was in a bit of a flutter was evident in the excessive claims it made:

> Nothing less than the reformation of England as regards the particular vice against which our efforts are aimed lies before us. There is humiliation in the thought that the chosen Anglo Saxon race, foremost in the civilisation and government of the world, is first also in the great sin of Gambling.[78]

At a time of grave national self-doubt, when British economic supremacy was being overtaken by the USA and Germany, and when some Dutch farmers in South Africa gave the British forces a bloody nose in the Boer War, the League's message found favour with many in the reforming middle class. Gambling was blamed amongst others things for lost industrial production, for military failures in South Africa,[79] and .

for a general disinclination to work which was seen to sweep through society. Beatrice Potter, later Beatrice Webb, wrote of the poorest 'leisure class', usually casually employed or unemployed, whose 'constitutional hatred to regularity and forethought' was expressed in gambling. Those who tried to live by gambling were 'parasites eating the life out of the working class, demoralising and discrediting it'.[80]

For the NAGL, however, gambling demoralised and discredited the whole nation. The solution was sought in an evangelical campaign against it, modelled partly on the temperance movement. Congregations at churches and chapels were encouraged to sign the pledge against gambling.[81] The League also published a *Bulletin* twice a year, quoting from the more influential tracts and tomes on the ills of gambling, reproducing the more tragic or shocking reports on the subject from the local and national press, and warning of worse to come in editorials and articles on all aspects of the vice. The anti-gambling views of labour leaders such as Ramsay MacDonald and John Burns, both Nonconformists, were featured regularly in the *Bulletin* to support the campaign amongst the working class. The chief result of this latter strategy was that labour leaders earned the pejorative title of 'faddist' from the sporting press. Such derision had hitherto been reserved for the campaigning middle-class critic of popular habits. Thus Lord Turnour, keen to make political capital out of Labour MPs' support for the Street Betting Bill, argued that labour representatives in parliament were supporting 'one law for the rich and another for the poor'.[82]

Whilst Nonconformity underpinned the critique of gambling from the left, the concern of labour leaders for the leisure preferences of the poor stemmed from a socialist desire to secure the spiritual as well as the material ascendancy of the working class. The title and argument of John Burns' Clarion tract – *Brains Better Than Bets or Beer* – suggests this. Burns addressed himself specifically to an upper working-class artisanal audience, 'the aristocrats of labour', whom he felt shared his repugnance at the economic harm working people did to themselves by betting.[83] Moreover, the desire for something for nothing was seen as antithetical to the co-operative and collective ideals of British socialism.[84] For Ramsay MacDonald, betting was a class disease, one which had 'spread downwards from the idle rich to the hard working poor'. In proposing this 'law of imitation', in fact, MacDonald was merely putting a socialist perspective upon the NAGL's analysis of the spread of gambling.[85] The earliest phase of the NAGL's campaign had been aimed at the wealthiest gamblers as a means of beginning the process of total abolition by removing their bad example.[86]

In addition to this and the aforementioned activities, the NAGL engaged with the authorities on a number of other levels. John Hawke, appeared as a witness on both Parliamentary Enquiries in 1901 and 1902 to make the case for greater prohibition. They were particularly active in the north west, the Lancashire and Cheshire Branch being supported by liberal papers such as the *Manchester Guardian* and the *Manchester Evening News*, and after 1900 by tireless campaigners such as Canon Green. The NAGL petitioned watch committees and chief constables suggesting the police be availed of further powers to enforce the bylaws against betting.[87]

To the Parliamentary Committee of that year, Chief Constable Peacock described police intervention under the Manchester bylaw. It required three persons to be assembled together to constitute obstruction, and the police only proceeded against the bookmaker or his agent, not the backers.[88] Peacock took the opportunity to ask Parliament for stricter legislation. He emphasised the difficulties the police faced in enacting the legislation, that is, in arranging and carrying out successful raids on the bookmakers. This was severely hampered by the lack of co-operation from the public due to the unpopularity of the laws.[89]

The Street Betting Act of 1906 was sponsored by the Liberal Peer, Lord Davey. It was intended to standardise the laws against gambling in an • attempt to control the increasing incidence and significance of popular betting. It was a product of the paternalistic strain in new liberalism as well as the moral panic of the time, and it reiterated the incipient bias of the 1853 Act. In this it elicited strong criticisms from sporting and gambling interests as a 'monstrous sample of class legislation' and ensured that betting would remain a political issue.

Organised opposition was orchestrated largely by the sporting press, most particularly by the *Sporting Chronicle* and the *Sporting Life*. The National Sporting League was formed in 1902, under the aegis of the • *Life*, to argue for the legalization of betting without the introduction of a betting tax. Like the NAGL, the NSL also lobbied those who made the law and those who upheld it. Thus Peacock had also to refuse a request by the League to be allowed to petition against the Act from a table outside the gates of Manchester Infirmary.[90] The League's 'sporting' title, as with the sporting press, was an attempt to legitimate pro-gambling interests in the eyes of the public, and coloured the rhetoric of its spokesmen, who were self-appointed from the ranks of bookmakers and journalists on the sporting press, and the sporting wing of the

House of Lords.

The League was mainly conservative politically, apart from the maverick Liberal Horatio Bottomley, MP for Hackney South. Bottomley was a friend of Thomas Henry Dey, a wealthy bookmaker operating from both London and Holland, who was a conservative borough councillor in Hackney, London.[91] Both were keen proponents of the sporting and betting ethos, and strongly opposed to the intervention of 'faddists' into the time honoured rights of sportsmen.[92] The League held public meetings up and down the country. At one 'enthusiastic meeting in Manchester' in October 1906 it was demanded that places be set apart for the purpose of street betting 'in the same way that the Stock Exchange was set apart, and what was the latter but a legalised form of gambling?' At the same meeting, Bottomley proclaimed his intention to rouse 'the working men of England' against 'the prevailing wave of puritanical and namby-pamby, goody-goody legislation' which 'struck at those fundamental principles of self-reliance and robust manhood which made the English race what it was'.[93] The tipster 'Augur' of the *Sporting Life*, wrote of his 'intense feeling of detestation at the inroads faddists are being allowed to make upon the sacred liberties of the people', and asked why the Davey Bill was confined to 'working men only' Augur himself provided the explanation for this as one of 'the line of least resistance' taken by anti-gamblers and politicians who knew they could never stop the betting of the rich and powerful.[94]

For those concerned with gambling, the sporting press was the gambling dimension of the 'cheap and sensational press' problem, which comprised not only the *Life* and the *Chronicle* but more pertinently the flood of tipping sheets and football coupon papers which had risen since the 1880s. As Lady Bell lamented, the 'crusade' against gambling 'encounters as ardent a propaganda in favour of it, in which a far greater number are engaged than on the other side'.[95] The liberal social commentator C. F. G. Masterman accused these papers of exploiting the 'excitements of gambling and adventure' and of directing the thoughts of the multitude 'away from consideration of any rational or serious universe'.[96] What follows is an attempt to open up the relatively unknown field of the tipster and coupon press, its promoters, and its effect upon the betting market.

V

The rise of bookmaking and the betting market was viewed eagerly by those who felt they could make money out of the demand for betting intelligence. The tipsters who surfaced on the racecourses were outnumbered by the growing number of 'advertising tipsters' who appeared in the sporting and more down-market local newspapers. The Manchester *Free Lance* in 1871 pointed to 'a certain description of advertisement (pushing) itself into greater prominence in the local and general press. 'Unfortunate young men', particularly clerks and assistants, were 'fleeced' by the turf 'prophets of the period'.[97]

The parliamentary enquiries into gambling in the early twentieth century identified the major cause of the spread of illegal cash betting as 'largely due to the great facilities afforded by the Press and to the inducements to bet offered by means of Bookmakers circulars and Tipsters Advertisements'.[98] Such advertising also extended to the publication of tipping sheets. For Liverpool, the social statistician A. J. Robertson observed that tipsters and bookmakers were usually behind those papers 'comprising the sporting and betting interest'.[99] To this, we should also add what might be termed 'adventurer-printers' who, big or small, made forays into the tipping and coupon-paper market.[100]

The catalogue of the newspaper archive at Colindale is a very general guide but it does appear that these various entrepreneurs decided to provide their own sporting sheets in late Victorian and Edwardian England, although it is extremely difficult to quantify accurately the growth and extent of this press because so much of it was ephemeral. · *Willing's Press Guide* and the *London Newspaper Directory* do not list some of the more short-lived publications, especially in the earliest flurry of the tipster press, which found their way into the newspaper archive. A few titles will illustrate this. The *Winner*, for example, was the ultimate of such ephemera, a London daily which started and finished in June 1900. It was a two or four sided buff-coloured fly sheet measuring less than five inches wide and just over ten inches deep. It offered tips and racing gossip by its publisher, the tipster 'Binocular', whose suggested powers of long-sightedness evidently did not extend into newspaper proprietorship. *Turf Tips and Bookmakers' Crack-Ups*, owned and edited by 'The Turf Dapster', an otherwise anonymous London tipster, managed to last from March to May in 1890. The title of this sheet echoes a common claim of tipsters: that it is possible to win a few shillings or pounds off the bookie, and be as shrewd as he is.[101] A London paper, weekly at one penny, it is not in *Willings*. 'The Wizard' tried out his *Sporting Tissue* on the Manchester public on 21 November 1890. It 'ran for two or three days'.[102] A. Dick Luckman, who was a friend of many bookmakers and also the tipster Robin Goodfellow of the *Daily Mail*, had tried to make a go of the *Sport Set*, a sixpenny monthly, in 1908, but he admitted he had neither the money nor the patience to see it through.[103] Two other tipsters who published their own sheets at the turn of the century were Tom Diamond of Glasgow and Jimmie Glover of Leeds. They could claim with some honesty that they were party to information from the stables as they were friends of the trainer John McGuigan. McGuigan argued that none of the 'flotsam and jetsam', the 'so called tipsters', made 'the same personal efforts to obtain information' as Glover and Diamond.[104]

Most of the smaller operators could not achieve the circulation to enable them to meet costs and to continue for more than a few months, or at best a few years. The rapid demise of most of these papers was not so much a result of the actions of the NAGL as of the intense competitiveness of the market. It may also be argued that punters who wanted to fill in a coupon trusted their money to papers with a longer history and a greater likelihood of paying-up.

Some of the papers offering tipsters and coupons which lasted a year or more do find their way into *Willings*. For example, *Turf Snips*, which lasted from March 1891 to November 1898, was published by E. R. Swindells of Manchester. According to *Slater's Directory of Manchester, Salford and Suburban* between 1894 and 1898, Swindells was a 'letterpress printer' in Withy Grove, which was near to the Hulton Press. *Lotinga's Weekly* ran from March 1910 to July 1914, when it was killed off probably by the racing restrictions imposed during the early years of the war. Lotinga had been the tipster 'Larry Lynx' in *John Bull* before his vicious row with that paper's proprietor Horatio Bottomley.[105]

Bookmakers also published tipping and coupon sheets to make money and to advertise themselves. T. H. Dey's friend and rival bookmaker Bob Siever ran the *Winning Post* in London from 1892 to 1894. Dey himself advertised in this and a number of sporting papers before establishing his own sheet, the *Turf Pioneer*, which lasted only a few months in 1894. It was aimed at the working-class starting-price cash-betting market, but it never achieved a large circulation and with other similar ventures, 'soon expired'.[106]

Most did. If wealthy backers such as Dey and Siever could not stretch their papers' life beyond a few months or years it was unlikely that gambits with less venture capital behind them could do better. The publication of starting prices, tips and coupon competitions in the local and national dailies wrecked the chances of most small sheets. However, in Manchester at least, the biggest operators also took direct and unfair action to stifle upstart competition. One north west tipping sheet was born out of an industrial dispute between the Printers' Typographical Association, associate members of the National Labour Press, who were engaged in a dispute with the Hulton Press over pay and working conditions. During the strike, the tipster W. G. Campbell, who was 'Galliard' of the *Sunday Chronicle* and 'Carlton' of the *Manchester Daily Dispatch*, both Hulton 'papers, left his employer to establish his own tipping sheet, *Racing Shares*. There was co-operation between him and the striking printers. In the *Evening Newspaper*, Campbell apologised to his readers for a suspension in the publication of *Racing Shares*, and promised that 'a well-known printing firm paying the full rate of wages' would print his 'go-ahead sporting sheet' soon.[107]

The striking printers themselves were shrewd enough to appreciate the addition to sales that betting intelligence offered. The first edition on 31 August 1920 promised its readers that tomorrow it was to publish 'a first edition giving a programme of the races for the day. This will be on sale in the street at 10.30.' They soon introduced their own tipster 'Master Herbert'. But both papers were killed off by the combined might of Hulton and Extel. Extel decided not to transmit any information to the National Labour Press, and in so doing incurred the following analysis of the situation from the striking printers:

> Arrangements were made yesterday by the Manager of the National Labour Press with the Manchester Representative of the Press Association and Exchange Telegraph Company's joint service for a general news service and racing and sports results. Tonight we are informed, not altogether to our surprise, that no news from this source will be supplied to us . . . It is another example of the power of capitalism, organised to break every attempt made to invade what it presumes to call its prerogatives.[108]

Such bitterness in the light of what was both strike breaking and also, in effect, censorship – the restriction of access to the news facilities of Extel – was also frustrated by the difficulty of entering a local and sporting press dominated by Hulton.

Alongside tipping sheets, there was an increasing number of football coupon papers jostling for the attentions of the punting public, and discussed in chapter 7. The coupon press like the tipster press is impossible to quantify accurately. As A.J. Robertson observed, bookmakers and tipsters themselves were often the proprietors of many papers comprising the football-cum-betting press.[109] This threw into sharp relief the symbiotic relationship between the growth of sport and gambling in the late Victorian and Edwardian years.

The appearance of these cheap tipster and competition sheets was viewed with alarm and distaste by the anti-gambling movement. In 1891 Seton Churchill accused newspapers with tipsters of promoting 'lies of the most barefaced character'.[110] This view of the tipster-as-liar found strong support among critics of gambling. 'Mr. Tipster and his dupes' was a common theme, and some thirty years after Churchill, E.B. Perkins derided 'the bad English covering an utterly stupid pretence at knowledge' which characterised the tipster press.[111] Equally hated were the various 'skill' competitions offered by newspapers to increase their readership. The NAGL decided to take legal action against them, and tried to use the indeterminacy of the lottery laws to their advantage. For example, one of the most famous papers offering 'skill' competitions at the turn of the century was *Sporting Luck*, a weekly owned by the enterprising Stoddart family of Manchester. *Sporting Luck*'s 'Racing Skill Competitions' were involved in an important test case successfully brought by the NAGL in 1900. Proprietors of such papers emphasised the application of skill and judgement, rather than a reliance upon pure luck, which kept gambling competitions on the right side of the law. The NAGL victory brought some sympathy for Mrs Ava Stoddart from the *Times* leader in November of that year over inconsistencies in the interpretation of the Lottery Acts. As Stoddart herself argued, a case brought against her by the NAGL in 1895 had found in her favour, so she continued on the same footing.[112] The downfall of *Sporting Luck* lay in the weekly offer of one free coupon to predict the winning horse in a forthcoming race, followed by a charge of one penny for subsequent coupons used in the paper. The free coupon was taken to infringe the law by inducing people to participate in a lottery. The issue of skill, her salvation in 1895, did not count in this case.[113] The Stoddarts could, however, also rely on the profits of *Football Record*, mentioned below in chapter 7. By January 1914 and the demise of *Sporting Luck* that paper was no longer offering its own competition but ran advertisements for racing coupons issued by a British bookmaker living in Switzerland, one of many who took themselves abroad to be able to accept cash as well as credit bets through the post.

Yet the *Sporting Luck* case was only one of a significant number of legal attempts by the NAGL to crush prize competitions. *The Sun* was fined twenty-five pounds plus costs for promoting a lottery in the form of its 'sun spots' competition.[114] *John Bull*, which was taken over by Horatio Bottomley from 1906, became his mouthpiece not just for the legalisation of off-course ready-money betting but also for the promotion of 'skill', that is, gambling competitions such as 'Bullets' where the readers had to invent witty sentences from suggested clues. *John Bull* was to be subsequently prosecuted a number of times for its so-called 'skill' competitions.[115] The Hulton press was an obvious target for the NAGL. In 1908 John Hawke, honorary secretary of the league, attempted unsuccessfully to prosecute Edward Hulton and Company at Manchester Court House as a 'rogue and vagabond' under the 1823 Lotteries Act for the *Ideas Limericks* paper.[116] Unfortunately, a limited company did not constitute a 'person' under the Act, and this left the field open for bigger promoters.

The NAGL was also prepared to contemplate the enforced opening of · mail addressed to advertising tipsters and to newspapers offering coupon competitions which might contravene the complicated provisions of the Acts of the lottery laws. But as the pro-gambling Marquis of Salisbury stated in a House of Lords debate upon Public Betting, it was impossible to 'stop newspapers from giving information upon a thing which is a matter of public interest, namely, the state of the odds on various races. I cannot conceive a state of society in which that kind of censorship of the press would be tolerated'.[117] Neither the banning of starting price odds in papers nor the opening of post occurred. Yet the · practice by the Postmaster General of opening packages under warrant from the Home Office, to monitor breaches of the Lottery Acts, was to occur later during the heyday of the Irish Hospital Sweepstake from 1930, discussed in chapter 8.

The Edwardian years thus witnessed the beginning of the strong · association of the popular press with gambling, which has continued to the present day. As the NAGL complained to the Royal Commission on Lotteries and Betting in 1932, the newspapers were now firmly associated with famous tipster names, and were still petitioning for readers via gambling competitions. The NAGL singled out the Hulton press, to wit the *Midday Chronicle*, the morning edition of the *Manchester Evening Chronicle* for 'special mention' to the 1932–3 Royal Commission. This came out in fact at 6 am and again at 1 pm, earning itself the colloquial title of the 'One o'clock'.[118] The *Manchester Evening Chronicle* was the most prolific of the more popular local newspapers who began to offer buff and other coloured editions containing purely sporting and betting information, tips, gossip, the past form of horses, and the results of all sporting events. It also offered the 'St. Leger' and 'Brighton Autumn Cup' competitions in September 1932, for prizes of £1,500 and £150

37

respectively. Canon Green was not far wrong when he argued to the 1923 Select Committee on Betting Duty that 'half the evening papers in the North of England would have to close down if it were not for their betting editions'.[119] National newspapers began to follow suit, establishing the famous tipster names in the national press of the twentieth century. The *Daily Mail*'s Robin Goodfellow along with 'Yeoman's Gossip', and 'Dalrymple' were all products of the Edwardian boom in tipping. The *Daily Mirror*'s earliest editions in 1904 contained 'Fancies for Today' from its tipster 'Arrow'. By 1914 the famous 'Bouverie' had been installed. The *Daily Sketch* also took no chances. Its first edition in March 1909 provided tips from the inside knowledge of 'Gimcrack'. The *Daily Express* contained the tipsters 'Scout' and 'Bendex'. The names of these tipsters spoke of inside information from the sporting world of the turf or reflected the names of succesful horses. Even labour and communist newspapers felt compelled to add tipsters. The communist *Daily Worker* for example tried to do without tips as it did not want to be part of a 'gigantic swindle' on the working class. It stopped them in 1930 but they were back again by 1934.[120]

A recent study of newspaper tipsters has shown that a great many of 'expert' tips are wrong, and that, not surprisingly, it is more difficult to pick a winner in the Grand National than the Derby.[121]

Competitions too became staple features of the national press during the Edwardian period. The *Daily Mail* promoted 'Crosswords' prize competitions for prizes of between £500 and £2,500. The *News of the World* had no competitions in the early years of this century but by the early 1920s it offered readers skill-based 'Crosswords' prizes or 'Fashion' competitions for potential rewards of £2,000 or £2,500 respectively. Coupon entry was one shilling and five pence. The *Daily Sketch* tempted readers with 'Fairwords' and 'Crosswords'.

Other newspapers, for example the *Manchester Evening News*, owned by the Nonconformist Russell Allen, tried to resist the dissemination of betting matters. Both Allen and Hulton gave evidence to the 1902 Select Committee of the House of Lords on Betting. Allen blamed newspapers publishing tips for 'holding out deliberate encouragement to people to bet who perhaps otherwise would not'. He felt that papers which carried advertisements for tipsters were peddling lies. He quoted from a letter he had received from 'employers of labour in Manchester' who alleged that slack work and lost production, the demoralisation of apprentices, and the impoverishment of workers, resulted from betting activities on the shop floors of the mills. He felt, as did the employers, that if the 'lower-class' newspapers stopped publishing tips and starting-prices, most people would cease betting.[122] In this, Allen was wrong. As Edward Hulton Junior told the same committee, if the newspapers stopped publishing starting prices bookmakers would simply 'have their own odds; it would not stop betting at all'.[123] He must have enjoyed telling Parliament that Allen and other editors had tried to suppress racing news some years earlier 'but [had] found that the public demanded it, and so they had to restore it again'.[124]

As the sociologist Guy Chapman argued, the rise of the sporting press had begun the 'long line' of 'Ajax' and other tipsters in the national press.[125] The infusion of, firstly, advertising tipsters into the local papers in the mid nineteenth century and, later, the flood of tipping sheets and coupon papers offered by tipsters, bookies and other entrepreneurs were the broader origins of this phenomenon. But in general, the popular press, both local and national, had incorporated tipsters and coupon competitions by or during the 1920s. These years witnessed both the climax and dwindling of the tipster and coupon press as the bigger papers consolidated their market.

VI

From the early Victorian years betting and gambling was designated as both a moral and social problem which offended the legitimate processes of money making and the acquisition of property. Socially, it was felt that whilst the rich might still be allowed to bet privately with luxuries, the poor could not be allowed to endanger their own economic interests, nor to cause a public nuisance, by betting away their scarce resources in cheap gambling houses. The laws passed between 1823 and 1906 attempted to institutionalise this status quo. But they were passed as mass betting took off into self-sustained growth. Their major consequence was a widespread evasion of the law. This failure of intention became increasingly exposed as the commercialised and nationalised mass gambling market flourished. An extended and transmuted 'sporting' interest – the sporting press and the bookmakers – provided the facilities for this market and supplied the most vociferous spokesmen for a permissive betting culture cast in the image of a great sporting nation. This appealed to the rising expectations of an increasingly, though by no means uniformly, wealthy working class, and defeated the intentions of an ill-conceived law. The voice of the punters, however, was evident in actions rather than words. They signalled their disapproval of the laws by continuing to bet regardless of police intervention. The social network which made this possible, and the nature of the betting itself, are the subject of the next chapter.

Notes

1 *Royal Commission on Gambling*, 1978, Report, Vol. 1, paras 12.9–12.35, pp. 164–71.
2 Peter Arnold, *The Encyclopedia of Gambling*, 1978, p. 90.
3 This discussion is based on T. R. Gourvish, *The Government and the Business of Gambling: State Lotteries in Britain, 1750–1826*, given at the Institute of Historical Research, 23 February 1989. Robert Woodhall, 'The British State Lotteries', *History Today*, July 1964.
4 *SC 1808*, First Report, Cmd 182, p. 7.
5 *Ibid.*, Minutes of Evidence (hereafter Minutes) Appendix A, pp. 41–3.
6 *Ibid.*, Minutes, p. 67.
7 *Ibid.*, Minutes, pp. 31–2.
8 *Ibid.*, Minutes, p. 11.
9 *Ibid.*, Minutes, p. 12. In *The Wealth of Nations*, Smith argued that a lottery over-valued the 'vain hope of gaining some of the great prizes' and undervalued 'the chance of loss', 1982, p. 210 (first published 1776).
10 D. E. D. Beales, *The Political Parties of the Nineteenth Century*, 1971, p. 7.
11 James Mott, 'Popular Gambling from the Collapse of the State Lotteries to the Rise of the Football Pools', 1975, p. 2.
12 Robert W. Malcolmson, *Popular Recreations in English Society 1700–1850*, Cambridge, 1973, pp. 42–3; 49–50. Robert Poole, 'Leisure in Bolton 1750–1900' unpublished dissertation, 1982, pp. 19–22, pp. 21, 28–30; held at Bolton Local History Library.
13 Cited in John Ashton, *A History of Gambling in England*, 1898, pp. 209–10.
14 *Bell's Life in London*, 5 January 1840.
15 Dennis Brailsford, *Sport and Society: From Elizabeth to Anne*, 1969, p. 216.
16 William Hazlitt, 'The Fight', in *Selected Writings*, 1985, pp. 78–97 (first published 1821).
17 Kellow Chesney, *The Victorian Underworld*, 1982, pp. 313–30.
18 *Bell's Life in London*, 17 January 1830; 24 January 1830.
19 Hazlitt, *op. cit.*, p. 321.
20 Johnson, *op. cit.*
21 Mott, *op. cit.*, pp. 19–21 Hugh Cunningham, *Leisure in the Industrial Revolution*, 1980, pp. 111–13.
22 Charles Booth, *Life and Labour of the People in London*, Third Series, *Religious Influences*, Vol. 2, 1902, p. 246.
23 Brailsford, *op. cit.*, p. 213.
24 Roger Mortimer, *The Jockey Club*, 1958, *passim*.
25 Anthony Trollope, *British Sports and Pastimes*, 1868, p. See also chapter 5, below.
26 Benjamin Disraeli, *Sybil,* p. 6, 1986 (first published 1845).
27 Discussed below, chapter 5, p. 109.
28 *SC 1844*, Minutes, qu. 2857, p. 184.
29 Harold Perkin, *The Origins of Modern English Society*, 1978, p. 277.

30 Brian Harrison, *Drink and the Victorians*, 1971, p. 318.
31 *PP 1844, III (219)* p. 8, Clause 17.
32 *SC 1844*, Report, p. iv.
33 E. C. Devereaux, 'Gambling', the *International Encyclopedia of the Social Sciences*, Vol. 6, 1968, p. 56.
34 *SC 1844*, Minutes, qu. 869, p. 75.
35 *Ibid.*, para. 2562, p. 168.
36 John Carroll, *Breakout From the Crystal Palace*, 1974, pp. 158–9.
37 *SC 1844*, Minutes, qu. 593, p. 46.
38 *Porcupine*, 17 May 1862.
39 W. E. Bear, 'Market Gambling', *Contemporary Review*, Vol. LXV, June 1894, pp. 781–94. George Eliot saw no difference between the results of such activity and pure gambling. She wrote that 'in gambling, for example, whether of the business or holiday sort, a man who has the strength of mind to leave off when he has only ruined others is a reformed character', *Daniel Deronda*, 1988, p. 125 (first published 1876).
40 *Porcupine*, 27 March 1875.
41 Johan Huizinga, *Homo Ludens: A Study of the Play Element in Culture*, 1949, p. 52.
42 E. B. Perkins, *The Problem of Gambling*, 1919, p. 65.
43 *HC Debs*, 11 July, 1853, col. 87.
44 *PP 1852–3, I (761)* , p. 135.
45 *Criminal and Miscellaneous Statistical Returns of the Manchester Police, 1843 to 1899*, held at Manchester Local History Library.
46 *HC Debs*, 11 July 1853, cols. 87–8.
47 Wray Vamplew, *The Turf*, 1976, p. 205.
48 *Free Lance*, 25 May 1867, p. 179. In 1852 Dickens described tobacconists in London which were really betting shops: *Household Words*, 'Betting Shops', 26 June 1852, pp. 333–4.
49 Hugh Shimmin, *op. cit.*, 1856, pp. 98–9.
50 J. M. Chenery, *The Law and Practice of Booking, Betting, Gaming and Lotteries*, 1963, p. 15.
51 *SC (Lords), 1902*, Report, para. 20, p. 457.
52 *Porcupine*, 10 March 1877.
53 *Porcupine, ibid.*; 31 March 1877.
54 *Liverpool Review*, 20 December 1884; 13 December 1884; 15 November 1884.
55 *Manchester Evening News*, 20 and 21 May 1885.
56 Booth, *op. cit.*, Vol. 2, p. 88. See also Vol. 1 pp. 89–90 and Vol. 5, p. 164.
57 Booth, *ibid.*, First Series, *Poverty*, Vol. 1, 1889, p. 94.
58 Ben Weinreb and Christopher Hibbert, *The Encyclopedia of London* 1986, p. 961.
59 Samuel Johnson, *op. cit.*
60 John Bee, *Sportsmans' Slang: A New Dictionary of Terms Used in the Affairs of the Turf* (&c.), 1825, pp. 111–12; Roger Longrigg, *The Turf*, 1975, text accompanying plates 141, 142 and 143.
61 Charles Sidney, *The Art of Legging*, 1977, p. 21.
62 *Ibid.*, p. 52 *et seq.*
63 The *Sporting Chronicle*, 22 April 1926, p. 1, contains advertisements for these firms, and others.
64 David C. Itskovitz, 'Victorian Bookmakers and their Customers', *Victorian Studies*, Vol. 32, No. 1, 1988, p. 25.

65 Dyke Wilkinson, *A Wasted Life*, 1902, pp. 32–6.
66 John Benson, *The Penny Capitalists*, 1983, p. 75.
67 E. J. Hobsbawm, *Industry and Empire*, 1979, pp. 162–3.
68 See R. E. Pahl, *Divisions of Labour*, 1983, *passim*.
69 *Free Lance*, 22 February 1868.
70 Canon Horsley, *How Criminals are Made and Prevented*, 1919, p. 169; *Free Lance*, 25 May 1867. *Porcupine*, 10 March 1877.
71 *Ibid.*, p. 38.
72 *SC 1901* pp. 356–7.
73 James Greenwood, *The Seven Curses of London*, 1985, p. 242 (first published 1869).
74 J. M. Scott, *Extel 100: A Centenary History of the Exchange Telegraph Company*, 1972, pp. 13–30.
75 *SC 1902*, Report, para. 7, p. 449.
76 Tony Mason, 'Sporting News, 1860–1914', in Michael Harris and Alan Lee (eds), *The Press in English Society from the Seventeenth to the Nineteenth Centuries*, 1986, pp. 170–1.
77 Mason, *ibid.*, p. 181.
78 *Bulletin* of NAGL, Vol 1, No. 7 1893, p. 1.
79 SC 1923, Minutes, qu. 601, p. 396; John Hawke, *The Extent of Gambling*, in B. S. Rowntree (ed.), *Betting and Gambling*, 1905, p. 8.
80 Beatrice Potter, 'The Docks', in Booth, *op. cit.*, *Poverty*, Vol. 4, pp. 31–2.
81 A copy of one such Pledge, signed in 1893, is kept at Manchester Local History Library.
82 *Times*, 14 November 1906.
83 John Burns, *Brains Better than Bets or Beer*, 1902; Will Crooks, *Working Men and Gambling*, 1906.
84 Stephen G. Jones, 'The British Labour Movement and Working Class Leisure, 1918–1939', unpublished Ph.D thesis, University of Manchester, 1981, pp. 218–28. Ross McKibbin, *op. cit.*, pp. 172–3, 176.
85 Ramsay MacDonald, 'Gambling and Citizenship', in B. S. Rowntree (ed.), *Betting and Gambling: A National Evil* 1905, p. 120.
86 David Dixon, 'Class Law: The Street Betting Act of 1906', *International Journal of the Sociology of Law*, 8, 1980, pp. 103–9.
87 Watch Committee Minutes, 4 December 1902, the Police Museum, Newton Street, Manchester. My italics.
88 *SC 1902*, Minutes, qu. 152–3, p. 9.
89 Peacock gave testimony to four parliamentary enquiries in 1902, 1908, 1918 and 1923.
90 Watch Committee Minutes, Manchester, 1906. Letter, 27 October 1906.
91 Julian Symons, *Horatio Bottomley*, 1955, p. 191.
92 T. H. Dey, *Betting in Excelsis*, 1908, *passim*.
93 *Sporting Life*, 9 October, 1906.
94 *Sporting Life*, 10 October 1906, p. 4.
95 Lady Bell, *At the Works*, 1985, p. 266 (first published 1907).
96 C. F. G. Masterman, *The Condition of England*, 1909, p. 83.
97 *Free Lance*, 20 May 1871.
98 *SC 1902*, Report, para. 5, p. 449.
99 A. J. Robertson, 'Football Betting', *Transactions of the Liverpool Economic and Statistical Society*, 1907, p. 3.
100 This discussion of the tipster and coupon press is based on Frederick Leary's

History of the Manchester Periodical Press, Vol. 4, 1880–1893, held at the Archives department at Manchester Central Library, and on the Newspaper Library Catalogue at Colindale, North London.

101 *Braddocks Guide to Horse Race Selection*, 1987. In the preface he writes of punters and bookmakers 'Never have so many owed so much to so few.'

102 Leary, *op. cit.*, p. 541.

103 A. Dick Luckman, *Sharps, Flats and Gamblers*, 1914, p. 224.

104 John McGuigan, *A Trainer's Memories*, in J. Fairfax Blakeborough (ed.), 1946, p. 158.

105 Symons, *op. cit.*, p. 189.

106 T. H. Dey, *Leaves From a Bookmakers' Book*, 1931, pp. 26–7.

107 *Evening Newspaper*, 10 September 1920.

108 *Evening Newspaper*, 2 September 1920.

109 Robertson, *op. cit.*, pp. 3–4. Football coupon betting is discussed in chapter 7, below.

110 Hugh Seton Churchill, *Betting and Gambling*, 1894, pp. 119–20.

111 E. B. Perkins, *The Problem of Gambling*, 1919, p. 77.

112 *Times*, 23 November 1900, cited in *Sporting Luck*, 30 November 1900.

113 *RC 1949–51*, Home Office Memo, para. 111, p. 10.

114 *Bolton Evening News* 7 June 1901.

115 Julian Symons, *op. cit.*, p. 141.

116 *Justice of the Peace*, 29 May 1909.

117 *HL Debs*, 20 May 1901, cols 553–4.

118 *RC 1932–33*, Appendix by NAGL pp. 196–8.

119 *SC 1923* Minutes, qu. 6800, p. 396.

120 Stephen Jones, *op. cit.*, p. 266.

121 Margaret Miers, 'Winning Selections: Reporter's Tips for the National and the Derby', *Society for the Study of Gambling Newsletter*, No. 17, July 1990, pp. 25–7.

122 *SC 1902*, Minutes, qu. 1588–9, p. 75; qu. 1612–23, p. 76; qu. 1650–1, p. 77.

123 *Ibid.*, Minutes, qu. 2536, p. 119.

124 *Ibid.*, Minutes, qu. 2572, p. 120.

125 Guy Chapman, *Culture and Survival*, 1940, p. 115.

Chapter 3
Street betting, *c.* 1906–1961

This chapter looks at the day-to-day activity of organised illegal off-course ready-money betting before the introduction of Licensed Betting Offices in 1961. The social and economic significance of street betting is examined and, finally, the reasons for and the immediate results of legalisation are discussed.

I

The network of off-course betting on horses came into full existence in the second half of the nineteenth century, as described in the previous chapter. This was made up of the street bookmaker (colloquially known as the bookie), his agents (the 'runners', touts and look-outs) and the punters. The betting transaction took place in a number of ways, and varied according to local custom and the size of the bookmakers' operations. The smallest bookmakers usually did business from a street pitch, in an entry or semi-conspicuous spot where 'he would make it known he would take bets'.[1] People would either take their bets directly to the bookmaker or his runner, who usually operated from a nearby house, or the bookie's runners would come and collect bets from the pubs, clubs, houses and workplaces on behalf of the bookmaker. The bookmaker usually had an agent in every local mill or workshop. Thus the term 'street betting' did not convey the whole picture.

In the north west, most appear to have worked from the front or back room of a house in a working-class district which was guarded by look-outs or 'dogger-outs' who warned by signalling of potential police raids. In Liverpool this was often called 'keeping nicks' or 'dousing'. Many houses, as we will see, were customised, or adapted to allow bets to be slipped quickly and quietly through a back window or a special flap. The social role of the public house made it a centre for the collection and paying out of bets, despite the possibility of a publican losing his or her licence. Canon Green stated that the police knew of only six public houses in Salford in the early 1920s 'where betting was not prevalent' and, because one licensed victualler refused to have betting on his premises, 'the man failed'.[2]

Contemporaries felt that gambling was more of a problem in the north west, especially Manchester, than elsewhere. To the 1923 Select Committee, for example, both a major bookmaker and Canon Green testified that betting was 'more rife' in Manchester.[3] Police statistics confirmed this impression, for it could only be an impression due to the lack of any hard statistical evidence on betting turnover, locally or nationally. The counties of London, Lancashire and, some way behind, Yorkshire, had the highest rates of convictions for 'Betting and Gaming' punishable under the 1853 and 1906 Acts. It is perhaps no accident that the National Anti-Gambling League (NAGL) had its English offices in Westminster, Manchester and York. Within Lancashire, Manchester overtook Liverpool after the 1906 Act to take top place in the county's convictions table. Thus in 1911, the peak year for betting offences in the two cities before 1914, the Manchester police took in 387 bookmakers or bookmakers' agents compared to 190 in Liverpool. During the 1930s, this figure rose to a peak of 1,034 in Manchester in 1932 (with a police district population of 766,300 in the mid 1930s) compared to 322 street betting convictions in Liverpool (with a bigger police district of 856,000).[4] In Salford, a city of 223,000 people in the mid 1930s, convictions were consistently higher than for towns of comparable size. In 1934, for example, the Salford courts made 414 convictions under the 1906 Street Betting Act compared to fifty-three in Newcastle.[5] Bolton, with a police district of 177,000 in the mid 1930s, was more typical nationally. Yearly prosecutions were often in single figures, and in its peak years of 1912 and 1933 they numbered ninety-nine and eighty-three respectively.[6]

Why were the figures so high in Manchester and Salford? It may have been a consequence of anti-gambling policemen there. In the 1880s and '90s, Detective Jerome Caminada had tried to suppress gambling by raiding gambling clubs and dealing with racecourse thieves and cheats.[7] From 1900 the new Chief Constable of Manchester, Robert Peacock, made clear his personal dislike of gambling in testimony to parliamentary enquiries. Moreover, the vigilance of the Manchester police was probably heightened by the presence of the north western office of the NAGL, at the Produce Exchange, which organised highly publicised meetings in the area. The police also had Canon Peter Green of Greengate, Salford, on their doorstep. He was perhaps the foremost national critic of gambling from the late Edwardian years to the 1930s.[8]

Green pilloried the authorities at public meetings for insufficient action against gambling, wrote urgently on the subject in tract and newspaper column, contributing regularly to the *Manchester Guardian* under the pseudonym 'Artifex'. Green made country-wide generalisations from his local anti-gambling activities. For example, he claimed to the 1923 parliamentary enquiry that gambling reduced the national output by 'at least twenty per cent per annum'. He based this unscientific estimate on the worried testimony of Lancashire mill and mine owners and foremen. He was fearful that workers were restless and unproductive on big race days. Signal boxes went unmanned and coal unmined.[9] Green also informed the 1923 Select Committee that it was common for machine operatives in Lancashire to ignore their work and talk of gambling, some even 'deliberately setting their machine tools one sixty-fourth of an inch from the job so that they can talk gambling and there was no chance of a mistake whilst they debated'.[10] The Report of the Committee argued from Green's evidence that there was 'scarcely a works in the country employing more than twenty workmen where there (was) not a bookmaker's agent'.[11]

Fears over lost production, and the related concern for the physical and mental well-being of Lancashire's industrial working class, were an important contemporary issue. They took on an added urgency during the first world war, when munitions production was central to the war effort. Another prominent Anglican, Bishop Welldon, the Dean of Manchester and Secretary of the Manchester Branch of the NAGL, claimed that gambling at local munitions works during the first world war was the height of selfish greed whilst thousands of British men were killed every week in the trenches.[12] The chief constable shared such views. He felt that the munitions workers, enriched by overtime and higher rates of pay, were 'extravagant'. He told tales to parliament in 1918 of workers paying to enter the more expensive enclosures at the Manchester Races, and of one workman who bought a piano for eighty pounds and 'because it was such a splendid piece of furniture', bought another one for the opposite side of the room.[13] Peacock claimed his views were supported by 'the protectors of the morals of Manchester', the Watch Committee. This, in 1918, was composed of magistrates, businessmen and local councillors, two of whom were Labour Members.

The anti-gambling lobby was particularly shocked at the spectre of women and children betting. Both were seen as particularly vulnerable to gambling, either to its temptation or as the victims of betting men. As oral testimony and autobiography shows, there were certainly cases of husbands gambling away the housekeeping money. This led not just to financial hardship for the family, but to lives made miserable by bad tempered husbands or fathers. Such cases put many people off gambling for life.[14] Women at work were also thought to be in danger. Canon Green told a meeting of the National Union of Women Workers in Manchester in 1913 that mill girls and women were 'forced to bet' by foremen.[15] Some parents allowed their children to take bets to the bookmaker or his runner, an aspect which worried many social workers and anti-gambling campaigners who were concerned that the habit of betting was being learned amongst the young by example and encouragement.[16] Female gambling was seen as proof of the great increase of betting in general. Green claimed that while gambling had grown by 50 per cent among men since 1895, it had increased 'fifty-fold amongst women'.[17] He felt that 'a betting woman was worse than a betting man' because she was setting a bad example to her children.[18] In a more extreme vein, a missionary from the Manchester City Mission claimed that mothers were pawning their childrens' clothes to bet.[19] During the Edwardian years and into the 1920s, anti-gamblers were convinced that the runner, or the 'back door tout', was a major cause of the increase of gambling amongst women.[20] In the 1920s, social workers for the Liverpool Council for Voluntary Aid (LCVA) estimated that in one poor district of Merseyside in the 1920s over 50 per cent of women 'have the betting habit'.[21]

Yet in general women betted less regularly and for smaller amounts than men, usually on the big classic races such as the Derby and the Grand National. A possible reason was that to be seen to frequent the bookmaker's house might have impeded some women's claim to respectability.[22] More importantly, perhaps, they were forced to balance the household budget as best they could, leaving them little money for a flutter.[23] In consequence, the most common bets for women appear to have been penny, twopenny, threepenny and sixpenny singles and doubles.[24] For the post-war years, the sociologist Bernice Martin remembers more occasional betting amongst her female neighbours in Lancashire. The social survey of betting published in 1951 confirmed that women during the 1940s and early 1950s liked a little flutter on the big races of the year. The Derby, betted upon by 31 per cent of the female sample was the most popular race, followed by the Grand National at 25 per cent and dropping to 11 per cent or less for other major races.[25] Yet some women liked to gamble frequently and seemed not bothered about so-called respectability. Rowntree and Lavers found a factory worker who bet most days with the bookmaker's runner and thought the excitement she got 'was cheap at the price'.[26]

In general, oral evidence from before the first world war to the 1930s shows that the stake money varied from one penny, two pence, three penny singles, doubles and trebles to bets for sixpence, a shilling, two shillings, two shillings and sixpence and sometimes above this. This does not contradict the sizes of the betting slips seized by the police and presented to parliamentary enquiries. The Chief Constable of Liverpool told the 1923 enquiry that most bets were between sixpence and two shillings and sixpence.[27]

The stake money itself was wrapped up in little slips of paper bearing a nom de plume to guarantee anonymity to the punter in the event of a police raid. Noms de plume, like nicknames, personalised the punter, for example 'Vick' the root of the surname Vickerman, or 'E. A. Ash', the alias of Jack Ashley's mother.[28] The police, however, almost always aimed at the bookmaker or his agent. In Lancashire at least, apprehensions of punters rarely occurred. As we will see, these raids were often arranged between the police and the bookmakers but genuine raids did occur, often stimulated by complaints or tip-offs from anti-gambling neighbours. The following newspaper report illustrates the nature and extent of street bookmaking in Bootle in 1915, and the difficulties involved in the operation of a genuine raid of a bookmaker's house:

Defendant had been engaged in betting at his house for a considerable time, but the premises were so well guarded by scouts that it was only the other day that Det. Serg. Bell, in company with Dets. Higgins and Rushton, effected an entrance. The house had a back entrance, approached by a passage, and the procedure had been for people making bets to enter by the rear and hand in bets to Defendant through a window which had been raised eighteen inches.

In consequence of complaints, the police kept the house under observation on October 27th and 28th. During the four hours 11 a.m. to 3 p.m. on the former date, the following persons entered and left by the back way: 139 men, eighty five women, forty four children total 268, many of them carrying slips of paper in their hands. By the front door, during the same hours eighteen men, ten women and three young girls and three young boys (aged between ten and fourteen) entered.

When the house was searched, 732 betting slips relating to the previous day were discovered. These slips represented 1,741 bets, amounting to £244 twelve shillings, the items ranging from three pence to six pounds. (Bench fined Defendant £100 and four pounds costs).[29]

A number of oral respondents have provided similar accounts of street betting at a nearby bookmakers' house. Walter M., speaking of Hulme, Manchester in the 1930s, said that bookmakers 'all lived in the houses and betted from the houses'. Alex M. of Salford remembered:

> The 'office' was in the rear room of a terraced house in each case, complete with a telephone and 'blower' . . . A simple cover over a back yard led to a door with a 'window' cut in, this window was just a hole with a removable shutter/cover and it had a small shelf on the inside. Bets were placed by knocking on the shelter if not open, and handing in the bet through the opening . . . look-outs ('dogger outs') were placed at strategic points to warn of police activities, these were usually assisted by enthusiastic local youngsters. The bookie usually had a 'mug' whose main job was to be caught by the police with nominal evidence only.[30]

This reference to the 'blower' referred to the London and Provincial Sporting News Agency's telephone service, established in 1929, which further encouraged bookmakers to set up operations indoors.[31] This relayed the odds formulated at the courses to the agency, from whence they were was phoned on a special line to the bookmaker subscribers, many of whom were running early betting shops in all but name.

Yet oral evidence, social surveys and contemporary newspaper reports for other parts of England illustrate that the street-betting arrangement varied from place to place.[32] In London, for example, bookmakers and their runners took bets more often in-the-street than in the north west or midlands. The metropolitan equivalent of the mug was known as the 'percher', and the police were well aware that bookmakers frequently put up such characters in the street to protect the real staff.[33]

Runners, as this point suggests, were vital to the day-to-day business of street betting. Many bookmakers, like the 'notorious Sam Grundy' in Walter Greenwood's *Love on the Dole*, had often moved away from where they first took bets to pleasant suburban districts, using a runner's house as a base. The runner also collected bets for those who were unable to get to the house. As well as receiving bets from an outdoor pitch in entries or alleyways, he or she would go to collect bets from pubs and workplaces. Dinner-time, before the afternoon's racing, was when most transactions took place, as a worker for Mass Observation noted:

> Midday, vault. The bookies runner comes in and has argument with the landlady about her yesterday's doubles. Betting slips and newspapers are produced. She then makes bets on day's races. The runner has a gill of mild.[34]

Tom M. of Whittle-le-Woods near Chorley, had a round of pubs from which he had to collect the bets in time for the 'off':

> Every pub in this village . . . the people used to hand the bets to the landlord, and I used to peddle in on me bike to see the right amount were backed, peddle off to the next pub and take the bets for 'em because there was no other way to get their bets on.[35]

The workplace was central to dinner-time betting and running. Gambling at work, whether office or machine-shop, mine or mill, reflected the dovetailing of work and leisure in areas where work and home were all but next door to each other, and in many cases the runner made this possible.

Many bookmakers had agents in factories who whilst employed there would take bets for the bookie or his runner. This was usually accomplished, certainly from the 1920s, by the use of the clock bag, a piece of equipment designed to eliminate cheating and ensure the safe facilitation of the bets to the bookmaker before the race. The clock bag was a canvas bag attached to an automatic clock which operated a time lock at the mouth of the bag. This clock was set to close the bag at the exact time of the first race of the day, when it would then snap shut and receive no more bets. The runner – in theory – could receive no more bets. The bookmaker had the key. The runner deposited the bag with the bookmaker as soon as possible after the race had started. Some runners assisted in the reckoning up or settling of the bets. Paying out took place that evening or the next day. Runners sometimes kept the names of the punters in a little notebook or diary, or if it was only a small round, committed the names of the punters and their nom de plumes to memory. A good memory was a qualification for the job.[36]

Not all runners were men. In 1919 the anti-gambler E. B. Perkins blamed female agents and back-door touts for the 'extraordinary increase of gambling amongst women' in the industrial areas.[37] Ethel Kay, of Harpurhey, began by taking bets for her husband to the bookmakers. She then began to collect bets as a favour for other relatives and neighbours, both male and female, until the bookmaker asked her to 'keep it up and put her on a fixed commission'.[38] As Joe Kay recalled, his mother had been illiterate until then but 'taking the growing number of bets and dealing with the neighbours' winnings did, to tell the truth, teach her to read and write'.[39] This supports Robert Roberts's claim that many ill-educated Salford punters made a breakthrough to literacy by studying the racing and sporting news in the *One o'clock*.[40]

A number of people have said that the bookmakers and their agents participated in the social and economic life of the community. The runner often devolved these extra-bookmaking activities, lending money, allowing bets 'on the strap' (on credit) and paying out towards charities, raffles, community trips and such events. For example, Joe K., remembering the Scotland Road area of Liverpool from the 1930s wrote that runners 'were genial characters who were to the forefront in helping people out in less fortunate circumstances.' Joe M. of St Helens said the bookie and his runners were 'very generous' and would often lend money to purchase food.[41]

Such generosity was not always based purely on friendliness. The runner also needed to maintain a standing with the punters in the neighbourhood. One Bethnal Green runner in the 1930s accepted payments of fish and fruit from the local market porters instead of the stake money proper. These were punters who already owed for strap bets and as he told his sister, 'If I don't do it, May, they're gonna go to somebody else then I'll never get my twenty [pounds] back.'[42]

Mass Observations' emphasis on the popularity of the runner – for example, it was customary for winning punters to give the runner the stake money – was at odds with that given by Robert Roberts for Edwardian Salford who writes that runners were perceived to be 'at the bottom of the social pyramid' along with 'idlers, part-time beggars and petty thieves'.[43] Yet it might be argued that Roberts over-emphasises the lowly disreputable character of the runner, as of the bookmaker, a result of the influence of his shopkeeper mothers' emphasis on self-improvement. The distaste he held for gambling was strongly in evidence in both *The Classic Slum* and *A Ragged Schooling*. Yet for many punters the runner was of the same class and economic circumstances as they, but had hit upon bad times. Many punters became runners in • periods of irregular employment or unemployment, and were thus usually supplementing poor relief or, from 1929, the Public Assistance allowance. The Pilgrim Trust emphasised this for Liverpool between the wars. George Hewins – The Dillen – ran bets for 'Brummagen Richard' in Stratford-Upon-Avon in the 1930s whilst unemployed. A number of ex-punters had become runners for the same reason during the 1920s and 1930s. Some had relatives who were runners for a while.[44]

A hard working runner with a big round could probably earn a substantial amount outside of formal employment. Oral evidence for different parts of England confirmed the statement of a street bookmaker from Plaistow, East London, to the Willink Commission that pay for runners had been one shilling and sixpence in the pound since the 1930s.[45] There were exceptions, however. E. W. Bakke, an American social observer of inter-war Britain, found one runner who was paid twelve pounds a week by his employer.[46]

The runner and his or her employer, but more usually the 'dummy' or 'mug', were the targets for the police strategy against betting. The bookmaker, furthermore, always paid the fine, which from 1907 was ten pounds for a first offence, fifty pounds for a second offence and a hundred pounds or three months jail for a third and repeated offences. Regular arrests were an unwanted interruption which was bad for trade. This was where the mug was useful. He was usually unemployed or a pensioner whom the bookie had offered a financial reward to stand in for the runner to be arrested. If a genuine police raid occurred, however, runners would of course try to escape. In this they often received help from the locals. For Middlesbrough in 1907, Lady Bell noted that a policeman might watch 'as much as he likes' but 'most of the cottages have back doors and a way out into a back street, and nothing is easier than to go in at one door and out at the other'.[47] A Salford woman gave a vivid account of how this happened:

> They had what they called a runner, that was all mi father could do, well they were lookin' out for the police, 'cos the police were on every so often, they'd all shout 'Charlie they're here', well everybody opened their doors then and whoever was the runner like he shouted to the other feller to come in, so they had an idea when they were coming . . . I were only a little kid, soon as they said they were coming everybody opened their doors and the runner ran through and you locked your gate, and they ran through to the house on the other side.[48]

Runners tried to destroy the evidence too, sometimes by flushing slips down the toilet.[49] Unlucky runners who were caught, and who were on the dole, faced the possibility of losing their unemployment allowance, as it was police practice to inform the Board of Guardians if a runner was caught with unemployment cards. Yet the police said they came across few cases of this,[50] as the bookmaker, now to be discussed, was often a better provider than the Board of Guardians or the Public Assistance Committee.

II

Official bookmakers' organisations protested too loudly that they were engaged only in legal credit betting, and had little or no connection with the bookmakers in the streets.[51] Yet the view of a clear-cut dichotomy between legal credit and illegal unrespectable cash bookmakers glossed over the sizeable middling strata of combined credit and cash • bookmakers. Charles Cautley, the erudite chairman of the 1923 Select Committee on Betting Duty, soon got to the bottom of it when questioning a credit bookmaker.

We have been told there are some men who do both credit betting and street bookmaking, but they are very few? Yes they are. You agree to that? Yes. I know quite a lot who do that. I know quite a lot of credit men who have agents in the streets. Well, it is not so few as we have been led to understand? No.[52]

Autobiographies by wealthier bookmakers clearly indicate that some of • them were involved in illegal cash betting. T. H. Dey, the London bookmaker, who also had an office in Middelburg, Holland, in the Edwardian years, built up a 'flourishing cash connection' in the streets of London as well as accepting ready-money bets by post at his Dutch base. In the later Victorian years, Dyke Wilkinson, an owner of a small and profitable jewellery manufactory in Birmingham, began on-course bookmaking at Walsall Races as an extension of his compulsive gambling and his affection for the spectacle of the races. After some mishaps he expanded his operations to an on- and off-course credit and ready-money trade.[53] Dey, who became a wealthy bookmaker, had begun his career as a bookmakers' clerk before poaching some of his employers' clients and setting up business himself during the 1890s.[54] Jack Hamer of Bolton took both cash and credit, and so did Tom M.'s employer in Chorley.[55]

There is, unfortunately, little documentary evidence for the vast majority of small operators. As Benson points out, 'penny capitalists' rarely kept records, and those who did 'are probably even more untypical than those rescued from larger business enterprises'.[56] This is particularly true of illegal street bookmakers, who did not keep records that could have been used as evidence against them in court.

In the nineteenth and earlier twentieth centuries, many costermongers began as bookmakers, using any extra capital they possessed to take a few small bets amongst friends in the street or at a racecourse or to hold the bank in card and coin games.[57] Their irregular work gave rise to surfeits and deficits of cash, and bookmaking offered a potential way of breaking the cycle. Yet oral evidence for the twentieth century confirms Bensons' suggestion that many bookmakers started out from the security of a regular job, often by organising sweeps or running small books for their workmates during the lunch hour before racing began. In closer-knit communities, many kept their original occupation whilst running a book for their friends and workmates. A miner from County Durham recalled that all the bookmakers he knew 'were miners, and they worked foreshift twelve midnight until eight a.m. so that they could take the bets through the day'.[58] During the 1950s, sociologists found that the ambition of many miners to become bookmakers stemmed from the physical uncertainty of and solidarities generated by their work which was favourable to a male culture of consolation based on beer and betting.[59] Barbers and other shopkeepers were well placed both socially and economically in working-class areas to run their own profitable sideline in bookmaking. In Southampton from the late 1940s a fish and chip shop owner ran a lucrative local trade in bookmaking, both jobs prompting such jokes as 'the shop for a win or a plaice'.[60] Jack Hamer, who became a successful local bookmaker in Bolton from the early 1920s, had been a window cleaner on the railways before 1914 before starting a 'penny book' amongst his workmates.[61] In London in 1903, the Irishman Christopher Fisher, a compositor, left his trade to begin bookmaking in Clerkenwell with his unemployed brother. They initially relied upon the capital he had saved from his work in the printing industry,[62] and also perhaps upon the Irish community in London, as in Liverpool, who were sometimes more inclined to make bets with a fellow countryman.[63] Members of other immigrant groups turned to bookmaking as a potentially profitable livelihood in a foreign country. Joe Coral, for example, a Polish Jew, came to Dalston in East London in 1912. He realised soon enough that 'the English will always back their fancy' and that the stake money usually stopped with the bookmakers. After a short spell as a runner he started his own ready-money business, and by the 1960s his shops were all over London.[64]

Unemployment and redundancy led a number of working-class self-helpers to begin bookmaking, as the Pilgrim Trust found in Liverpool during the 1930s: 'Some have tried running "books" of their own, a more risky undertaking than the taking of betting slips for established firms, by which means, to judge from the sample, a substantial number of men supplement their unemployment allowance.'[65] As Chinn notes, the occupation of bookmaking was egalitarian in the sense that no qualifications were needed in order to enter it.[66] But this view should be qualified by the consideration that the more money an aspiring bookmaker possessed, the better were his chances of making even more.

A run of wins by the favourites, those horses where the odds are shorter because they have been heavily backed, could seriously deplete a bookmakers' capital by the demand on outgoings. For Barnsley in the post-war years one punter remembered that poorer bookmakers were more vulnerable in this situation: 'The smaller bookies used to dread the Royal Ascot meeting with such long prices in the betting. A lucky punter with a few pounds could put them out of business.'[67] The wealthier T. H. Dey, however, 'plodded along for some time' until a rank outsider won the Derby, providing Dey with a couple of hundred pounds of unsuccessful stakes on the favourite, and 'the heart to launch out still further'.[68]

Another important consideration for a would-be bookmaker was the nature and extent of the established local trade. At the outset the new bookmaker did not possess the support of, and often rivalled, the network of existing bookmakers who helped each other by accepting bets which were 'laid-off', that is, devolved by one bookie to another to offload some of the expense in the event of a pay-out. The aforementioned Irish bookmaker in East London, for example, who set up his pitch 'without any communication with any other bookmaker' could not engage in laying-off.[69] This problem must have confronted many beginners. The wealthier local bookmakers may have refused to accept lay-off bets from the smaller operators, confirming and per- petuating their lower economic status. More directly, the established or the bigger operators were in a more favourable position in the struggle to offer the most attractive odds to the punters. Most bookmakers had a top limit as to what they would offer, which varied according to their personal wealth. For the Scotland Road area of Liverpool during the 1930s, Joe K. stated that the 'maximum one could win regardless of the amount staked was usually around three pounds ten shillings.[70] A Glasgow bookmaker told the 1923 enquiry that he originally had a ceiling of five pounds, but as he grew more successful he could offer bigger winnings.[71] But the most effective way to deal with competition was through violence or the threat of it.

The race-gang warfare of the 1920s was in large part based on the struggle to monopolise pitches both on and off the racecourse. The intimidation of bookmakers and their agents took the form of protection, which in a similar way as the mob in Prohibition America, meant that a bookmaker was blackmailed into paying for his own protection against his aggressors. If he refused to pay he was beaten up or cut up or worse. One bookmaker talking of the difficulties of starting out on the courses stated that 'in addition to the running expenses (which included clerk's fees and their fares) there was the protection money you had to pay too if you didn't want to be beaten up and have your stand wrecked'. He also remembered an associate who 'got beaten up for not going into a protection racket'. Jack Spot, 'the king' of the London bookmakers during the mid 1950s, was not averse to some extra-competitive activities.[72]

A literary insight into petty bookmaker violence both on and off the racecourse is given in Brighton Rock, Graham Greene's 1930s novel about the small-time criminal fraternity in Brighton. This was made subsequently into a film by the Boulting Brothers in 1947. The psychopathic and sexually frustrated teenage gang leader 'Pinky' manipulates a protection racket both on and off the course by carving up rival bookmakers and touts. During the 1920s, one of Arthur Harding's many illegal and violent occupations was to defend Hymie Davis 'the big Aldgate bookmaker' from the notorious Italian mob the Darby-Sabini gang.[73] In Sheffield between the wars a number of bookmakers involved in organising the highly profitable pitch-and-toss gaming rings employed henchmen not only to keep watch for the police but also to intimidate and assault other bookmakers.[74] This problem resulted from the criminalisation of ready-money betting and bookmaking. As the Rothschild Commission noted in 1978, bookmakers lived at the edge of the law or beyond it, and were thus 'prey to protection rackets and gang violence'.[75] This gave bookmaking a bad name, although it has been argued strongly elsewhere that the thugs were not proper bookmakers at all.[76]

Once established, bookmakers often passed on their business to a son or another member of the family. Oral and autobiographical evidence for the twentieth century confirms the view of a recent anonymous but 'established bookmaker' that bookmaking was usually 'passed on from father to son, uncle to nephew, and it is very rare for an "outsider" to break into the trade'.[77] After 1945, Steven Hamer, following a spell as a jockey, took over the father's business with his brother. In Birmingham, Dennis P.s' brother took over his father's trade during the 1960s. The hereditary dimension reflected two family-based economic strategies. Firstly, that bookmaking had demonstrated its security and profitability over other local occupations, and that the son was better off as a bookie. Secondly, the inheritance of the trade was the strongest expression of the wider family involvement in the enterprise. As an activity central to the informal economy and the leisure culture of the poorer working-class communities, the wives and children were easily involved in the day to day acceptance and settling of bets. A number of punters and ex-bookmakers testified to this. For example Cynthia M., whose widowed bookmaker father also ran a fish and chip shop in Southampton during the 1940s and '50s remembered that she and her grandmother helped their father in the collection and settling of bets, as did Jack Hamers' wife in Bolton during the 1920s and '30s.[78] Relatives provided the bookmaker with free and presumably agreeable and • trustworthy labour, as they shared an obvious interest in the success of the family business.

As a working-class entrepreneur, the bookmaker fascinated middle-class observers, who provided most of the contemporary descriptions and images of him. Mass Observation for example, gave this description of the remarkable 'Humpty Dumpty', a bookmaker in Radcliffe, Bolton:

> This is a man of medium height, thick set, rather corpulent with thick gold chain very prominent: he also has the usual cigar and a very prominent display of gold rings on his fingers: I personally have counted as many as six rings on both hands and when he is drinking usually rests one hand on the counter to display the same.[79]

Even Tom Harrisson, a founder of MO, felt that the writer of the report had exaggerated his findings.[80] The grosser aspects of the bookmaker caricature were also to be found in literature, such as the hearty bowler-hatted fellow at the beginning of Michael Arlen's *The Green Hat* (1924), 'Piggy White' in Howard Spring's *Shabby Tiger* (1934) and most notably Sam Grundy in Walter Greenwood's *Love on the Dole*, first published in 1933. Greenwood painted an unfavourable picture of 'Honest Sam' who frequented pubs, smoked fat cigars, and had a rapacious eye for women and working-class punters. Robert Roberts wrote that bookmakers' 'morals, flash suits and bedecked wives usually put them beyond the pale of proper respectability'.[81] This unflattering stereotype given by • Greenwood and Roberts was in part the response of two working-class writers who had lived amongst the poor and were frustrated by their condition. They sought out those whom they saw as the villains who profited from poverty, and the appearance of certain bookmakers must have given them an impression of garish characters parading among the have-nots. Many on the left shared this view. *Northern Voice*, the organ • of the Independent Labour Party in the north west, depicted bookmakers as 'those who wax in their opulence and corpulence'.[82] Cartoonists, such as Tom Webster of the *Daily Mail* from the 1930s, and films like *The Belles of Saint Trinians* (1954) starring George Cole as the dapper bookies' runner 'Flash 'Arry' perpetuated this image. Such images transmitted the idea of the bookmaker as a 'spiv', 'one who lives by his wits', especially in the black market or the racing game.[83]

There were two shortcomings with this parody. First, it ignored female bookmakers. The NAGL kept up a running commentary on what it saw as the scourge of women bookmakers. In 1900 it gave the case of Theresa Butcher, a greengrocer of Clarendon Street, Hulme, who was fined ten pounds for taking bets at the shop. She was described as 'an elderly white-haired woman' who was 'respectably dressed'.[84] In 1912, a Mr Lister was shocked to be called from work following a police raid on his wife's secret betting business, which she ran from the front room of their house in Collyhurst, Manchester. She did most of her trade with women and children, apparently without her husband's knowledge. As a little boy, who inadvertently knocked on the back door during the raid told one policeman: 'I come every day for my mother, and I give it to the missus or the girl.'[85] This further suggests, given Greenwood's emphasis on Sam Grundy's tendency to leer at women, that many preferred to bet with another woman.

Yet the major problem with the bookmaker caricature was its exaggeration, and its subsequent inability to see the bookmaker as working-class punters might have done. As Benny Green writes, not all bookmakers fitted 'the cliche bookmaker, a florid profligate in a check suit'.[86] Moreover, for a number of reasons, bookmakers were important contributors to local economic and social life. Firstly, perhaps, the bookmaker as employer was the most direct contribution to the local economy. As one rather boastful 'sportsman' and bookmaker wrote in the mid 1930s, the bookmaker 'causes employment, clerks, runners, and he has got a good name by not being too hard on his clients'.[87] Secondly, many bookmakers kept up a gift relationship with their punters, buying drinks in pubs and often allowing bets 'on the strap' or 'on tick', that is, credit bets wherein the punters were entrusted to pay up the stake money when they could afford to do so. Hamer, furthermore, helped people who were having trouble with the means test, the loathed system of having one's belongings valued before dole money was paid out. Hamer nominally purchased their furniture and, because it was his, the local authorities could not arrange for its sale.[88] He also made a more symbolic contribution which spoke of a shared experience with his neighbours and peers. After 1918, he paid 125 guineas for war memorials in the form of rolls of honour to the dead of Clarendon Street School, of which he was a former pupil. These were unveiled by the Mayoress of Bolton in

1920.[89] Such activities did not go unnoticed by the police. The Chief Constable of Manchester informed parliament in 1932 that bookmakers were 'rather good to some of the poorer about them'. He said he knew of examples of bookmakers paying rents and doctors' bills, and presenting banners to churches.[90] Their largesse even earned the respect of Roberts.[91]

However, because bookmakers were better off than many around them, they were prone to a significant pressure within the community of street betting which worked to the advantage of the punter. Firstly, as the sociologist Robert Perrucci has argued, whilst bookmakers were expected to validate their success with gifts and gestures, they retained most of their profits. Bookmakers also had to be careful not to be too generous. Either way, they were a target for 'the group response of envy'.[92] Secondly, and related to this, bookmakers were compelled to honour their bets. A known 'welsher' or defaulter would never receive a · halfpenny stake. Yet conversely, the punters would try on a corrupt bet, a fiddle, if they could. After all, the bookmaker could afford it. He was an aggregator who paid winnings from unsuccessful bets, or whose losses were often offset by other unsuccessful stakes. But the punters, now to be discussed, were in a straight win or lose situation.

III

The fiddle against the bookmaker by both runners and punters stemmed · from their relative prosperity based on a realistic appraisal that the odds favoured the bookmaker, and that consequently he could afford to pay out in fair bets or foul. A fiddle was basically the safest bet, a bet on a horse or dog which had already won. As Joe M. put it, 'we always used to say tek it off them as 'ave it.'[93] There are a number of oral and autobiographical examples of this outlook. The most common way, perhaps, involving both runners and punters, was the example given by Joe M. of St Helens: 'The main rule was if you had a friend, a settler, he would slip you a bet in when he was settlin' and he'd write you a couple of winners in and put your nom de plume on. And then next time he could put you in a couple and put another nom de plume on'.[94]

Another fiddle used pigeons. For example, Walter M., answering the question 'Can you remember when they first set up White City or Belle Vue?', a question intended to elicit his memories of the first big grey-hound meetings, answered:

Yeah, oh I could tell you a tale about that. When they first started at White

City, the only bookie in that area of Manchester – Alf Birds – was the only bookie with a 'phone. So we'd send a chap to White City dogs with a basket to put the pigeons in. You could get a bet on at the bookies' up to the second race, so we had a lad at White City first race, a five dog race, you'd have five dogs written out; the dog'd'd won, on the pigeon and away, the name of the
· winner, and the pigeon loft was right near the bookies', so we'd wait for this pigeon comin' in and if we got it down right away we'd get the first winner.[95]

Bookmakers knew they were going to be fiddled from time to time. According to Steven Hamer: 'it was catch as catch can. If they could do you they would. To them you were fair game, the bookie were fair game'.[96]

The appreciation of the punters that the odds favoured the bookmaker was given little or no recognition by anti-gambling propagandists who
· portrayed the punters as unsuspecting prey to the bookmakers' intentions. The fiddle against the bookmaker was justified not only by the realisation of the bookmaker's financial superiority. It was, especially for the poorer punter, a minor aspect of a wider strategy of 'getting by', one of many opportunities which were seized when available. To explore this further, an analysis of the punters is necessary.

Unfortunately, before the 1940s no objective quantitative study of the class basis nor of the nature and size of the punting public was undertaken. The Parliamentary Enquiries of 1902, 1923 and 1932–3 were convinced that the increase in betting was located within the artisan and working classes but short of the 'scarifying figures'[97] of the NAGL there was no exploration of those sections most likely to bet. Unfortunately,
˙ there is no hard information on punters' jobs before the post-war surveys of betting. Yet these found that the incidence of betting did not vary greatly across the manual or blue-collared working class. From a sample of 1,600 in the mid 1940s MO found that the most frequent gamblers on horses were unskilled workers (38 per cent), administrative grades (37 per cent), and skilled workers (34 per cent). (At this time skilled worker was replacing 'artisan' as a vocational description.) The least frequent gamblers were clerical workers (26 per cent) and retired or unoccupied (15 and 26 per cent respectively). Not surprisingly, MO found that the poorest gambled least frequently and for the smallest amounts. More affluent skilled workers placed higher stakes.[98] In common with MO, the *Social Survey of Betting* found in 1951 that 44 per cent of their sample of over 2,900 punters betted on horses. They noted that the average stake for ready-money punters was eight shillings compared to the three pounds ten shillings of credit punters. They found a small

majority of punters were middle-aged and middle-waged, but few bet more than forty pounds per year, less than one pound a week. Most bet · 'comparatively small sums'.[99]

Working-class gambling was thus conducted in a more moderate · fashion than the accusations levelled against it. Canon Green for instance told the Select Committee of 1923 that one million 'cases of demoralisation' resulted from betting, a view treated with some caution by the questioner.[100] Except in extreme cases, no causal link between · gambling and poverty was ever established. Pauperism was more likely to result from low wages and inadequate poor relief, or what the sociologist B. S. Rowntree called primary poverty. For a family of five in · Lancashire in the mid 1930s, unemployment benefit amounted to thirty-three shillings a week, a quarter of which went on rent.[101] This automatically placed them below Rowntree's minimum standard of thirty-five shillings, crucially after rent was paid, required for the purchase of food, warmth and clothing. As Dixon shows, Rowntree was hesitant in blaming people for pushing themselves into what he termed secondary poverty by useless expenditure on drink or gambling. He wanted to focus public attention upon the greater tragedy of inadequate income.[102]

Rowntree knew that economic insecurity was the real problem, and that most expenditure was constrained by it. Thus Orwell, pointing to the appeal of gambling for the poor, saw it as the 'cheapest of luxuries' in such circumstances, allowing people to buy a bit of hope, which was · sometimes realised.[103] Thus Joseph Toole, who grew up in Edwardian Salford, and later became a socialist and the mayor of Manchester, remembered that a big win by his father gave new clothes to the whole family and a trip to Blackpool, the first time he had seen the sea. Harry Hardcastle, in *Love on the Dole*, also bought clothes and went to the seaside.[104] Gambling winnings could provide in one instant what months or years of saving were aimed at. It was a realistic economic response to the impossibility of long-term saving, which was a problem for both the poorest and those in regular but low-paid work.

Along with lack of money, lack of stimuli was often ascribed to · working-class life in the poorest areas. For Lady Bell, gambling amongst poor housewives was 'horribly undesirable' yet explicable by their 'sordid daily life' to which gambling contributed 'constant moments of alternating hope, fear and wonder'.[105] Bell's argument applied with equal force to the unemployed. The psychological role of gambling as a source of hope and tension release was compounded, for many of the poor, by its economic dimension. Unlike most other items of leisure expenditure, gambling offered a chance of economic return. The study of form and the anticipation of the results were an inexpensive use of time, and the means for this were available in the form of a cheap and accessible sporting, local and national press, all of which carried racing intelligence. As McKibbin notes, the Pilgrim Trust in their investigation of Liverpool in the 1930s emphasised the 'intellectual' importance of studying the past form (performance) of horses and football teams,[106] and women as well as men studied the form of horses.[107] This exercise was an attempt to reduce the element of chance from the bet, a view which casts further doubt on the anti-gambling definition of gambling as involving the abandonment of reason. The 'Turf Ready Reckoners' listed in the British Library Catalogue also aided the mathematical calculation of odds and potential winnings from stake sizes.

Another strategy for winning beyond the perusal of form or fiddling was anchored in fatalism. The insecurity of working-class life in the poorer areas was conducive to a fatalistic attitude to life, and the belief in luck. Superstition, with its pre-scientific belief system, was a strong component in the world view of many people. It was part of an outlook and set of practices intended to mitigate against the worst environmental and personal contingencies. Bernice Martin sees gambling as both an expression of these insecurities and of the strategies to offset them. Superstitions are 'framing devices in a culture of boundary and control'.[108] Mass Observation noted the widespread cultural paraphernalia of such practices, which was both product and perpetuator of it. For example, horoscopes in newspapers, *Old Moore's Almanack*, fortune-telling gypsies at the seaside and the devices marketed ostensibly to eliminate chance from the pools. These were 'constantly urged by the press, pools and music hall.[109] They were also a feature of some tipping and form publications. For example, Ariels' *Astronomy Applied to Horse Racing* (1919) or Star Faith's *Planetary Influences on Racing* (1925), listed in the British Library catalogue, spoke to the mystical side of the punter. One ex-punter remembered his mother would only write her bets on tea paper, 'that's what you got your quarter pound of tea in. She said it was lucky'.[110] Anthropologists have noted this use of charms in other cultures.[111] In *Esther Waters* (1894), George Moore linked gambling behaviour with fatalism, which he saw as a hopeless belief system. Towards the end of the book, a horse race allegorically determines whether William Latch, a bookmaker, will live or die. Fate, not medicine or alcohol abuse, decides his end.

The fancy too was built into the ostensibly non-rational determination of betting choice. To 'fancy' a horse after studying its form is common speech, but it speaks of predilection and symbolises an inclination as well as a mechanistic perusal of form. Punters knew, in the last analysis, that the results were not predictable and so deployed a whole range of superstitious devices to try, as Bernice Martin puts it, to 'frame' the result. And these of course are not necessarily inimical to the random results of much gambling. Keith Thomas's concluding statement about magic is especially true of both the superstitious outlook and of gambling itself in times and places characterised by economic insecurity: 'If magic is to be defined as the employment of ineffective techniques to allay anxiety when effective ones are not available, then we must recognise that no society will ever be free from it'.[112]

When an income was too low and intermittent to leave any or hardly any disposable income, it was a more realistic and certainly a more enjoyable use of money than saving, but it did not always compromise it. Charles Booth pointed to the difficulties of conserving money in the uncertain environment of dockland in East and South London in the 1880s and 1890s. Yet he described the communal thrift and loan clubs to which a minority of casuals contributed on a regular or semi-regular basis depending on income, and which paid back the money before Christmas or at holiday times.[113]

In Lancashire, too, many on similarly precarious incomes saved in small collective self-help schemes known colloquially as 'diddlums' or 'tontines'. These were perhaps run by a local publican or matriarch who assumed responsibility for them. Diddlums were so called because the person running it might 'diddle off' with the money before the Christmas holiday.[114] In Bolton in 1938, MO noted that 'diddlum clubs' had recently declined in popularity since a number of cases of treasurers doing such 'moonlight flits'.[115] The 'tontine' was a similar arrangement, the name and principle of which was derived from an insurance system based upon share investment which had been popular in the eighteenth century.

Such clubs were useful to pay into and draw out of throughout the year, and along with pawning helped people to get by within a cycle of debt and occasional credit. They were a symptom of the poorest areas where, as Melanie Tebbut has written, the insecurity of poverty led to a 'distinct outlook' in which the need for bridging credit and its provision by local traders was central. This was especially true of more settled communities, 'where credit dependence mitigated against mobility and reinforced relations with local traders, including the pawnbroker'.[116]

Including, too, the bookmaker, who employed people and helped people out. The prominence of these savings schemes and credit arrangements illustrates that gambling did not preclude saving for many who possessed the distinct outlook of the poor. John Barron Mays, in his study of juvenile delinquency in Liverpool during the 1950s, found one son of the casual poor who was a regular gambler and saver:

> His pocket money is seven shillings and six pence a week, and this has to cover fags, pictures, bets and club dues but he manages to save about two shillings and six pence towards a summer holiday at a Butlins Camp. About six pence goes each week on horses, six pence on the pools and six pence on the sweep. He has won the sweep twice lately and added considerably to his savings.[117]

His grandmother ran a tontine. It has been argued that gambling for poor casuals in nineteenth-century London was a 'more congenital form of self-help than saving' but this perhaps polarises the issue too much.[118] From the nineteenth century up to the end of the 1950s, from Booth, through the Pilgrim Trust to Mays, there is evidence that gambling coexisted with saving amongst the casual poor. Together, they were part of a strategy of self-help for those who could not bring themselves to conform to what George Orwell called 'Smilesian, aspidistral standards'.[119] As Paul Johnson puts it, in criticism of some social investigators for misunderstanding the working-class economy, most people were motivated by 'self-help sometimes, self-interest always'.[120] This perspective was enough to prevent most betters from ruining themselves and their families through excess.

IV

The failure by some middle-class observers and by government to understand the reality of the extent and nature of gambling informed the prohibitive tenets of the laws, and caused resentment amongst punters, who saw betting in moderation as harmless. As the sociologist Richard Hoggart noted in the 1950s, many working-class people felt that: 'the law is in some things readier against them than against others. Their street corner betting, it is often remarked, is a risky business. If they ran an account with a 'Commission Agent' it would not be.'[121]

Like Hoggart, sociologists of the 1950s and 1960s and historians since were concerned with working-class consciousness and political behaviour. They attempted to tease it out from the social and economic experience of working-class people. Elizabeth Bott, for example, argued that 'the ingredients, the raw materials of class ideology are located in the individual's various primary social experiences, rather than in his position in a socio-economic category'.[122] Thus the experience of police intervention was viewed by punters as farcical, corrupting and biased. Here are three examples to illustrate this:

> I am convinced from what I heard and saw that police activity was known in advance of it occurring; on too many occasions the bookie had ample evidence to remove proper evidence and set up the 'mugs' with nominal paraphernalia only.

> It was all a farce really. The bookies were never licensed but the police gave them written permission.

> They'd nothing against the police really but the gambling laws and the by-laws and that was made by people with money, masons and the Pilkington family; they was all magistrates and freemasons and all kind o' things . . . They run the town.[123]

The 1906 Act reinforced a sub-political 'us and them' feeling, described in some detail by Hoggart. People felt that police–bookmaker collusion was a necessary but unjust symptom of a bad law. Thus, when police action was genuine, bookmakers and their customers closed ranks against the law. The Deputy Commissioner of the Metropolitan Police told Parliament in 1932 that police in uniform were unable to make arrests for the offence, and he felt the bias of the law caused a 'general lowering of respect' for the police, 'putting them in a position of antagonism to a very large part of [the public] which is quite law abiding in all respects except those arising from the taste for gambling'. The Chief Constable of Manchester told the 1933 Enquiry that 'no one is with us, everybody is against us'.[124]

The failure of the law to reduce working-class betting, its unpopularity, and the potentially corrupting position in which it placed the police, had been pointed out by some police chiefs in the Edwardian years, most notably to the Royal Commission on the Metropolitan Police in 1908.[125] In some cases, it led to direct financial gain through bribery, as bookmakers paid policemen to let them alone or to tip them off about any forthcoming raids. In the north west, there were a number of cases of policemen taking payments from bookmakers, for example in Preston in 1909 and most notably in Liverpool in 1928, which became a national scandal and resulted in a number of dismissals of indicted policemen.[126] In 1932 Canon Green greatly offended the police by his accusations of corruption, although this was only a few years after the Liverpool case.[127] As Dixon notes, the potential and actual problems of corruption were played down by police and governmental officials, but was an important element in disenchantment with the betting laws. Yet policemen doing their duty could fall foul of corruption. One, speaking of the Metropolitan Police in the late 1950s, has described how he interrupted a bookmakers' runner's pitch one day, only to be told that his superior would hear of it. He was immediately posted to another, more mundane, beat.[128] Similar experiences happened to other policemen who learned not to interfere with the bookmaker's liason with a superior officer.[129] Most policemen simply adopted the more convenient blind eye approach, as they often did with prostitutes, taking in one or two of them every so often in order to give an impression of law enforcement.[130]

Little, however, has been written about those policemen who were looking to promotion, and for whom a betting arrest was a means to a career end. Police personnel registers and warrant books record the commendations from the chief constable or the bench and the wage rises if a policeman secured a betting conviction. In August 1917, for example, a detective sergeant of the Kent County force was: 'commended by the Chief Constable for the exceptional care and skill shewn [with other officers] in detecting and carrying through the case against Fredk. W. Knight, Licensee of the Prince Albert P.H. Gillingham, for allowing his house to be used for betting'.[131] Such policemen were the source of genuine raids. Yet despite such boosts to their chances of promotion many policemen probably felt that 'there were far better tasks to perform than chasing bookies', but as this London policeman lamented, they were 'duty bound to enforce the law, however unpopular'.[132]

In contrast to the 1932–3 enquiry, by the late 1940s police spokesmen were with one voice calling for the removal of the laws. The Police Federation of England and Wales told the Willink Commission that: 'we have achieved nothing except perhaps the arrest and conviction of many hundreds of otherwise ordinary respectable citizens who perhaps abide by every law in the land except the Betting Act of 1906'.[133] In 1960, the joint Under-Secretary of State highlighted the need to 'revise laws which have fallen into disrepute'.[134] Marwick views this as 'the sound conservative principle of restoring respect and credibility to the law'.[135]

Yet legalisation also followed on from two further developments. Firstly, Winston Churchill as Chancellor of the Exchequer had tried to tax legal credit betting from 1926 as a belated but, as Dixon and Hood show, a blinkered implementation of Cautley's proposals.[136] The tax on dog-race totalisators from 1934 and football pool betting from 1947, discussed in chapters 6 and 7 respectively, made it morally difficult to ʼ resist growing calls for the legalisation of ready-money betting.

Secondly, although this is a more difficult phenomenon to pin down, there was a general change in official attitudes, a realisation that Vic- ʼ torian paternalism was now inappropriate to a wealthier working class. The Willink Commission, unlike previous enquiries, was more responsive to the view that betting was not the excessive arena of waste and emiseration beloved of anti-gambling tracts, but an activity enjoyed by the vast majority of punters within a consciousness of self-regulation, or moderation. The statistics, by then, proved it. About £70 million was spent annually on gambling, representing a total annual stake of less than two pounds per person, a 'comparatively unimportant sum'.[137] This represented a minute burden, if that, on the national economy. Expenditure on gambling was considerably less than on alcohol or tobacco. In terms of the family economy, as the economist Geoffrey Crowther told the Commission, the impact of personal gambling was more difficult to assess, but he was unable and unwilling to make a gloomy diagnosis about family finances.[138] A year later, the sociologist Michael Young wrote that there was little hard information on the distribution of income within the family.[139] On a different level, the Report of the Commission also concluded in the light of Crowther's evidence that gambling did not interfere with industrial efficiency, and might in fact have a positive effect on industrial morale in some cases.[140]

Another significant realisation during these years was that gambling · did not preclude saving. Enoch Powell, in a paper for the Institute of Economic Affairs in 1960, argued that gamblers were also savers, and that big winnings were often saved.[141] Social investigations in the 1950s showed gambling often coexisted with short-term saving for specific items such as the holiday or a labour-saving device. This was a time of higher wages and the more optimistic outlook of the post-war years. This facilitated an extension of financial freedoms and expectations which undermined the paternalistic logic of the gambling legislation. This view was most clearly stated by the Conservative MP William Deedes, in the debate over R.A. Butler's proposed Bill to legalise off-course cash betting on horses:

> Much of our former social legislation, now being repaired, reflects a state of mind which saw an obligation to protect the working class from its own excesses and follies. The law that we are replacing is typical of that. If one has a telephone one can be entrusted to bet to the limit [but] if one has to rely on a

pub one cannot do so.[142]

Deedes saw the bill as 'a positive imposition of self-restraint and individual responsibility', Tory tenets of individual and social behaviour. Yet this was no libertarian kicking-over of the traces. Before this new betting dispensation could be introduced a number of moral and practical objections and alternative suggestions, in the form of amendments to the proposed legislation, had to be negotiated.

V

The betting offices introduced on to the streets in May 1961 were considered by a number of MPs, mostly Labour, to be a bad idea, and they raised objections to the Bill as it passed through the House. Douglas Houghton echoed Ramsay MacDonald when he argued that betting shops would be 'a reproach to our society. It shows that many of our people are bored and frustrated and do not know what to do with their lives'.[143] Bob Mellish, the Labour member for Bermondsey, along with Reginald Paget, the Labour member for Northampton, proposed to legalise the existing local networks of bookmakers and runners. These were viewed as a reflection of community solidarities which had evolved according to differing patterns of work. Eric Johnson, on behalf of Blackley in Manchester, felt that in an industrial manufacturing area such as Trafford Park the workers would still rely on the runners to get their bets on for them.[144] Mellish's proposal was simply that agents and runners should become paid legitimate employees of the bookmakers, and that accepted places for laying and paying out bets, such as the street and the public house, should be recognised. To support his case he argued that the biggest bookmakers would monopolise off-course cash-betting outlets and that the Conservatives, as the party of the small family business, were ignoring a major part of their natural constituency.[145] A few Tories were sensitive to this view, pointing to the Irish experience of legalisation since 1926, where a Dublin bookmaker owned nearly half the shops in his city.[146]

For different reasons, large-scale bookmakers also opposed the legalisation of their smaller counterparts. William Hill argued that Butlers' Bill was 'a charter for small bookmakers' which would undermine the basis of the credit trade.[147] As we will soon see, the large bookmakers had nothing to fear and much to gain from the legalisation of cash betting, especially those who ran an under-trade in off-course ready-money betting anyway.

Another argument used by Mellish and others was that the new system would tempt the young and 'women going shopping' into the betting shop.[148] Mellish, proud of his cockney credentials and knowledge of the East London working class, must have known that it was common already for women and teenagers to lay their own bets, as well as those of their husband's or father's, with the street bookmaker. Accusations and fears about reckless or incredulous punters, once directed at the entire working class, were now reserved largely for women and, especially, the young. The government, in the final drafting, did not worry any further about women but it felt compelled to outlaw the employment of people under eighteen in the proposed betting shops. Reginald Paget pointed to what he saw as a double standard. Invoking the father to son lineage of many bookmaking families, he stated:

> If we legalise in this case the use of great sums of new capital and new resources of the nation, why, on the other hand, must we say that the business is so disreputable that apprentices and young people may not be introduced to what is the living and business of their parents? That sort of idiotic hypocrisy I find it difficult to put up with.[149]

But such idiocy was quickly agreed to by the House. However, it is worth pointing out that a number of MPs were prepared to contemplate youthful betting and gambling without gloomy or pessimistic prognoses. George Wigg, later Chairman of the Horse-race Betting Levy Board, told the House what most working-class mothers and fathers had long known, that ' the business of having a little bet is not regarded as terribly evil and starts long before the age of eighteen'.[150] It can be argued that the hypocrisy which Wigg pointed to was ironed out by the general sense of compromise which infused the parliamentary debates. A silly and biased law was to be removed and betting was to be legalised, but it was not to be encouraged. Betting and gambling were still not regarded as admirable activities in themselves. The continuing resonance of this view was not a historical consequence of the anti-gambling lobby's efforts. Rather, the toleration of gambling was a necessary consequence of the realisation which Marwick describes and which Deedes had articulated to Parliament. The betting shops were a logical outcome of this qualified liberalisation, because such establishments could be more easily monitored than activities which took place in smoke-filled back rooms and in bars, clubs and alleyways. For similar reasons, a move to legalise postal cash betting as the major form of off-course betting was rejected.[151]

During the third reading of his Bill, and in the light of the foregoing discussions and amendments in the House, Butler was sensitive to the issues and problems arising from the introduction of legal outlets for ready-money betting. 'The street', he argued, 'is not the proper place in which to bet'. On a practical level it would involve licensing and registration difficulties with the local magistrates and planning authorities. More importantly, any relaxation in favour of the status quo 'would allow further solicitation to take place'. He also felt it would make it more difficult to prevent betting with young persons. He thus favoured licensed betting offices, yet he accepted the use of runners where the needs of the working population dictated.[152]

Betting shops were introduced in May 1961. They were to be licensed by the local licensing authorities who conferred approval under guidelines laid down by the Town and Country Planning Acts of 1947 and 1959. The interior of each office reflected the finger-wagging behind the new permissiveness, but this was not enough to assuage critics of the new dispensation. A Methodist spokesman lamented that 'all legislation to do with gambling must of necessity be a compromise': 'the sort of compromise that permits the opening of a betting shop but insists that it be as cheerless and sombre as possible'.[153]

Each office was to contain only the counter, books, slips, and the lists of starting price-odds pinned up from the racing pages. No stools and no television or radio was allowed, only the blower and a board to chalk up the changing odds. These interiors were supposed to prevent loitering. As the *Times* correspondent noted, shops could open as early as 7 am, but most business would, as it always had, be done at lunch time.[154]

Street bookmakers were given a six-month transitional period in which to re-establish their external trade in a betting shop. Although runners could collect bets from workplaces, it appears that the runner declined in popularity throughout the 1960s. Runners had died out for similar reasons in the Republic of Ireland from the late 1920s.[155] Many simply became clerks. One large London bookmaker who had four runners on the street told the *Times* that they had cost him '£400 each in fines, but they took 2,000 bets a day. Now I shall use them as clerks'.[156]

It is difficult to know the punters' opinion of all this. Many in retrospect report a feeling of gladness, but also felt a sense of loss for the more informal, illegal and therefore exciting street betting. Clarence M. of the Elephant and Castle in London missed the element of a possible raid and seeing the bookmaker get 'nabbed', but he thought that the new law was a good one.[157] Joe K. of Liverpool thought shops:

not as exciting as the old time betting as it was always considered a great thrill putting one over on the bookie (impossible now with modern technology) and a bigger thrill was putting one over on the cops. The difference now I believe is that it has become stereotyped like going to the supermarket.[158]

Such perceptions were also shaped by other changes in society which divested people of the 'known and familiar' and a sense of belonging they once felt.[159] The end of street betting coincided with a number of important general changes which directly affected the experience of working-class people. This was a time of the comprehensive redevelopment of many urban working-class areas in which 'Coronation Streets' of slum terraced houses were replaced by tower blocks and 'streets in the sky'. The allure of a house and garden in the suburbs tempted many, especially the more affluent workers, to vacate the inner urban areas.[160] Mass immigration into the older inner-urban areas during the 1950s also changed the social tone and created new tensions as well as allegiances in local life. In the end of course, a complex of cultural and economic changes did more to undermine the social meshing of people in the towns and cities than the abolition of the street betting network. Butler's Act was but a single aspect of many influences, national and local, social and economic, shaping the pattern of working-class recreation in the post-war years.

There was certainly little resistance to the betting shops among punters. The Chief Constable of Liverpool was able to report to the Watch Committee in 1962 that 'the majority of betting offices are well conducted'. There were, however, a number of infringements over the use of television on the premises. Independent television had transmitted starting price odds since the mid 1950s, and the BBC did the same from 1958.[161] There were also prosecutions for advertising too loudly, and for betting with under-age persons. There were eighty arrests in Liverpool for the continuation of street betting from May to December 1961. The fines were then increased to finally stamp this out and 1962 saw only five arrests on this count. The chief constable could conclude with relief that the establishment of licensed betting shops 'has eliminated a long-standing complaint, and with it the necessity of providing special police patrols'.[162] These teething troubles were short lived on Merseyside. It is difficult to know just how many new outlets opened up there after May 1961, as the annual police report in Liverpool does not give the number of bookmakers' permits applied for, and the entries in the trade directories were only for the biggest bookmakers. In Bolton borough, however, 222 bookmakers permits, representing 272 shops, were in force by December 1961.[163] In Bolton the transition to licensed offices produced similar problems to Liverpool. In 1961 there were three cases of television sets being used in betting shops, seven cases of unlawful advertising and thirty-three cases of resorting to unlicensed betting premises.[164] In Manchester between May and December 1961, there were two cases of unlicensed betting offices, fifteen cases of resorting to unlicensed betting offices, one case of allowing a betting office to be used for gaming, one case of under-age betting and one case of unlawful advertising. Fifteen persons were prosecuted for continuing street betting but twelve of these cases were in the new estate of Wythenshawe, 'where the number of licensed betting offices is small'.[165]

The chief constable also pointed to the beginnings of what was to become a major future development:

> Perhaps the most startling result of the new Act has been the popularity of 'Bingo' competitions, many of them as serious business enterprises and others conducted to provide financial assistance to clubs and charitable organisations. Very few have given cause for police action.[166]

In all, there were about 13,340 betting shops nationally by 1962. In the early 1960s sociologists found that bookmakers' profits were highest per head in the north, especially Yorkshire and the north west, a phenomenon they ascribed to the prominence of mining and the related dearth of opportunities for social mobility in the poorer parts of these counties.[167] The fears of the big bookmakers like William Hill before 1961 proved groundless. Between them, the large scale bookmakers like Ladbroke's, Coral's, Hill's and Mecca owned 0.2 per cent of all outlets in 1962. This had risen to a market share of almost 24 per cent. by 1977.[168] Smaller local chains like Stanley Racing of Liverpool and Dones of Salford also grew from this time.[169] Apart from these big chains, the other major consequence of the 1960 Act for both bookmakers and punters was the inevitability of a tax on off-course betting, introduced in 1963.

VI

The Act of 1960 was only possible under the more permissive and wealthy years of the post-war period. This was a qualified liberalisation, brought about painfully slowly in response to the failure of the previous legislation and its consequences. The new dispensation also had to be structured to provide a system which could be monitored by the police and taxed by government. Otherwise street betting could have carried on in the terms Mellish and most of the smaller bookmakers desired. Yet the key word in trying to explain the punter's disregard for the legislation, and the undoing of the laws, is moderation. For most of our period the majority of punters had been in control of their betting, so they saw it as harmless. Government perceptions, however, had been obscured by the rhetoric of the anti-gambling lobby and inadequate statistics. When it was realised that most gambling was not damaging to most people, legalisation was contemplated; it would not have been so without it. A similar realisation also stimulated the reform of the lotteries legislation in 1956, and led to the introduction of premium bonds in the same year, discussed in chapter 8.

The next chapter, however, moves away from the world of organised betting to explore the world of coin and card gaming, and small-scale betting on local sports. These activities were also illegal, yet widely practised.

Notes

1 Charles Sidney, *The Art of Legging*, 1976, p. 77.
2 *SC 1923* Chaired by Charles Cautley, Minutes, qu. 6770, p. 394.
3 *Ibid.* Minutes, qu. 6858–72, pp. 339–400; qu. 8609, p. 493.
4 'Returns for the Police Districts of Liverpool and Manchester', in *Judicial Statistics for England and Wales*, Vols 1912–13, Cmd 6650 cx. 537; 1932–3, Cmd 4450. xxv. 991. Please note that these figures are for 'Betting and Gaming', not 'Gaming &c.', punishable under the Vagrancy Acts.
5 Andrew Davies, 'The Police and the People: Gambling in Salford, 1900–1939', *Historical Journal*, Vol. 34, No. 1, 1991, p. 98.
6 'Returns for the Police District of Bolton', in *Judicial Statistics for England and Wales*, Vols 1914, Cmd 7267 c. 187; 1934–5, Cmd 4977 xxii. 763.
7 Jerome Caminada, *25 Years of Detective Life (in Victorian Manchester)*, Vol. 2, Manchester, 1985, pp. 7–17.
8 H. Beecher Cooke, *Anti-Gambling Demonstration in Manchester, October 26, 1904*, Manchester, cited in David Dixon, *From Prohibition to Regulation: Bookmaking, Anti-Gambling and the Law*, Oxford, 1991, p. 357.
9 *SC 1923*, Minutes, qu. 6858–72, p. 400; qu. 6848, p. 399; Peter Green, *Betting and Gambling*, 1927, pp. 29–33.
10 *SC 1923*, Minutes, qu. 6769, pp. 393–4.
11 *SC 1923*, Report, para. 14, p. xii.
12 NAGL *Bulletin*, November, 1916.
13 *SC 1918*, Minutes, qu. 2386, p. 94; qu. 2428, p. 96.
14 Mary Bentley, *Born 1896*, Manchester, 1985, p. 25. Alex Granger, *Life's a Gamble*, Bognor Regis, 1983.
15 NAGL *Bulletin*, Vol. 5, No. 53, August 1913.
16 C. E. B. Russell, *op. cit.*, 1980, p. 113 (first published 1913). Liverpool Council of Voluntary Aid, *Report on Betting in Liverpool*, 1926, p. 5.

17 NAGL *Bulletin*, August 1913.
18 Green, 1927, p. 36.
19 NAGL *Bulletin*, August 1913.
20 Green, 1927, pp. 30–6.
21 LCVA, *op. cit.*, p. 7.
22 Bernice Martin, a sociologist who grew up in Lancashire in the post-war years suggests this for the 1940s and 1950s: *A Sociology of Contemporary Cultural Change*, Oxford, 1985, p. 73. It was doubtless true before then.
23 Elizabeth Roberts, *A Womans' Place*, 1984, pp. 148–68.
24 *Manchester Evening News*, 27 August 1912; Clapson, 1989, pp. 78–82.
25 Martin, *op. cit.*; W. F. F. Kemsley and D. Ginsburg, *Betting in Britain*, 1951, p. 17.
26 B. S. Rowntree and G. R. Lavers, *English Life and Leisure*, 1951, p. 12.
27 Writer's Oral Project: C. E. J., born Waltham Cross, Hertfordshire, 1915, Qre.; A. S. M., born Salford, Lancashire, 1932, Qre.; Steven Hamer, born Bolton, 1921. Tape 1, Side 1; *SC 1923*, Minutes, qu. 768–71, pp. 38–9.
28 Writer's Oral Project: Mrs M. Vickerman, born Huddersfield, Yorkshire, 1918, Qre. Jack Ashley, *Journey Into Silence*, 1973, p. 30.
29 *Liverpool Daily Post*, 5 November 1915.
30 Writer's Oral Project: Walter M., born Hulme, Manchester, 1919, Tape 6, Side 1. Alex M., *op. cit.* See also Richard Heaton, *Salford, My Home Town*, Manchester, 1983, p. 10.
31 Writer's Oral Project, John A., born Barking, Essex, 1913, Tape 7, side 2. He was an employee of the Agency from 1929.
32 Writer's Oral Project, Clarence M., born Walworth, London 1909; Qre.; Rowntree and Lavers, *op. cit.*, p. 128; Carl Chinn, 'Betting Shops and Race by Race Betting Before the Betting and Gaming Act, 1960', *Society for the Study of Gambling Newsletter*, No. 17, July 1990; *Picture Post*, 12 November 1949.
33 Harry Cole, *Policeman's Progress*, Bath, 1985, p. 99.
34 MO, *The Pub and the People*, Welwyn, 1970, p. 263 (first published 1943).
35 Mark Clapson, 'The Social Significance of Working-Class Gambling in Lancashire, 1900–39', unpublished MA dissertation, 1983, University of Lancaster, p. 21.
36 Hamer *op. cit.*; Joe M., *op. cit.*
37 E. B. Perkins, *The Problem of Gambling*, 1919, p. 19.
38 Joe Kay, *The Chronicles of a Harpurhey Lad*, Manchester, 1987, pp. 61–2.
39 *Ibid.*, p. 61.
40 Roberts, *op. cit.*, p. 164.
41 Writer's Oral Project: Joe K., born Liverpool, 1923; QU; Joe M., *op. cit.*
42 Writer's Oral Project: May S., born 1913, Bethnal Green, London, Tape 7, Side 1.
43 Robert Roberts, *The Classic Slum*, 1983, p. 21.
44 The Pilgrim Trust, *Men Without Work*, 1938, p. 157. Angela Hewins (ed.), *The Dillen: Memories of a Man of Stratford Upon Avon*, Oxford, 1983, p. 173. Writer's Oral Project: Harry B., born Nottingham, 1899, Tape 10, Side 1. Joe M.'s uncle was a runner.
45 Hamer, *op. cit.*; Harry B., *op. cit.*; *RC 1949–51*, Minutes, qu. 1155, p. 81.
46 E. W. Bakke, *The Unemployed Man*, 1933, p. 199.
47 Lady Bell, *At the Works*, 1985, p. 255, (first published 1907).
48 *Bolton Oral History Project*, Bolton Local History Library, Tape Transcript No. 157a.

49 Harry B., *op. cit.*; *Writers' Oral Project*, Tape 5, Sides 1 and 2, Dennis P., born Harborne, Birmingham, 1925, and Ted J., born Handsworth, Birmingham, 1907.
50 *RC 1932–33*, Minutes, qu. 8920, p. 508.
51 *SC 1923*, Minutes, qu. 3289, p. 191.
52 *SC 1923*, Minutes, para. 4725–7, p. 250.
53 Dyke Wilkinson, *A Wasted Life*, 1902, p. 60.
54 T. H. Dey, *Leaves from a Bookmaker's Book*, 1931, pp. 18–19.
55 Hamer, *op. cit.*; Clapson, 1983, diagram of the business drawn by Tom, in Appendix.
56 Benson, *op. cit.*, 1983, p. 2
57 *Fraser's Magazine*, Vol. XVI, July, 1877, p. 80; see also chapter 6, below; Jerry White, *The Worst Street in North London*, 1985, p. 86.
58 Writer's Oral Project: A. S., born County Durham. 1918, Qre.
59 Norman Dennis et al., *Coal Is Our Life: An Analysis of a Yorkshire Mining Community*, 1956, pp. 148–9, 158–62, 190, 193.
60 Writer's Oral Project: Cynthia M., born Southampton, 1937, Qre.
61 Hamer, *op. cit.*
62 *Royal Commission on the Duties of the Metropolitan Police*, 1908, Minutes, qu. 43217–9, p. 985.
63 Joe K., *op. cit.*; see Carl Chinn, *Better Betting With a Decent Fella: Bookmaking, Betting and the British Working Class, 1750–1990*, 1991 (but forthcoming at time of writing.)
64 *Licensed Bookmaker*, October 1962.
65 The Pilgrim Trust, *Men Without Work*, 1938. p. 157.
66 Carl Chinn, 'Social Aspects of Sparkbrook, Birmingham, in the Twentieth century', unpublished Ph.D thesis, University of Birmingham 1988, p. 146.
67 Writer's Oral Project: Leonard T., born Barnsley, 1925, Qre. See also George Moore, *Esther Waters*, 1985, p. 65 (first published 1895).
68 Dey, *op. cit.*, p. 19.
69 *RC 1908*, qu. 45247, p. 987.
70 Joe K., *op. cit.*
71 *SC 1923*, Minutes, qu. 4852–3, p. 286.
72 Alan Wykes, *Gambling*, 1964, p. 272; on Jack Spot see *Times*, 6 March 1956, 27 March 1956.
73 Raphael Samuel (ed.), *East End Underworld: Chapters in the Life of Arthur Harding*, 1981, pp. 184–5.
74 J. P. Bean, *The Sheffield Gang Wars*, 1981.
75 *RC 1976–78*, Report Vol. 1, para 6.2. p. 24.
76 Carl Chinn, *op. cit.*, 1991, but forthcoming at time of writing.
77 R. A. Wooley, *op. cit.*, foreword by 'An Established Bookmaker', p. 1.
78 Cynthia M., *op. cit.*; Hamer, *op. cit.*; Dennis P., *op. cit.*
79 MO Archive, *Worktown*, Box 1, File D., dated 25 July 1937.
80 MO, 1970, p. 265.
81 Walter Greenwood, *Love on the Dole*, 1983, p. 113 (first published 1933). Robert Roberts, *The Classic Slum*, 1983, p. 37.
82 *Labour's Northern Voice*, 10 July 1925.
83 Eric Partridge, *Penguin Dictionary of Historical Slang*, 1988, p. 889.
84 *NAGL Bulletin*, Vol. 2, No. 21, November 1900.
85 *Manchester Evening News*, 27 August 1900. Elizabeth Dawson's *Mother Made a Book*, 1962, *passim*.

86 Benny Green, 'Uncle Was a Street Bookie', *Guardian*, 1 May 1991.
87 John Hilton, *Why I Go in for the Pools* 1936, p. 70.
88 Hamer, *op. cit.*; Dennis P. and Ted J., *op. cit.*
89 Correspondence held at Bolton Local History Library. Hamer, *op. cit.*
90 *RC, 1932–33*, Minutes, qu. 736, p. 59; see also John Hilton, *op. cit.*, p. 70.
91 Roberts, *op. cit.*, pp. 36–7.
92 Robert Perrucci, 'The Neighbourhood Bookmaker', in Paul Meadows and Ephraim Mizruchi (eds), *Urbanism, Urbanisation and Social Change: Comparative Perspectives*, New York, 1968, pp. 307–8.
93 Joe M. *op. cit.*
94 Joe M., *op. cit.*
95 Walter M., *op. cit.* For an identical episode in Bolton at the time see Jeremy Seabrook, *Unemployment*, 1983, p. 43.
96 Hamer, *op. cit.*
97 Geoffrey Gorer, 'British Life: It's a Gamble', in R. D. Herman (ed.), *Gambling*, 1967, p. 81.
98 Mass Observation, *Mass Gambling*, 1948, p. 32;
99 Kemsley and Ginsburg, *op. cit.*, pp. 1–3.
100 *SC 1923*, Minutes, qu. 6824–5, p. 398.
101 Stephen Constantine, *Unemployment in Britain Between the Wars*, 1980, p. 28.
102 Dixon, 1991, pp. 65–7.
103 George Orwell, *The Road to Wigan Pier*, 1976, pp. 79–81 (first published 1937).
104 Joseph Toole, *Fighting Through Life*, 1935, p. 56; Walter Greenwood, *Love on the Dole*, 1983, p. 119 (first published 1933).
105 Bell, *op. cit.*, p. 258.
106 Pilgrim Trust, pp. 98–100, p. 157; Ross McKibbin, 'Working Class Gambling in Britain, 1880–1939', *Past and Present*, No. 82, 1979, p. 156.
107 Jeremy Seabrook, *Working-Class Childhood*, 1982, p. 83.
108 Martin, *op. cit.*, pp. 73–4.
109 MO Archive, *Moneysworth*, Box 48, File F, p. 22.
110 Joe M., *op. cit.*
111 George J. McCall, 'Symbiosis: The Case of Hoodoo and the Number's Racket', *Social Problems*, Vol. 10, No. 4, 1963.
112 Keith Thomas, *Religion and the Decline of Magic*, 1978, p. 800.
113 Charles Booth, 'Life and Labour of the People in London', *Poverty*, Vol. 1, 1889, pp. 43, 111.
114 Bob Edwards, oral testimony in Tony Lane's Oral Project on the street life of Liverpool since the 1900s, Department of Sociology, University of Liverpool.
115 MO Archive, *Moneysworth*, Box 48, File F, p. 22.
116 Melanie Tebbutt, *Making Ends Meet*, Oxford, 1985, p. 19.
117 J. B. Mays, *Growing Up in the City*, 1964, p. 193.
118 Jeffrey Richards, introduction to James Greenwood's *The Seven Curses of London*, Oxford, 1981, p. xii.
119 George Orwell, *Keep the Aspidistra Flying*, 1989, p. 60 (first published 1936).
120 Paul Johnson, *Spending and Saving: the Working Class Economy in Britain 1870–1939*, Oxford, 1985, p. 232.
121 Richard Hoggart, *The Uses of Literacy*, 1968, p. 73 (first published 1957).
122 Elizabeth Bott, *Family and Social Network*, 1957, p. 163.
123 Alex M., *op. cit.*; Heaton, *op. cit.*, p. 10; Joe M., *op. cit.*
124 *RC 1932–33*, Memo of Deputy Commissioner of the Metropolis, para. 10, p. 34; Minutes, qu. 708, p. 58.

125 *RC 1908*, Report, para. 4156, p. 131.
126 *Preston Herald*, 18 September 1909; *Times*, 14 February 1928.
127 *Manchester Evening News*, 21 November, 1932.
128 Writer's Oral Project: Tape 7, Side 1: John T., born Cymbran, 1928.
129 Harry Cole, *Policeman's Progress*, Bath, 1980, p. 97; Arthur Battle, 'This Job's Not Like It Used to Be', p. 36 of unpublished and undated manuscript copy held at the European Society for the Study of Policing Archive, the Open University, Milton Keynes.
130 Testimony of Bill Hudson, an ex-Liverpool policeman, unpublished, in Tony Lane's Oral Project, Department of Sociology, University of Liverpool; Dixon, 1991, pp. 7, 243–5.
131 Kent Count Constabulary, *Record of Service*, Vol. 2, p. 87, held at Maidstone Local History library. See also City and Borough of Peterborough Police, *Register of Officers and Constables*, for PCs William Covill and William Jakel. This is held at the Police Museum, Peterborough.
132 Edward Lyscom, *London Policeman*, p. 184. Manuscript copy held at the European Centre for the Study of Policing archive, the Open University, Milton Keynes.
133 *RC 1949–51*, Memo., para. 2, p. 158.
134 *HC Debs*, 11 May 1960, Cols 426–7.
135 Arthur Marwick, *British Society since 1945*, 1987, p. 145.
136 Dixon, 1991, pp. 269–97; Christopher C. Hood, *The Limits of Administration*, 1976, pp. 169–89.
137 *RC 1949–51*, Report, para. 170, p. 49.
138 *Ibid*.
139 Michael Young, 'Distribution of Income Within the Family', *British Journal of Sociology*, Vol. 3, 1952, pp. 305–19.
140 *RC 1949–51*, Minutes, qu. 169, pp. 48–9.
141 J. Enoch Powell, *Saving in a Free Society*, 1960, p. 117.
142 *HC Debs*, 11 November 1959, cols 934–5.
143 *HC Debs*, 16 November 1959, col. 910.
144 *HC Debs*, 11 November 1959, col. 905.
145 *HC Debs*, 5 May 1960, cols 1314 to 1399. Small bookmakers were grateful to Mellish: *Licensed Bookmaker*, May 1963.
146 *HC Debs*, 16 November, 1959, col. 830.
147 *Sporting Life*, 16 November 1959.
148 *HC Debs*, 5 May 1959, cols 1333–4.
149 *HC Debs*, 10 May 1960, col. 214.
150 *HC Debs*, 18 May 1960, col. 223; col. 222–6.
151 Dixon, 1991, p. 332.
152 *HC Debs*, 5 May 1960, col. 1339.
153 *Times*, 6 May 1961.
154 *Times*, 2 May 1961.
155 *HC Debs*, 16 November 1959, cols. 915–916.
156 *Ibid*.
157 Writer's Oral Project: Clarence M., born London, 1909, Qre.
158 *Ibid*., Joe K., *op. cit.*
159 This is Richard Hoggart's term, *op. cit.* Jeremy Seabrook, *City Close Up*, 1971. *Unemployment*, St. Albans, 1983, p. 81. It can be argued however that Seabrook is far too morbid about the effects of social change upon the post-war working class.

160 Michael Young and Peter Willmott, *Family and Kinship in East London*, 1958.
161 *Times*, 25 August 1958.
162 *Annual Report of the Chief Constable of Liverpool*, 1963, p. 48.
163 *Annual Reports of the Chief Constable of Bolton*, 1962, pp. 72–3.
164 *Ibid*.
165 *Annual Report of the Chief Constable of Manchester*, 1962, p. 57.
166 *Ibid.*, p. 56.
167 'Note on the Reasons for the Variation between County Boroughs in Betting Shop Profits for Thousand Population', 1967, *Titmuss Papers*, File 320. Special Reading Room, British Library of Political and Economic Science.
168 *RC 1976–8*, Report, Vol. 1, para. 611, p. 27.
169 *Kelly's Directory of Liverpool*; Davies, op. cit., p. 115.

Chapter 4
Coins, cards, birds and bowls

Beyond the development of commercialised off-course betting on horses lay a hinterland of informal and uncommercialised games and sports played for money. These were mostly, but not always, free from the intervention of bookmakers and other entrepreneurs. A single chapter on gaming cannot hope to deal with all those activities which fall under the term, nor all those pastimes which were conducive to a little friendly wagering. Cruel sports, for example, despite their survival,[1] have been excluded. This chapter focuses on coin gaming, most notably pitch and toss, card gaming, and the local sports of pigeon racing and bowling. Gambling was central to these activities, and determined their organisation.[2] Slot machines are included here rather than in the chapter on lotteries because of their close relationship with coin gaming, although slot machines played in order to win cash, and some amusements with prizes machines have been described as a lottery, and might have been included in chapter 8. The experience of all these activities is recreated through Mass Observation materials and oral testimony.

I

Gambling with coins must be as old as gambling and the coinage. It was popular in pre-industrial Britain despite being punishable under the Vagrancy Acts from the reign of Elizabeth.[3] These Acts have been applied against gaming and betting since, as against drunkenness and begging and other outdoor nuisances. Pitch and toss was the most common form of coin gaming, and was played at least since the eighteenth century.[4] In London during the 1840s a magistrate described a game of pitch and toss thus:

> a hole is made in the ground, or some object is placed there, and the players pitch at same with pence or halfpence; he who pitches nearest the hole or object is entitled to the first toss into the air of all the pence played with and

claims every piece of money which falls with head uppermost; he who pitched second best has the second toss and so on till all the players have successively tossed, or the money is exhausted. Sometimes, young boys play for cakes, but generally for money.[5]

Coin gambling had long been associated with the male poor, especially the young. To the 1844 Select Committee a number of magistrates and police witnesses pointed to the association of boys and young working men with coin and card gaming, especially 'boys of loose habits and irregular propensities'.[6] During the mid nineteenth century social investigators into London's poor and criminal population emphasised the popularity of coin and card gaming amongst the casually employed, most notably the costermongers or barrow boys who sold fruit and vegetables, fish, meat and pies in the streets of the capital. Gambling was an exciting if precarious way to spend the time when selling was slack. It threw into relief the 'easy come easy go' fortunes of the casual labour market. As Henry Mayhew wrote:

> If a costermonger has an hour to spare his first thought is to gamble away the time. He does not care what he plays for so long as he can have a chance of winning something . . . Nothing will damp his ardour for gambling, the most continuing ill-fortune making him even more reckless than if he were the luckiest man alive.[7]

Such gambling on the public highways posed problems for police intervention, and for the magistrates who had to pass sentence. This is evident in the testimony of spokesmen for the police and the magistracy to parliamentary enquiries, and also in *Justice of the Peace*, the magistrates journal, which began in 1837. In 1844 the Chief Magistrate for Bow Street Courts complained that gaming was brought to the attention of the police by

> persons who being obstructed in the streets by children playing at pitch-and-toss or other games of chance, have required the police to take them into custody and convey them before a magistrate; the parties so charging have very seldom appeared to support the complaint, but have left it to the policeman to support what he saw.[8]

Those convicted for the first time could be fined a few shillings, with subsequent convictions threatening larger fines or the spectre of hard labour for three calendar months. Somebody caught playing pitch and toss was very much at the mercy of the individual inclinations of the magistrate. As questions to *Justice of the Peace* illustrate, magistrates were unsure of when to convict under the various Elizabethan and Georgian statutes that made up the Vagrancy Acts.[9] Certainly, the Vagrancy laws were tightened during Queen Victoria' reign, and by the Vagrants Act Amendment Acts of 1873 and 1876, the offence of gaming was extended to include more types of 'instruments of gaming' and most locations (including the inside of a railway carriage), and also to make it easier to convict the young.[10] The young, especially in relation to crimes against property, were subject to more punitive sentencing in the second half of the nineteenth century as the general facilities for summary jurisdiction were tightened up and expanded by the Justice Act of 1856, and later by the Summary Jurisdiction Act of 1879.[11] Paternalistic concern for the · young, especially after the 1880s, was stimulated by a fear of the social consequences of a distinct and alienated culture of the young poor. as John Gillis, Paul Thompson and Geoffrey Pearson have observed, contemporary middle-class social reformers were fearful at the rise of juvenile delinquency as the worst edge of an increasingly dissolute and independent layer of young working-class people.[12] Pitch and toss and other forms of gaming in the streets were viewed as symptoms of a wider crisis of morality amongst the young expressed in disobedience of the law. This view became a 'moral panic', one of the scapegoats for the alleged social fragmentation and economic decline which the later Victorian and Edwardian middle class feared.[13] For example, in 1902 Charles Booth described a game of pitch and toss amongst some west London lads who used 'horrid oaths' and threatened violence to a preacher who strode amongst them and seized their pennies.[14]

Magistrates usually fined offenders for street gaming. For example, in Bolton by 1900 most lads or young men caught gaming were fined two shillings for a first offence, and two and six, five shillings, seven and sixpence or seven days imprisonment for subsequent offences. The unlucky Samuel Mayoh of Church Avenue, who was arrested twice in July 1901 for 'playing by way of gaming with coins at a game of chance known as Tossing', was fined two shillings for his first offence. For the second he was given the choice of paying a five shilling fine or going to prison for a week.[15] This was no doubt a considerable blow to the household economy. Elizabeth Clapson remembered her uncle Billy, who lived with her family, was caught by the police playing pitch and toss in Jubilee Square, Reading, just before the first world war.

> If they was trying to catch 'em gamblin' they used to come up in plain clothes. You used to get fined about five shillins, that was a lot of money them days, five shillins. My dad used to go to work for about two pound a week, 'od carryin', labourin' an' that.[16]

Due to the economic burden of such penalties, whip rounds amongst the gamesters often helped to pay fines.[17]

As this quote also shows, most were usually caught by lightning raids. One Mancunian, speaking of the 1930s, remembered a crowd of policemen tumbling out of a furniture van to arrest a gaming school.[18] Robert Roberts described the physical violence of one such episode, and thought it left youngsters with a suspicion of authority which stayed with them all their lives and shaped the attitude 'of a whole working-class generation toward civil authority'.[19] Unlike the street betting laws, which aimed for the bookmaker and his employees, here the punter directly experienced arrest. Subsequent appearances in court were used by some parents, for example by Jack Ashley's mother, to warn their offspring of the dangers of mixing with a rough lot.[20]

Such gatherings were almost always male, although Madeline Kerr's enquiry into Liverpool slum life in 1953 came across a twelve-year-old girl called Peggy, and her friend Betty, who regularly played 'toss' with the boys in the streets. Peggy won two and sixpence one week and seven and six a fortnight later, and told Kerr that 'the boys do pay up when they lose.'[21] Yet although it is necessary to modify the view that coin gambling schools were wholly male,[22] it would be foolish to deny its broad truth. Oral testimony shows that girls usually watched the gaming or performed the role of scout or look-out. These sentinel and spectatorial positions symbolised both a general exclusion from, and disinclination to become involved in, boisterous street games involving money.

For their male participants, coin games were regarded as manly, part of a peer group culture based on risk and bravado. As Rudyard Kipling put it, 'If you can make one heap of all your winnings, And risk it in one turn of pitch and toss . . . You'll be a Man my son.' Jerry White has argued that gaming assemblies were part of a gender-based learning process, and that proving one's manliness helped to compensate for the lack of a steady job and the humiliations and deprivations associated with poverty.[23]

However, excessive displays of manliness or indulgence in these gatherings could have tragic effects for the wives and children of the punter. Sheila H. , of Leigh in Lancashire, remembered the worry and despair caused by her fathers' heavy gaming at a local organised pitch and toss school. Please note that the police were tipped off in this episode:

There was a so called 'top field' at the end of our street which was the beginning of the meadows I suppose. In this field was 'The Hollow' . . . My mother used to go on about 'pitch and toss' and various card games to my father, and once reported the 'Hollow' to our local police station. This, in turn, made more upset in our family as the gamblers took it out on my father for his wife 'shopping' them. If my father had a good day in the 'Hollow' he would not go to work the next day. If he had a bad day in the Hollow then he would take it out on my Mother, Brother and myself. Many's the time we have trudged through the streets looking for lodgings.[24]

As Davies argues, also from oral evidence, such cautionary episodes reminded many of the dangers of excess, and characterised the 'bad husband' or father.[25]

Oral testimony for the twentieth century illustrates the great local diversity of coin games. 'Nudges' for example, seems to have been peculiar to Manchester, particularly Hulme, as the local name for the game of 'fives'. William L. , the son of a docker, remembered the game clearly from his boyhood in the late 1920s and 1930s:

And what you used to do was you'd get five coins, old English pennies, the big pennies. They would toss them up on the thumb and finger of the left hand if you were so left handed, and you would catch them in your right hand. So you toss up five pennies, and you've got five pennies in your fist in the other hand. Now, then you would turn your fist over so that your knuckles were down to the floor and you'd got five pennies in your hand. You would then open your left hand and people would bet on the amount of heads that you had showing when you opened your fist, the five coins.[26]

Nudges was very popular amongst the lads and men of Hulme and the Golden Eagle public house on Stretford Road was probably nicknamed 'the Nudger' due to the incidence of the game in its vicinity.[27] 'Pitch in the Scrapper' was played in the north east, the scrapper being the metal channel in the footpath to take away water from the guttering pipe.[28] 'Shaking in the hat', played in Boston, Lincolnshire, and the rural east midlands, was an indoor or under-cover game. Coins were placed in a hat and then everyone in turn would shake the hat and turn it over on a flat surface, preferably a hessian sack to stop the coins rolling. The winner had the most heads facing upwards and took all the coins.[29] 'Heads and tails' was probably the simplest form of tossing played with one or more coins. These were tossed into the air and the players predicted how many would land facing heads or tails up.[30]

Pitch and toss gained a greater notoriety during the inter-war years because, as the most common form of coin gaming, it was used by bookmakers and other petty entrepreneurs to make money. Bookmaker rivalry over organised pitch and toss rings in Sheffield led to the infamous wars between gangs of henchmen hired by bookmakers to protect or expand their grip over the tossing rings.[31] Yet not all bookmaker involvement led to violence. Bert W. remembered that local bookmakers organised surreptitious games on the beach at Seaforth, near Bootle, on Sunday mornings, complete with paid look-outs to warn for the police, and minders to fend off trouble. Other lads who wanted to make some money saw an opportunity in pitch and toss. The following quote from Peter M. of Birkenhead illustrates this, and both the spontaneous yet structured elements in a game of pitch and toss. A lad would

> place a certain amount of money on the ground and invite anyone to bet against him tossing two coins in the air and landing on the ground with the two heads facing up. First of all two men or young schoolchildren would be posted as look-outs, this was known as being on douse as in scouse or keeping nicks. Then somebody would be selected to pick up, his job was to make sure the money was covered by the right amount and who had struck a bet, it was usually done by the local hard cases so there would be no cheating going on. Whoever had put the money on the ground then placed two coins on the palm of his hand tail side up and toss them above his head, if he didn't throw them high enough anyone who had put a bet on could stick a hand or foot out before they hit the ground and shout 'BAR THEM' they were then tossed up again. If they landed with two heads facing up he won, if they landed two tails up he lost, if they landed one head and one tail, known as 'two ones' they had to be tossed again. If the tosser won he would give the picker-up a small amount of his winnings and a coin or two to the lads on 'nicks'.[32]

Such economic adventurism often took the form of some ingenious fiddles. Bert W. of Bootle made double headed pennies on his lathe to ensure the success of his ventures:

> If there were people who you knew didn't play a lot you could use your double headed pennies – you couldn't lose. 'Cos when you tossed them up they either came down what they called two 'ones', a tail and a head, or two 'heads', 'cos one had to be heads anyway, so that you couldn't lose.[33]

Bert would only pull this trick four or five times, before it became too suspicious, then he would start an argument and slip the coin into his pocket whilst the others were distracted. Skill was often an essential factor in the enactment of a fiddle. An experienced tossman was skilled in the art of 'butterflying', making the coins look as if they were spinning when they were just 'wiggling rapidly', same side up.[34]

After 1945, it appears that the incidence of coin gaming in the streets began to decline, although it was still popular in poorer areas well into the 1950s.[35] It was probably marginalised by the growth of alternative distractions, such as the television set, rock music and milk bars. It is possible, although doubtful, that slot machines displaced coin gaming in the streets.[36] This is because they had already been around since the Edwardian years.

The question of whether these slot machines broke the lottery laws • was inconsistently dealt with in a number of cases from 1903. The issue was one of 'chance or skill', and on the nature of the prize, as some amusements with prizes machines were not played for cash and were defended on this principle, although they certainly took cash. In 1903, a machine in which a penny was inserted into any one of seven compartments, two of which gave the penny back, one of which entitled the winner to two pennyworth of goods from the shop, and four of which kept the penny, was found to infringe the lottery laws because it was based on pure chance. However, from 1914 magistrates had some difficulty with the 'clown machines' in which a marble rolled around between pins in a vertical bagatelle-like structure, and either did or did not end up in a little cup held by a clown. Some thought it a game of pure chance, others did not.[37] The 'diversity of the types of automatic machines' caused the police 'considerable difficulty'.[38]

The 1908 Select Committee on Lotteries made no provision for new legislation on slot machines. Moreover, despite concern expressed by anti-gamblers to inter-war enquiries, there was no new attempt to restrict access to slot machines, despite the fact their popularity appears to have been growing between the wars, when an increasing number of amusement arcades were opened in seaside towns and in the bigger cities. It was claimed in court in Manchester during the late 1920s that there were 2,000 slot machines in one police division.[39] In Manchester and other parts of the north, shopkeepers were also instrumental in introducing machines to the public. Some shopkeepers had installed 'bell fruit' machines, invented in America in 1895, from which winners received tokens to exchange for goods in the shop. The Chief Constable felt that slot machines were a 'menace' to the poor, 'particularly to women and children'.[40] The Chief Constable of the Metropolitan Police told parliament in 1932 that 'By far the most troublesome form of gaming [in] recent years is the automatic gaming machine of the "fruit" variety'. Here, the player put a penny in a slot and pulled the handle on the side of the machine, which set three reels spinning, each of which contained pictures of different types of fruit. If winning combinations of fruit synchronised in the window at the front of the machine, for example

* three cherries or three oranges, the player won a prize. These were kept 'in large numbers' in refreshment shops and cafes and in working men's clubs 'and in other clubs of good standing where they prove a useful source of profit to the management, and are to a large extent beyond the control of the police'.[41] Police proceedings could be taken under the Metropolitan Police Act of 1839, and by all forces under the Betting Houses Acts of 1853 and the Gaming Houses Act of 1854, as well as under the Lottery Laws. Yet, as with bylaws to do with other forms of gaming, the police were critical of a state of affairs which was uneven nationally, and felt the 1932–3 Commission should 'remove the foolhardiness of the law' which allowed gambling on certain machines on one side of the road but not on the other, in a different local authority district.[42]

The distribution of slot machines seems to have been through a middle firm who let them to shopkeepers. When asked by Mary Stocks how machines intended for arcades ended up in shops, the managing Director of Essex Auto Manufacturing Company Ltd, who made the 'Diddler' machine and other gambling gadgets stated that 'the machine is sold outright to somebody and that is the only thing we know about it'.[43] At the local level, these were probably small amusement catering firms, often with fairground connections, who were prepared to rent machines to anyone. Two such companies were the Amusement Equipment Company Ltd of London, registered in 1937, whose directors included a managing director of some arcades, a 'merchant', and two 'amusement caterers'. In Manchester, from 1957, the Amusement Catering and Equipment Company was managed by a hotelier and an accountant. An oral history of Stockton on Tees between the wars, refers to the enigmatic 'Italians' who distributed slot machines to local shops.[44]

In 1936 *The Economist* estimated that turnover on slot machines was £15 million a year. In 1938 the Christian Social Committee on Gambling estimated that between two and three hundred thousand automatic machines were taking up to £15 million annually.[45] These machines came in all shapes and sizes. In Blackpool during the late 1930s Mass Observation undertook a little census of the types of slot machines at the Olympia and Winter Gardens, and at the Central Pier Arcade in Blackpool. In the first two establishments, amongst the grip tests, football games, fortune telling machines and the 'What the Butler Saw' peep shows, there were 113 'Allwin' machines, twenty-three 'Shooting Machines', nineteen 'Merchandisers', eighteen 'Steer-A-Ball' machines, fourteen 'Sky Jumps' and so on. Most of the fruit machines and slot machines were constructed to make a profit. They could not run out of money, so the reels were fixed to pay-out only on certain combinations. Some occasional players were lucky to hit the bigger payouts with just one or two coins, others who fed the machines and kept winning were often putting in more than they took out.[46]

Mass Observation described the buzzing and clattering of the seafront arcades, and the young working-class couples and groups who flocked to them, especially on rainy days. A player who won frequently was a centre of attention, and was usually male. More recent research on young people and slot machines at seaside resorts illustrates that about 70 per cent of boys play machines in arcades compared to 40 per cent of girls.[47] Yet arcades were meeting places not just for holiday makers but also for the local young, 'for the majority of whom sociability rather than sustained machine playing is the real reason for being there'.[48]

Many Blackpool arcades employed 'G-men', 'or more often G-women' during the summer. They were usually young; one of them was an Oxbridge student. This was a decoy job, in which the Gs were given money to play to win, shouting out their successes and creating a noisy impression of money gushing into the tills of the machines. This was illegal, so, in the same way that bookmakers' runners memorised the faces of policemen who might come up in plain clothes, the Gs 'know the police better than the police know them, and when the detectives are about they play to lose.' A seasonal job, the pay was thirty-five shillings to two pounds a week, depending on the number of hours worked. Many poorer residents could supplement their normal wages or dole money by 'putting in a couple of hours in the evening'. Even one of MO's principal observers in Blackpool did this.[49]

The Blackpool pleasure beach site, the biggest in the country, Blackpool central pier, Brighton pier and other major sites were owned by the Amusement Caterers Association (ACA). To the 1932-3 Royal Commission on Lotteries and Betting, they claimed to hold three hundred amusement sites at the seaside, on piers and on fairgrounds.[50] This grew slightly from then, and to the 1949-51 parliamentary enquiry, the ACA claimed to own 350 arcades, about 80 per cent of permanent and semi-permanent amusement arcades. About 300 A. C. A. arcades were at the seaside, the other fifty were in 'other urban areas'.[51] The ACA said that there had been a great increase in the number of arcades during the early years of the second world war, but that they had dropped off in the later 1940s. Evidence from the London County Council appeared to support this view, as the number of arcades in the

County of London dropped from fifty-three in 1948 to twenty-five by 1950.[52] Perhaps because of this decline, and because of local differences in the levels of provision of slot machines, the Willink Commission was prepared to leave individual local authorities to decide their own bylaws on gaming machines.[53]

The fear amongst the authorities about arcades was two-fold. Firstly, that they were meeting places where all sorts of perverts might gather to prey on the young.[54] Secondly, that children's pockets fed the machines and introduced them to the gambling habit for life. In the latter case, in 1915, Birkenhead Education Committee passed a resolution denouncing 'the harm done to children' by such machines, and felt that some children were 'in possession of more pocket money than was good for them'.[55] In 1916 the NAGL felt that 'there had been a large increase in the number of automatic machines all over the country' since the start of war and called for tougher sentences on those promoting 'these gambling snares for young children'.[56] In 1927 the Lord Chief Justice stated that the slot machine 'was a pest and a most mischievous pest, because it operates on the minds of young persons and corrupts them in their youth'.[57]

Fears about the relationship of young people not only to slot machines but to all gambling seem to have grown in the late 1940s and early 1950s. Police statistics, with due acknowledgement to their problems, give an impression of this. In Liverpool, under the general category of 'gambling', the number of juveniles proceeded against rose from nineteen in 1945 to fifty-six in 1954, before its jerky slide to fifteen by 1960. In Manchester, the offence of 'gaming' for children and young people rose from single figures in the 1940s to twenty-one in 1954. These were hardly big figures, however, and misdemeanours such as wilful damage, being found on enclosed premises, or 'railway offences' were often far higher.[58]

Social investigations provided varying estimates. In 1946 it was estimated that 32 two per cent of eleven- to fourteen-year olds in Lancashire regularly visited the arcades.[59] In 1950 a survey for the Cadbury's Charitable Trust of leisure habits amongst adolescents in Birmingham found that only 5 per cent of girls and 13 per cent of boys spent money weekly on all forms of gambling. Occasional gamblers numbered 12 per cent of girls and 23 per cent of boys, and amounts ranged from one penny to ten shillings per week. The average amongst those who gambled was about eighteen pence per week.[60] From 1951, John Barron Mays undertook his study of juvenile delinquency in Liverpool in order to dampen down the moral panic about working-class youth which he detected in the local and national media. He found that pitch and toss and card gaming were still common amongst lads, and were part of a pattern of recreation handed down from the parent generation, rather than a new crisis of morality and crime. Mays made no mention of slot machines.[61]

There was a general decline in the number of juvenile gaming offences throughout the 1950s, reflecting the national trend. Although Gambler's Anonymous from its inception in 1964, the Home Office, anti-gamblers and youth workers have since maintained vigilance about young people gambling,[62] popular concern about miscreant behaviour from the mid 1950s had increasingly turned to the potential disorders associated with sex and drugs and rock and roll, reflecting changes in the leisure choices of the young.[63]

The place of the development of slot machines in the qualitative experience of coin gaming, whether for young or old, is no easy matter upon which to conclude decisively. They represented the mechanisation of penny games, and threw into sharp relief the commercialisation of informal coin gaming. Whereas play in the streets re-circulated the money amongst the local poor, the machines took the cash into the coffers of the Amusement Caterers Association, or the Showmen's Guild. Yet they shared certain features of pitch and toss: the sociability of the gathering and also the association with 'action', the flirtation with pure luck. All gaming gatherings were 'where the action is'. To throw a coin into the air, or to watch the drums of a fruit machine spin around, was to risk money on an uncertain outcome.[64] Yet the battle between player and machine was a more intensively individualised experience than tossing with a few mates. Various theories have been advanced as to why people played them. From some of Mass Observation's descriptions it seems that players, for example on ball steering games, were evaluating their own quickness.[65] A French sociologist has stressed the vertiginous aspects of play which can be viewed as particularly relevant to slot machines: the sense of disequilibrium and the vicarious experience of letting go, until normality is restored when the game is over.[66] Mott suggests that playing the slots is an attempt to beat the machine in a machine age. It allows a reciprocity with technology which is impossible in routinised tasks. The machine symbolises the workers' 'precise location in a complex division of labour', and thus an ideological resistance to it.[67] To attach relative weights to these explanations is a difficult exercise, yet there is probably an element of truth in all of them which depends on the social background of the players.

This section has been suggestive rather than conclusive. More historical work is needed on the social and economic impact of slot machines on coin gaming, particularly as an aspect of the Americanisation of English popular culture. Now, the attention shifts to cards.

II

Like coin games, card playing was often the first experience of direct participation in gambling for the young. As Mass Observation noted in 1948, card playing for small nominal stakes often took place within the family.[68] Unlike coin games, however, card games for money have been played by all social classes, although different games have become associated with different social groups and classes. The size of stakes involved has also reflected differing levels of wealth.

During the early nineteenth century gaming salons for the wealthy offered such card games as hazard, chemin de fer and whist as well as roulette, rouge et noir, backgammon and other games combining a small element of skill with chance. White's Club, established in the 1690s in St James's Street, London, and Brooks's Club, during the high days of Regency gaming in 1754, also of St James Street, were notorious as the gambling dens of the landed upper class.[69] As evidence by the proprietor to the 1844 enquiry revealed, Crockfords, begun in 1828 by an ex-military horse trainer, was perhaps symptomatic of both the established culture of gentlemanly gaming and the slow infusion of respectable bookmakers into these sumptuously appointed salons. Besides the dealing of cards and the spinning of the wheel, the acceptance of bets on horse races and other competitions from the wealthy patrons was commonplace. Crockfords was held to be responsible for an upsurge of gaming amongst the young gentlemen of the metropolis, an impression perhaps justified by Crockford's unwillingness to divulge details of the extent of betting on his premises to the Select Committee on Gaming in 1844.[70]

Yet the committee of 1844 was more concerned with the rise of 'common gaming houses', as locales for the sins of the multitude, than with the excesses of an elite. These establishments, run in situ by public house owners, coffee shop owners, cigar shop proprietors and others central to local social life, allowed card playing, bagatelle, quoits, backgammon, dice and a variety of instruments of gaming. A chief of police in London in 1844 felt that the difference between a common gaming house and a respectable establishment was simple, as 'the Berkeley Club would not let a Jew into it, nor a common fellow that has hardly a shoe to his foot'.[71] Some witnesses to the committee admitted to doubt over whether some houses for gaming were open to subscribers only, or let in all and sundry and were thus common gaming houses. The 1845 'Act to amend the law concerning games and wagers', working on the latter principle, made it illegal to keep a common gaming house, which included a 'house, room or place' and gave the police powers to enter, search, find evidence in the form of instruments of 'unlawful gaming' and prosecute. Later the 1854 Act increased these powers and made it an offence to own or keep a house, room or place for the purpose of unlawful gaming. Penalties ranged from £20 to £500 depending on the expense and scale of the operation, previous offences, and obstructions to the police.[72]

Of particular concern to the committee were the social consequences resulting from the use of deceit in gaming, such as false dice, false roulette wheels and card sharping. A superintendent of police for London drew the distinction between the harmlessness of gamesters 'playing amongst themselves' and the dangers 'when two or three sharpers get among them, and the subsequent ruination of the hapless victim's family. Some wives had 'not a halfpenny for their maintenance'.[73] Social investigators too were mindful that fiddlers preyed not only on their own gambling groups but also on 'those strangers who may have the misfortune to be in their company'. Mayhew warned his readers of the criminal elements – the 'magsmen' and 'sharpers' – who perpetrated frauds on unsuspecting passers-by using not only cards but also skittles and the 'thimble and pea trick', whereby the pea, instead of remaining under one of the thimbles which the sharper moved about on the table or floor was 'secreted under the thumb nail of the sharp'.[74] Sharpers were part of the sub-class of travelling poor and seasonally employed labourers who went to race meetings to whistle up a few shillings. Gipsies exhibiting coconut shies (whom Charles Hindley, a self-confessed member of 'the fraternity' of 'cheap jacks', called 'Romanees') were typical of this peripatetic group of marginals. For London in the 1880s Charles Booth noted that gipsies, card sharpers and people who sought work at the racecourses lived in the lowest streets of the 'vicious semi-criminal poor'.[75]

Sharpers, also known as 'nobblers', worked in groups, and travelled to race meetings and country fairs as far apart as Manchester and Maidstone.[76] 'Three Up' or 'Five Up', betting on which downturned cards would be turned upwards was also common, and 'Find the Lady' (the Queen) was a favourite trick, the sharpers shuffling the cards and playing amongst themselves before inviting someone to bet on where the card was hidden in the hand. The card had been removed from the pack by sleight of hand. These tricks were often pulled on trains against racegoers. In Lancashire County Court in March 1901 four 'Sharpers in a railway carriage' of 'no fixed abode' were, with the full support of the Lancashire and Yorkshire Railway Company, sentenced to one month hard labour each for playing a game of chance in a public place:

> In a way well known to the Magistrates, several passengers were beguiled into the affair. When Jones was searched, four 'flash notes' were found in his possession, Jeffries had also four 'flash notes' and three cards and a pocket book which contained four other 'flash notes', and Geary had six playing cards and three blank cards. The railway company felt very strongly in the matter that this class of passenger could not be stopped travelling. It interfered with the comfort of the passengers and it was a danger and a disgrace to the travelling class at large.[77]

A few days later in Bolton four 'sharpers in a railway carriage' at Westhoughton were given three months hard labour each for playing a game of chance in public and stealing seven pounds by deception.[78] In the 1940s, MO found that card sharpers and makeshift gaming booths were still part of the fun of the fair, as we will see in the next chapter.

Newspaper reports, and also the court of summary jurisdiction records for Bolton and Manchester, held at these respective local libraries, illustrate that from 1900 to the 1930s pontoon, banker, brag and whist were the most common activities for which lower-class gamesters in the street or in pubs were prosecuted. Oral evidence and Mass Observation material also illustrates the popularity in pubs of shove 'appeny boards, dominoes, darts, dice games, billiards and quoits. Indoors, especially in public houses, sidestake wagering on cards, crown and anchor, dominoes, darts and a variety of pub sports was a significant social activity in public houses and working men's clubs, although such establishments ran the risk of being prosecuted as common gaming houses.[79]

Police intervention in gatherings held behind closed doors where games of chance were played for money was also difficult. Offenders would protest that they were playing for love rather than money. John Monk, as a detective superintendent in London's East End during the early years of this century, had to confront this and other problems in attempting to raid and prosecute the instigators of spielers and other 'dens of infamy' which went on in, amongst other places, the back of a restaurant, lodging houses and model dwellings. Moreover, under the Betting Act of 1874 warrants for searching premises also had to be applied for, and as Monk laments 'it was weeks before I could find my man and execute the warrant'. He was also warned by a magistrate for illegal entry.[80] This state of affairs existed throughout the rest of the period under consideration, and led to an unwillingness both by many police chiefs to plan raids and prosecute offenders, and by magistrates to convict them.[81]

The problem was that it was legal to play games for money at private parties at home, provided that these parties or family gatherings did not spill over into a 'common law nuisance'. What was illegal was the keeping of a 'common gaming house', in which unlawful games were played for private profit, and where the general public or 'habitual users' went to play.[82] In a famous case in 1958, John Aspinall and his mother Lady Osborne, who used to arrange parties amongst London's wealthy aristocrats for baccarat or chemin-de-fer, were raided and charged with this offence. Following observation during which an Inspector clung onto a grille outside the window of a room in Hyde Park Street, and espied a dealing shoe and 'chips in a bowl' for chemin-de-fer, Aspinall and others were charged under the 1854 Gaming Houses Act, but eventually cleared because there was 'not sufficient evidence to prove unlawful gaming'. In other words, it could not really be proved that 'Aspers' was keeping a common gaming house for private profit.[83] This • case illustrates two points. Not only were the gaming laws full of holes, but the location of the game, whether in a club or at home, and the type of card game played, reflected social exclusivity, as it always had done. This has been true from the Georgian gaming salons such as Brooks and White's Clubs, mentioned above. For the inter-war years Graves and Hodge pointed out, with their tonges partly in their cheeks, the class alignments attached to a game of cards, and the increasing popularity of bridge with the upper middle classes. The lower middle class 'continued to play the less skilful whist'.

Yet the much maligned lower middle class could achieve some wonderful things from a few games of whist. As Political and Economic Planning (PEP) discovered, on the inter-war new estate at Watling in north London, whist drives were held by local religious and community associations in order to raise money for meeting places. A church hall built in 1930 'was provided largely from the proceeds of weekly whist drives'.[85] Such facilities had not been provided for the tenants by the London County Council, so this was a particularly apposite example of gambling as self-help.

Mass Observation found in the 1940s that whist drives were attended more by women than men, but that men turned up in greater numbers to drives with biggest prizes. For example, at a regular London suburban whist drive, not unlike Watling's, held on a weekday afternoon for a five pounds prize, men made up 42 per cent of the audience. But at church and village hall whist drives in northern towns, where prizes were smaller, male attendance was between 2 and 13 per cent. MO put this down to men gambling more 'seriously' than women for money, but they did not fully explore the sociable side of whist drives for women who did not go out to work.[86]

Games of cards for money could be played by anyone, but where they were played usually revealed the social, ethnic and class identity of the gamesters. Beatrice Potter, describing the assimilation into London's Jewish community of a Polish 'greener' (a recent immigrant) noted that he soon became 'an habitue of a gambling club'.[87] Walter Besant observed that dominoes gatherings had a similar role amongst Chinese immigrants in east London around 1900.[88] In Manchester, Benny Weingard emphasised the social function of card gambling amongst the poorer Jews of Choir Street. His parents 'used to like a social evening, a card evening. They used to start after two, after dinner, until about twelve o'clock at night. You couldn't get a meal, it was only two up two down, they was playing cards'.[89]

Amongst the wealthier local Jews, a Mrs Gaster, who later married Neville Laski, remembered that she and her husband played bridge, and joined a tennis club in Palatine Road, Parrs Wood. She emphasised the social network of the sephardic Jews in Manchester, who, from an Iberian mercantile background, felt socially superior to the Ashkenazi Jews from Eastern Europe. The membership of the club was predominantly Sephardic. Parties held there would begin with dinner or an expensive buffet supper and end with bridge. Bridge evenings were also held at friends' houses,[90] and were part of the increasingly popularity of bridge to which Graves and Hodge pointed.

Betting on cards, as with coins and crown and anchor, was also an exciting way to kill boredom in total situations of enforced or inescapable captivity where so-called leisure time was circumscribed by inexorable routine or confined environment. Soldiers based at barracks or in prisoner of war camps during the first and second world wars have testified to the distracting and escapist appeal of gambling in these most uncertain circumstances.

Such gaming was probably common where there was little or no access to bookmakers. It was against Queen's (or King's) Regulations, however. In the three years 1888 to 1890, out of thirty NCOs tried by court martial for allowing or participating in gambling, twenty-three soldiers, mostly corporals, were reduced to the ranks, and six sergeants were demoted to corporal. Only one man, a sergeant, was let off for previous good conduct.[91] 'Housey housey', now more commonly known as bingo, appears to have originated amongst soldiers sent to fight in the first world war. Harry B., who was a private based at Catterick Bridge Barracks prior to his departure for France, remembered the exploitation of the game by the corporal and sergeant who organised it:

> Well we used to go in the canteen at night and they'd run what's called bingo now. Well, we called it 'housey housey' but the trouble was there was these old soldiers, and we youngsters, and they'd got their own mates calling out 'bingo' and the cards was never checked so you never knew. It was all a dead twist and that was beer money for them . . . If you started to try any business you found yourself a real mug – they'd pick you up and mug ya.[92]

Every so often, Harry remembered, they would let someone win to keep up the pretence of fair play. Illegality was as much a breeding ground for corruption in high places in the army as well as amongst the civilian betting fraternity. Sergeants also took advantage of card games:

> And then at night in the hut we used to play at brag and that. And then when lights were out we used to have candles and if the orderly sergeant came in we'd drop a blanket over there and into bed quick. But they began to rumble that, and all they did they just picked up all the cash that was in the kitty and walked out. We couldn't do anything about it.[93]

Whilst incacerated in a Italian POW camp in the second world war, the author and journalist Eric Newby noticed that class distinctions amongst the soldiers were clearly reflected in the separate baccarat tables and exclusive bookmaking amongst the 'temporarily expatriate members of White's Club' which went on over running races.[94]

'Crown and Anchor' was another popular gambling game amongst the soldiers, and usually organised by the more economically adventurous individuals, or what Harry B. Called the 'spivvy types'. It was played by betting on whether the crowns or anchors on the die would land face up on a makeshift board or cloth marked out with the same. Mick Burke, from Ancoats in Manchester, who fought at Ypres, saw an opportunity to make a few shillings in this game:

In the summer of 1918 I found myself in a place called Trescault, where there were a lot of Australian troops. I were a bit in credit so we clubbed together to start a Crown and Anchor board. The Aussies loved it and we were having a burster – we lived like lords for a short time. People were asking for our rations because we could afford to dine in the local estaminets.[95]

Anti-gamblers such as E. B. Perkins were concerned at the indiscipline and crisis of morale amongst soldiers which they feared might result if the gambling fever got a hold amongst the lower ranks. An army chaplain during the Great War was aware of the extent of housey housey amongst the ranks, but viewed it as both a symptom of widespread gambling from top to bottom in the army, and as useful in preventing more virulent forms of gambling spreading amongst the soldiers. He knew that officers could not stop gaming in the ranks because 'the latter know that it is equally prevalent amongst the officers'.[96] This was the long-standing message of the NAGL: if superiors did not set a good example, they had no moral basis on which to attack the betting of others.

Like the routine of barracks and the oppressive regime of POW camps, prison conditions were conducive to a need to ameliorate enforced boredom through the risk and excitement of betting. A recent report of the Prison Governors Association has pointed to the widespread habits of betting for currency such as drink and drugs.[97] Beneath the excitement and sociability which gambling offers in such circumstances is an economic function: if free from corruption, betting serves as an egalitarian system for the random accumulation and distribution of scarce valuable items in an illicit and informal market.[98] All are equal on the throw of a dice or the dealing of the cards.

As with other forms of gambling, there were those who played cards and those who did not. Oral history archives, for example, Elizabeth Roberts's *North West Regional Project*, contain examples from the early twentieth century. Mrs. H.2.B's family of Hindpool, were Methodists. Her father, a manager of a bakers' shop, was a staunch believer and she 'never saw playing cards until I was grown up'. Another woman's father, a foreman in a brass finishing shop in Barrow, played cards but never for money, as gambling 'was wrong and he wouldn't have anything like that . . . Dad used to wear a medal, Church of England Temperance Society'.[99] It may, however, be possible to exaggerate the antipathy towards card playing amongst some of the Nonconformist church members. Clive Field's sample survey of 106 English Methodists, analysing retrospective attitudes towards leisure, found that whilst 74 per cent spurned dancing as 'next to the devil', and 47 per cent opposed the consumption of alcoholic beverages, only 25 per cent personally prohibited gambling, and only 15 per cent opposed card playing.[100] There is a problem with this finding, as many may have played cards for sweets or buttons only, but it is significant that card playing was viewed as less morally corrupting than dance or drink. This point was not lost on anti-gambling campaigners. Canon Green, for example, castigated his fellow churchmen and women for using raffles and whist drives and other forms of gambling to raise money for churches and chapels, and for failing to understand the principle that all gambling was wrong.[101] No doubt the residents of Watling would have disagreed with him.

It is difficult to quantify the amount of card betting and gaming which occured indoors, in pubs and clubs or at home. It is also impossible to assess changes in the incidence of such activities over time. This, however, is not true for informal but organised local sports which were vehicles for mutual betting amongst those of a shared enthusiasm, or 'fancy'.

III

Informal local sports may be defined for the purposes of this section as competitive hobbies organised collectively amongst friends, neighbours and peers on a non-commercialised basis. Two such sports, pigeon racing and bowls, were popular in Lancashire as media for betting until 1960. Whilst local sports like pedestrianism and prize fighting declined throughout the second half of the nineteenth century, pigeon racing, like whippet racing, was established as a working-class hobby. Both sports were outlets for friendly rivalry, for the individual pursuit of the perfection of the animal and its performance, and for petty wagering.[102]

IV

In 1898 the newly launched newspaper the *Racing Pigeon* felt that the 'enormous growth of the Racing Pigeon fancy during the past ten years, and its ever increasing popularity, convinces us that there is room for this journal'.[103] The directors and shareholders of the paper, who declared themselves as 'well-known fanciers' from all over England, were right. Both the paper and the sport were still going strong by 1960. Moreover, in the *Racing Pigeon* it is clear from reports of club meetings, lists of forthcoming races, advertisements for lofts and the birds, and correspondence that there was a small but noticeable bias in favour of the north west and Yorkshire before 1914. In the *Homing Pigeon Annual* in the 1890s, of about 140 individual homing pigeon clubs and federations of clubs in England and Wales, thirty-five names were in Lancashire and Cheshire. Most were formed in the 1880s, 1890s and 1900s. The West Lancashire Saturday Federation, for example, was formed in 1897 from six clubs. One year later it was composed of fifteen affiliated clubs, with 474 members.[104]

Pigeon racing was of two types, short distance and long distance. In Lancashire at least there was a clear status division between the labour-aristocratic long-distance flying clubs, often based at hotels, and the short-distance clubs run, as we will soon see, from pubs. The City of Liverpool Flying Club, formed in 1894, met at a hotel in Lime Street. Manchester Flying Club met at the Castle Hotel, Tyldesley. Long-distance flying was particularly popular amongst the artisans and lower middle classes of the north west. The *Annual* and the *Racing Pigeon* advertised 'squeakers' and 'homers' from the largest lofts for ten shillings or more, and both the *Annual* and the *Racing Pigeon* show photographs of comfortably-off artisans standing proudly in collar and tie by their own lofts in spacious suburban gardens. Entry fees were usually five shillings per race and an annual subscription of ten shillings and sixpence was required to keep out the unrespectable. As the Secretary of the Blackpool Long Distance Flying Union told the *Homing Pigeon Annual*, every member of his club paid their subscription by cheque, 'evidence of the superior class of men who now compose the fancy'.[105] This of course echoed sharply the distinction between more respectable credit betters and the lower-class street betters. The columnist 'Flying Beauty' was keen to emphasise the rational and improving qualities of this 'upper branch' of the fancy and to distinguish it from the inferior branch associated with low-life activities:

> We are classed with the men who go about from pillar to post with a significant dirty bag or basket on pigeon flying bent, and who spend most of the rest of their time in low pot-houses, gambling, practices which are most abhorrent to the real fancier.[106]

Yet the self-consciously better long-distance clubs did bet: they went in for pool betting, using collective stakes to boost prize monies got up from entrance fees to races. The Rules of the National Flying Club instructed members to time the bird's performance and record its leg-ring number on return, and to state 'all the pools and special prizes for which the bird was competing'. In 1914, birds flying back to a club in southern England from Marennes, Pons or Bordeaux, entered at four shillings each, could win their owners part of a total of £596 and eleven shillings in pools and prizes.[107]

Pigeon racing in the poorer areas was short-distance, more rough-and-ready, and less well-endowed with cash. For those in poor streets there were no large gardens or airy lofts. From the window of a railway carriage passing over a viaduct above 'two-storied London' one could see 'small rough-roofed erections' for the pigeons in the little yards and gardens of the workers' cottages.[108] Anywhere such as a small back yard or garden where a loft could safely be looked-after was suitable for keeping pigeons. MO's study of pubs in Bolton between the wars noted that short-distance pigeon clubs still met in the tap room or the rooms above pubs. The biggest local bet was the annual sweep, 'the most important and elaborately organised race' where members could bet in cash or in kind. As one fancier told the observer:

> I have seen the landlord of the R-- Tavern have a side bet of 100 black puddings. This is of course in addition to the money bets that have been wagered over a course of several weeks . . . I have seen side bets of sacks of potatoes, a sack of corn, flour, case of oranges, joints of beef, legs of pork etc.[109]

These side bets are a good example of the random distribution of 'treats' amongst the fanciers. The usual formalities and expense of purchasing such goods from tradesmen were subsumed to the vagaries of a race. Most clubs were organised on the pool system, with stake monies put in the kitty to be paid out as winnings or expenses after the race. As Mott argues, the 'pool' system often reflected the solidarities of mining areas and was as much a product of bird racing as the *pari mutuel* in horses or football betting.[110] For example, in Ashton in Makerfield between the wars, Joe Gormley's father kept pigeons for short-distance racing. It was an exciting group activity which took place on Sundays, with the draw for the positions to release the birds taking place in a pub.[111] Yet short-distance pigeon-racing was popular amongst other groups of workers. Harry B's brother in law, a farm labourer, was a pigeon fancier in a society run by farm labourers and local workmen in Boston, Lincolnshire between the wars. This was amongst fanciers only:

> he was a pigeon fancier and there was big races. Well they put so much in a pool, every entrant put and it went into a pool. *Was this called a pigeon pool?* A pigeon pool. The first pigeon home scooped the pool. But there was no bookie betting as you understand it. It was just amongst their own pigeon societies.

Their entrant was charged so much and that went into the pool. And there was so much taken out for expenses.[112]

In a race the pigeons were set off at the same time on the moors or nearby fields, and timed by using a clock bag under the jurisdiction of an umpire. Of the clock bag, Walter M. of Hulme explained that 'the pigeon fanciers used to have 'em – you clocked the pigeons time coming in'.[113] The clock bag, used widely by bookmakers from the 1920s to prevent cheating, may well have had its origins as a device for fair play in the pigeon pools.

Short-term pigeon racing perhaps started to decline between the wars. In Bolton, the Secretary of the local Short Distance Union blamed 'circumstances over which we have no control' namely 'bad trade and depression'. One collier, when asked if the local pigeon club was still in existence replied: 'Nor, they are broken up, what wi' one thing un another, un't pubs not doin' so well, thee get short o' money, un this started 'em falling out among themselves.' The observer agreed, blaming changing social habits and leisure preferences for the demise of bird betting as part of a general decline of 'local forms of culture that are skilled, active and communal in favour of newer and passive forms of leisure activity'.[114]

To some extent this decline was reflected in the pigeon press. For example, the sport's second-longest running paper *Pigeons and the Pigeon World*, formed in 1912 from *Pigeons*, and published in Bradford, was incorporated into a weekly paper called *Fur and Feather* from 1939. Pigeons were subordinate to rodents in this publication, usually meriting only a two-page feature. *Fur and Feather*, though, is an interesting read. By 1960 it was still redolent with the language of the fancy, and its regular 'Voice of the Fancy' frequently mentions the virtues of sociability, gentleness and homeliness of pet keeping, let alone 'the wholesomeness and generosity that go to make the Fancy'.[115] Moreover, the paper *Racing Pigeon* was still going strong, and serving the long-distance racers, who were still forming new clubs and pools. There were still over three thousand long-distance local clubs in 1960.[116] The *Racing Pigeon*, moreover, was taking up cudgels on behalf of poorer fanciers on council estates whose local authorities were refusing planning permission for lofts in the gardens, suggesting that status distinctions amongst the feathered fancy counted for less than in the Edwardian years.[117] McKibbin has clearly pointed to the reasons for the attraction of pigeon racing, and why it and other hobbies survived despite the alleged pacification of leisure mentioned by Mass Observation. For all participants, pigeon breeding and racing, as with other animals, was a shared enthusiasm, a hobby which provided 'acceptable competitiveness'. This was true for relatively wealthy skilled workers and those whose lives were often constrained by a mechanised work routine and '(less certainly) by the demands of group loyalties'.[118] To some extent, the same goes for bowling, another gentle and communal sport which did not take too kindly to the attentions of bookmakers.

V

Like pigeon racing, bowling was associated with pubs and local hotels with blowling greens. Bowls clubs were formed locally from the 1880s to the 1900s until they were brought together under the auspicies of national organisations.[119] The English Bowling Association was formed in 1903, with the cricketer W. G. Grace as president. In 1907, the British Crown Green Amateur Bowling Association was formed. 'Crown green' was and is a northern game, so-called because the green was 'slightly raised in the centre and falling away in every direction from the Crown'.[120] Most greens in Lancashire used for both amateur and professional bowls were next to a public house or hotel, often within its grounds. Unlike pigeon racing, which was and still is the preserve of men,[121] women participated as players, mostly in works or church teams, although there is little evidence of female betting. Locally, 'crown green' games were sponsored by local companies such as the breweries and textile and engineering firms. Flat green matches were held not just in pubs but also in parks such as Leverhulme Park in Bolton. The Mass Observation archive contains some detailed descriptions of the smaller matches between church school teams and works based teams, such as St Andrews versus St Georges Road Congregational women, and Barlow and Jones Ladies versus Moss Bank Ladies held at Moss Bank Park. The English Women's Bowling Association was formed in 1931. Admission to these smaller games was usually free or a couple of pence if held for charity. Gambling was slight or non-existent, it appears. Crown green bowls were the medium for betting amongst the players and spectators.[122] This was a similar distinction to that between long- and short-distance pigeon racing.

Professional bowling was controlled in Lancashire by the Lancashire Professional Bowling Association (LPBA). By the late 1940s the county possessed forty-five crown greens. The nature and extent of bowling on these greens was confused by the 1934 Betting and Lotteries Act which outlawed betting on athletic tracks, which were not defined properly in relation to horse and dog racing stadia. As the Chief Constable's Association of England and Wales told the 1949–51 Royal Commission 'it is not known if the intention of the Betting and Lotteries Act, 1934, was that bowling greens should be accepted as tracks' although the police treated them as such. This rendered the Professional Bowling Association liable to prosecution for allowing betting at athletic 'and other sporting events,' if the requirements of the legislation were not observed: 'The organisers, players and bookmakers move from green to green all the year round and give notice to the police as required by the [1934 Act], limiting the matches to eight on any one green in a year.'[123]

But oral evidence and MO materials show that the status of these 'bookmakers' at bowling matches is more intriguing than this quote suggests. Mr P., a supervisor at Singer Sewing Machines in Halifax, travelled regularly to Bolton in the 1930s both to bowls and sometimes to make books on crown green matches:

> They bet amongst theirselves, there was no such thing as bookmakers Y'see, as the game fluctuated, say one fellow went four or five in front 'e would then be about six to four on like, and you'd have to lay six pound to win four, or thirty pound to win twenty. There was lots of very big money bets in them days.[124]

John Summerfield, a founder of Mass Observation, has left a vivid account of a match he saw which supports this recollection. The match was a Crown Green Infirmary Handicap between Barnes of Horwich and Molyneaux, a Wigan champion, in July 1938. On some old wooden boards at the ground was chalked '41 Up. Admission 6d., No Betting':

> Man in front, at edge of green, immediately calls out 'six to four, six to four' then 'I'll tak fourteen bob to eight'. Another man says 'George Barnes can't win this game'. Chap at edge now says 'I'll tek five to four', another 'ten bob to eight', man passing 'ten bob to nowt'. Around the stand this calling of odds goes on all the time, not steadily but being taken up by several chaps, and then dying away again. *However, no one did any actual betting.*[125]

* The system worked like this: in much the same way as pub pals or workmates made little books for friends to have a bet, so a member or members of the local club laid odds and accepted bets on the results on the results of matches in progress. The club committee, or 'panel', regulated this:

> It was a gambling game as was instigated by theirselves . . . a committee to see

as it weren't unfair, and there was no people taking a dive and that sort of thing. It was kind of run for the benefit of people who were interested in having a gamble.[126]

All of this steered clear of ready-money betting, enabling legal mutual betting policed by the bowlers themselves. The sport did not need the attentions of real bookmakers. This was still true of northern Crown Green bowls in the 1950s and 1960s. As one Huddersfield bowler put it, 'Once you get that element creeping in, you get nasty stories about bowlers not bowling their best.'[127]

VI

The sports of bowls and pigeon racing were not destroyed or corrupted by betting. Rather, a flutter gave these sports a more exciting edge and was part of the sociability of the occasion. Playing cards at home or in clubs was still a favourite pastime of many, although the game itself and where it was played usually revealed the social class of the players. Coin or card gaming in the streets, however, appears to have been declining, although, as argued above, this cannot be blamed convincingly on slot machines. It was rather the result of wider social and economic changes interacting to the detriment of these activities. They were aspects of a recreational culture which, partly, dissipated in response to the combined effects of rehousing and changing leisure preferences during a time of relative affluence. For example, the percentage of homes with TV sets rose from less than 1 per cent in 1947 to over 80 per cent by 1960.[128] This signified a shift to more home-based entertainments, which was perhaps one of the influences that reduced the incidence of coin gaming in the streets, except perhaps in the poorest areas.[129] At this time, furthermore, an older generation of working-class gamesters settled into middle age and retirement and also, perhaps, into the games of dominoes or cribbage which the 1960 Act now permitted in public houses if authorised by the licensing authorities.[130] The betting shop, too, provided a new legalised meeting place for gambling from 1961. The commercialisation of gaming accelerated most markedly during the 1960s and 1970s, which is beyond the scope of this study, but is described elsewhere.[131]

Notes

1 Andrew Davies, 'The Police and the People: Gambling in Salford,

1900–1939', *Historical Journal*, Vol. 34, No. 1, 1991, p. 109; Lyn Murfin, *Popular Leisure in the Lake Counties*, Manchester, 1990.

2 Whippet racing, also a local sport with a thriving betting culture, became more heavily commercialised, and is discussed in chapter 6.

3 A. B. Gomme, *The Traditional Games of England, Scotland and Ireland*, New York, 1964, Vol. 2, pp. 43–4.

4 Gomme, *ibid.*

5 *SC 1844*, Minutes, qu. 203, p. 19.

6 *SC 1844*, Minutes, qu. 838 p. 73.

7 Henry Mayhew, *London Labour and the London Poor* (1861), Vol. 1, pp. 16–17.

8 *SC 1844*, Minutes qu. 119–201, pp. 18–19.

9 *Justice of the Peace*, 13 September 1873.

10 *Justice of the Peace*, 5 November 1892.

11 David Jones, *Crime, Protest, Community and Police in Nineteenth Century Britain*, 1982, p. 136.

12 John Gillis, 'The Evolution of Juvenile Delinquency in England', *Past and Present*, No. 67, 1975, pp. 96–126. Paul Thompson, *The Edwardians*, 1984, pp. 215–17.

13 Geoffrey Pearson, *Hooligan: A History of Respectable Fears*, 1983, pp. 196.

14 Charles Booth, 'Life and Labour of the People in London', *Religious Influences* notebooks, B262, pp. 201, 206–7, LSE collection.

15 *Register of the Court of Summary Jurisdiction*, Bolton, 1900–1930. Earlier records were destroyed in 1941 as paper salvage for the war effort.

16 Interview with Mrs E. Clapson, the writers' grandmother, born Reading 1899. Tape in possession of writer.

17 Alice Foley, *A Bolton Childhood*, 1973, p. 18; see also Jerry White, *The Worst Street in North London*, 1986, pp. 76–7 on whip rounds.

18 Walter M., *op. cit.*

19 Robert Roberts, *The Classic Slum*, 1983, p. 162.

20 Jack Ashley, *Journey into Silence*, 1973, p. 30.

21 Madeline Kerr, *The People of Ship Street*, 1958, pp. 33–4.

22 Davies, *op. cit.*, p. 110.

23 White, *op. cit.*, p. 186

24 Writer's Oral Project: Sheila H., letter.

25 Davies, *op. cit.*, p. 113.

26 Writer's Oral Project: William L., born Hulme, Manchester, 1922. Tape 9, Side 1.

27 Bob Potts, *The Old Pubs of Hulme, Manchester*, Manchester, 1983, p. 18.

28 Writer's Oral Project: Mr S. L., letter.

29 *Ibid.*, Mr G. R., letter.

30 *Ibid.*, Clarence M., for London between the wars, *op. cit.* Peter M., for Liverpool between the wars, letter.

31 J. P. Bean, *The Sheffield Gang Wars*, Sheffield, 1981.

32 Writer's oral project: Bert W., *op. cit.*; Peter M., *op. cit.*

33 *Ibid.*, Bert W.

34 Writer's Oral Project: Paul M., Leeds, letter.

35 J. B. Mays, *Growing Up In the City*, 1964, p. 193; Appendix C, pp. 189–201, contains a number of examples of pitch and toss and other forms of petty gaming and gambling in Liverpool.

36 The following discussion on slot machines owes much to Mott, 'Popular Gambling from the Collapse of the State Lotteries to the Rise of the Football

pools, 1975', unpublished paper at the History Workshop Conference on the working-class and leisure, pp. 64–9.

37 C. F. Shoolbred, *Lotteries and the Law*, 1932, pp. 60–4; *RC 1932–33*, qu. 6143–5, p. 409.

38 *RC 1951*, Report, para. 153, p. 43.

39 *RC 1932–33*, Minutes, qu. 83, p. 193.

40 *Ibid.*, Minutes, qu. 34, p. 54.

41 *RC 1932–33*, Minutes, qu. 15, p. 35.

42 *RC 1932–33*, Memo of Chief Constable Association (Cities and Boroughs of England and Wales), para. xii, p. 449.

43 *Ibid.*, Minutes, qu. 6192, p. 409.

44 Amusement Equipment Company Ltd, registered 1937, company number 00282503; Amusement Caterers and Equipment Company (Manchester) Ltd, company number 00580936; Armstrong, *op. cit.*, p. 25.

45 *Economist* cited in Mott, *op. cit.*, p. 66; *Times*, 4 March 1938.

46 The following information is taken from MO's 'Moneysworth', *op. cit.*

47 Sue Fisher, 'The Use of Fruit and Video Machines by Children in the UK: An Analysis of Existing Research', *Society for the Study of Gambling Newsletter*, December 1989, p. 18.

48 *Ibid.*, p. 22.

49 MO 'Moneysworth', *op. cit.*

50 *RC 1932–33*, Minutes, qu. 6154–6155, p. 407.

51 *RC 1951*, Report, para. 155, p. 43.

52 *Ibid.*, Minutes, qu. 147 p. 42.

53 *Ibid.*, Report, paras. 30–3, pp. 141–2.

54 D. B. Cornish, *Gambling: A Review of the Literature*, 1978, pp. 64–5.

55 *Liverpool Daily Post*, 30 September 1915.

56 NAGL *Bulletin*, November 1916.

57 *RC 1932–33*, Memo of Home Office, para. 113, p. 14.

58 Chief Constables of Liverpool and Manchester, *Annual Reports*.

59 Community Council of Lancashire, *Gambling Amongst Young People*, 1946, in Mott, op. cit., p. 66.

60 Bryan Reed, *Eighty Thousand Adolescents: A Study of Young People in the City of Birmingham*, 1950, p. 39. J. D. Willcock, *Report on Juvenile Delinquency*, 1949, pp. 12–13; pp 73–5.

61 Mays, *op. cit.*, pp. 100–2; 189–201.

62 National Council for Social Aid, *Christians and Gambling*, 1983, pp. 19–20; David Spanier, *Easy Money*, 1988, p. 105; on the question of delinquency and dependency versus moderation amongst young amusement machine players, see Mark Griffiths, 'An Analysis of "Amusement Machines: Dependency and Delinquency" ', *Society for the Study of Gambling Newsletter*, December, 1989, pp. 34–9.

63 Ray Gosling, *Lady Albermarle's Boys*, 1961, Marwick, *op. cit.*, pp. 151–3.

64 Erving Goffman, 'Where the Action Is', in Jack Dowie and Paul Lefrere (eds), *Risk and Chance: Selected Readings*, 1980, p. 255.

65 MO, 1947, pp. 210–11.

66 Roger Caillois, *Man, Play and Games*, 1964, pp. 181–4.

67 Mott, *op. cit.*, pp. 68–9.

68 MO, *Mass Gambling*, 1948, p. 239.

69 Ben Weinreb and Christopher Hibbert, *The Encyclopedia of London*, 1987, pp. 961 and 98.

70 *SC 1844*, Minutes, qu. 82–8, p. 9.
71 *SC 1844*, Minutes, qu. 485, p. 89.
72 C. F. Shoolbred, *The Law of Betting and Gaming*, 1935, p. 206. *Bill for the Suppression of Gaming Houses*, 1854 (86), III.
73 *SC 1844*, qu. 427, pp. 35–6.
74 Peter Quennell (ed.), *Mayhews' London*, 1983, p. 334.
75 LSE, Coll U: B45, *Poverty* Notebook, Windsor Road, Hackney, pp. 152–9.
76 Charles Hindley, *Life and Adventures of a Cheap Jack*, 1876, pp. 192–7.
77 *Bolton Evening News*, 7 March 1901.
78 *Ibid.*, 11 March 1901.
79 MO, archive, Worktown, Box 1, File D. See also the 'Pub Compilation Tapes', Manchester Tape Studies Collection, at Manchester Polytechnic. On the conviction of a publican in Liverpool for allowing card playing for money see *Liverpool Daily Post*, 30 November 1915.
80 *The Memoirs of John Monk, Chief Inspector Metropolitan Police; 1859–1946*, p. 112. (ms edited by the author's son in the possession of Clive Emsley, History Dept, The Open University.)
81 *Annual Report of the Chief Constable of Manchester*, 1938, p. 17.
82 *RC 1932–33*, Minutes, footnote. by Chief Magistrate, p. 182.
83 Brian Masters, *The Passion of John Aspinall*, 1988, pp. 89–92; *Times*, 11 January 1958; 13 February 1958; 20 March 1958.
84 Robert Graves and Alan Hodge, *The Long Weekend*, 1985, pp. 233–4.
85 PEP, *Planning*, No. 270, 15 August 1947, p. 67.
86 MO, 1948, pp. 241–3.
87 Beatrice Potter 'The Jewish Community', in C. Booth, (ed.), *op. cit.*, p. 583.
88 Walter Besant, *East London*, 1901, pp. 205–6.
89 Ben Weingard, Tape J253, Side 2, *Manchester Jewish Museum Tape Studies Collection*, Cheetham Hill Road.
90 Mrs Neville Laski (nee Gaster) Tape J144, Tape 1, Side 1. See also Rosie Levy, Tape 164, Tape 1, Side 2, on the Didsbury Country Club.
91 *Return of NCO's Court Martialled for Allowing Gambling and Cards*, 1888–90, PP, 1892, Vol. L., 269.
92 Writer's Oral Project: Harry B., born Nottingham, 1899. Tape 10, Side 1. Histories of the camps and trenches point to the role of gambling, and the popularity of brag, nap, whist, poker, crown and anchor, etc. See, for example, Lyn MacDonald, *They Called it Passchendaele*, 1983, pp. 75 and 148; John Ellis, *Eye Deep in Hell*, 1976, p. 151; Jeremy Seabrook, *Working-Class Childhood*, 1982, pp. 92–3.
93 Harry B., *op. cit.* See also Arnold Wesker, *Chips With Everything*, 1962, p. 45, on card playing at night in barracks during the 1950s.
94 Eric Newby, *Love and War in the Appenines*, 1983, p. 43.
95 Mick Burke, *Ancoats Lad*, 1984, p. 38.
96 In E. B. Perkins, *The Problem of Gambling*, 1919, p. 143.
97 Paul Bellringer, 'Gambling and Crime: A Prison Perspective', *Society for the Study of Gambling*, Newsletter, No. 8, 1986, pp. 9–12.
98 John Altman, 'Gambling as a Mode of Redistributing and Accumulating Cash among Aborigines: A Case Study from Arnhem Land', in Geoffrey Caldwell et al. (eds), *Gambling in Australia*, NSW, 1985, pp. 50–67.
99 *North West Regional Project*, University of Lancaster, transcripts for 'Working Class Barrow and Lancaster, 1880–1930' (1982) Mrs H.2.B., p. 87; Mrs M.10.B., pp. 14–16.

100 Clive Field, 'A Sociological Profile of English Methodism, 1900–1932', *Oral History*, Vol. 4, No. 1 1976.
101 Green, *op. cit.*, pp. 82–3.
102 Mott, *op. cit.*, pp. 19–25; see also 'Miners, Weavers and Pigeon Racing', in S. Smith et al., *Leisure and Society in Britain*, 1973, pp. 86–96.
103 *Racing Pigeon*, 20 April 1898.
104 *Racing Pigeon*, 20 April 1898.
105 *Homing Pigeon Annual*, 1906.
106 *Ibid.*
107 *Racing Pigeon*, 4 February 1914.
108 Booth, *op. cit.*, 'Poverty', Vol. 1, 1889, p. 31.
109 MO archive, *Worktown*, 'Gambling', Box 1, File D.
110 Mott, 1975, p. 48.
111 Joe Gormley, *Battered Cherub*, 1982, pp. 2, 3 and 7.
112 Harry B., *op. cit.*
113 *Writer's Oral Project*: Walter M., born Hulme, Manchester, 1919. Tape 6, Side 1. See also Frank Chapple, *Sparks Fly: A Trade Union Life*, 1985, pp. 25–6, on East London in the 1930s.
114 MO archive, *Worktown*, Box 1, File D.
115 *Fur and Feather*, 14 January 1960.
116 *Racing Pigeon*, 6 August 1960, 3 December 1960; Mott, 1973, p. 92.
117 *Racing Pigeon*, 3 December 1960.
118 Ross McKibbin, 'Work and Hobbies in Britain, 1880–1950', in J. Winter (ed.), *The Working Class in Modern British History*, 1983, p. 144.
119 This discussion is based on Phil Pilley, *The Story of Bowls*, 1987, and the MO materials.
120 Pilley, *ibid.*, p. 101.
121 Ian Sutherland, 'Playing the Doos', *New Socialist*, No. 20, October 1984. See also Jeremy Seabrook, *Unemployment*, St Albans, 1984, p. 43.
122 MO archive, *Worktown*, Box 2, File c, Folio lxix on Bowls.
123 *RC 1949–51*, Memo, para. 19, p. 373.
124 Writer's Oral Project: Mr. P., Tape 3, Side 1.
125 MO archive, *Worktown*, 'Gambling', Box 1, folio lxix 'Bowls 4'.
126 Mr P., *op. cit.*
127 Brian Jackson, *Working Class Community*, 1972, p. 105 (first published 1968).
128 A. H. Halsey et al., *Trends in British Society Since 1900*, 1974, p. 552.
129 Anonymous letter to writer on pitch and toss at the Eagle and Child public house, Liverpool, in the 1980s.
130 *RC 1976–78*, Report, Vol. 2, para. 16.6, p. 268.
131 *Ibid.*, paras 16.7–16.9, pp. 268–9.

Chapter 5
Horse racing and on-course betting,
c. 1839–1960

From its alleged origins as the 'sport of kings' to the sport of 'kings, bums and businessmen'[1] (not forgetting working-class punters) horse racing has maintained a prestigious status central to a shared national culture of sport and betting. Thus, following the Betting Act of 1853, horse races were the only sporting events where ready-money betting was legal, before the introduction of commercialised greyhound racing in 1926.

It is difficult to say something new about horse racing. Wray Vamplew has made a number of excellent historical studies of the economics and the social significance of the sport,[2] and there is a massive popular literature which emphasises its Englishness and its glorious past and present. This chapter will try to synthesise this with a discussion of mass betting on horse racing, which is concerned mostly with the Liverpool and Manchester racecourses. Firstly, it will discuss the commercialisation of horse racing in Lancashire and its relationship to mass betting. Secondly, betting both with bookmakers and, from 1928, the tote, are discussed in relation to the self-consciously English sporting tradition which has crystallised around the sport.

I

Manchester Central Library contains a 'Book Rarity' collection of late eighteenth- and early nineteenth-century race programmes for Lancashire and Cheshire.[3] The locations for these races, such as Heaton Park and Kersal Moor near Manchester, or Knutsford in Cheshire, were in the countryside. The origins of horse racing in field chases and hunting, and the patronage of the local aristocracy in terms of jockeyship, horse ownership, the provision of training facilities and land for the use of racing is clearly evident in these programmes. At the Heaton Park steeplechase meeting in 1834, for example, the horses were 'to be ridden by Gentlemen Members of the Racing or Fox Hunting Club' for two major trophies, the Stanley Stakes of ten sovereigns and the Heaton Park Stakes of twenty-five sovereigns. Prizes were got up between the contestants and sponsored by wealthy peers and owners such as the Earl of Sefton, Lord Stanley, Lord Derby and others. The races were one and a half miles long, the horses were three-year olds, and carried weights of between nine stones and seven pounds to ten stones and five pounds. Prominent amongst the owners were Lord Stanley, Lord Derby and a host of other gentlemen. This landed influence also dominated the composition of the Jockey Club, the unelected ruling body of the sport,. which was established in 1750. The landed Stewards of the Jockey Club 'took no cognisance of any disputes or claims with respect to bets', but devolved this dispute-settling role to the Tattersall's Committee, the adjudicating wing of the Jockey Club. Tattersall's, based at Knightsbridge and Newmarket, were the betting rooms of the horse racing aristocracy, and 'Tatt's' as it became known, also lent its name to the most prestigious enclosure, or 'Ring', at racecourses. The Jockey Club nominated two of its members to sit upon Tattersall's Committee, one of whom is its chairman.[4]

Since the end of the Napoleonic Wars in 1815, the 'hallowed Turf', a symbol of a free and fair England, had been upset by a series of legal actions caused by swindles and frauds which culminated in the debacle of the 1844 Derby, when older horses masqueraded as two-year olds, and a jockey pulled up his own mount in favour of the horse he had backed to win.[5] Then, as since, jockeys liked to bet on races, and there was nothing to stop them in Tattersall's Rules on Betting, as long as it did not lead to corrupt practice.[6] But the 'running rein' scandal was seen as evidence of the so-called 'demoralization of the Turf'. Admiral Henry John Rous, the leading member of the Jockey Club, was called upon to give evidence on behalf of that body before the Select Committee of 1844, a precedent followed by all parliamentary enquiries into gambling since. Like his predecessor, Lord George Bentinck, Rous was of the aristocratic pedigree required for such an esteemed position, yet he was less given to the gaming excesses of Bentinck and other Jockey Club members. Rous subsequently engaged in a prolonged campaign to rid the turf of corruption, which, unlike Disraeli, he was more inclined to view as much as symptomatic of the vices of the wealthy as of the growth of mass betting. But, as illustrated in chapter 2, he was unwilling to curtail the wagering of the class to which he belonged.[7]

The problem for the turf was its increasing association with big money · and business practices, harbingers of mass betting on the sport. A number of untitled names also appear on the racing programmes before 1850. These reflected not only the contribution of both local smallholders who kept a nag or two in the paddock for racing, but the increasing influence of industrial and commercial money. Thomas Houldsworth, for example, an MP and 'the founder of a great cotton business', had been racing horses since the end of the French wars in 1815.[8] He was one of the first in a long and growing line of businessmen who also sought to participate in horse racing by owning and running horses. Some famous examples since have been the banking Rothschild family from the late nineteenth century, the newspaper publishers Lord Beaverbrook and Edward Hulton from the 1900s, and William Hill from the 1930s. The sporting members of the middle class thus illustrated their willingness to participate in this established landed pattern of recreation, as racing horses were an extension of their competitive acumen, and symbols of social status.[9] Thus the role of horse racing in elite sociability was extended to those sections of the middle class whose sporting inclinations differentiated them from their more Nonconformist peers.[10] Owning horses was an expensive hobby of course, and less well-endowed racing enthusiasts such as publicans and smaller bookmakers formed partnerships to buy, maintain and race horses.[11]

The fusion between old and new wealth was to become instrumental in changing the spectacle and experience of the sport by the establishment of bigger enclosed meetings in Lancashire which came to largely replace open meetings such as Kersal Moor and Heaton Park throughout the rest of the century. The Heaton Park meeting in fact left its original location in 1838 for Maghull near Liverpool, where a local licensee with the support of local landowners had established a course during the 1830s. In 1839 these races were taken over and moved to Aintree by a landowner-dominated 'Aintree Syndicate'. The total capital in shares of this, the first proprietary racecourse company, was £1,000, owned by Lord Stanley, Sir T. M. Stanley, and members of the Blundells, a colliery owning family of the Catholic gentry, and the mill owning Hornby family.[12] The Earls of Sefton, Derby, Lord Grosvenor, Lord George Bentinck, Lord Stanley, Mr E. G. Hornby and others made up the race committee, which was responsible for the proceedings on race days. The directors of the company were drawn from these two groups and managed the course and its finances.[13]

From the outset the races at Aintree established themselves as the most exciting and enjoyable event of the year's racing calendar. The first horse to win the new race was named, appropriately, 'Lottery', as the uniquely high, wide and difficult fences tend to reduce the likelihood of favourites coming home first. This has made the race, traditionally, anybody's race. In the days leading up to the race the correspondents of the *Times* noted the early and 'immense number of arrivals'. Every room at the Adelphi Hotel was engaged a fortnight before the races, and most of the smaller hotels were full. Many legs had ensconced themselves in these rooms where they pinned up the lists which offered their odds and prices.[14]

Despite its wealthy instigators and evident popularity, the syndicate ran into difficulties in attracting enough capital to pay for the new course. They ran the Liverpool Steeplechase in the best traditions of the chase as a glorified open access country meeting, and the money for prizes and costs came from within the enterprise itself rather than from an external source from which it was possible to mobilise capital. It was left to the handicapper E. H. Topham, who took over the reins of the business in the early 1840s, to put the course on a more entrepreneurial and businesslike basis. He did this with the help of most of the existing executive and, more pertinently, the establishment of a local railway network which enabled a racegoing public to come from farther afield than previously. The Manchester to Liverpool line had been opened in 1830, and the local railway network spread apace in the 1840s.[15] Topham handicapped the race by grading the horses according to their ostensible merits, and renamed it the 'Grand National Steeplechase' in 1843. He is credited with ensuring that the course was better laid out. The course established at Aintree was over two and a half miles long with fourteen fences, some of them formidable obstacles for the less experienced jockeys and horses. The horses ran the length of the course twice.[16]

That Topham was a handicapper is important. Handicapping horses for racing, along with the development of selling-plate races where the horses were auctioned, were the earliest manifestations of a new type of competition for money in the early Victorian years. As Vamplew shows, from the 1840s the number of selling-plate races grew. They were really excuses to get money from the prize fund 'whilst at the same time giving owners a chance to get rid of relatively poor horses', and were a vital source of revenue.[17] Bigger prizes tempted more owners to enter their horses, and contributed to the cycle of capitalisation. Nationally between 1837 and 1869 the number of horses racing rose from 1,213 to 2,534. The number of courses holding meetings of longer than one day rose from fifty-six in 1848 to eighty-two by 1870.[18] The Aintree course was 'properly laid to grass, and railed in', that is, enclosed and entry fees charged, in 1885. (The enclosure trend had been set by the Sandown Park executive from 1875).[19] The first prize in the Grand National was three thousand sovereigns by 1907.[20]

The Manchester Races were placed on a commercial footing in 1847, with the formation of the Manchester Racecourse Company. The composition of the company executive appears to have been made up largely of small local landowners. They opened the new Castle Irwell course on the land of a Salford colliery proprietor who had married money in Miss Frances Fitzgerald, daughter of a wealthy and entrepreneurial local landowner. A twenty-four-year lease was granted.[21] Due to religious objections to the renewal of the lease for Castle Irwell in the early 1870s, apparently because the Nonconformist son of the colliery owner refused to allow betting on his land, the course was established at New Barns in Salford. It was moved back to Castle Irwell from New Barns in 1902, when the Manchester Ship Canal project bought the land to extend their waterway thorough Salford. The Company was re-registered in that year. By now, the composition of the executive is clearer. The leading businessman was John E. Davies of Sale, Cheshire, who gave his occupation as 'Gentleman', a title suggesting lots of free time and money, which was shared by four other members of the executive, one of whom was from London, one from Middleton, Lancashire, and two from Manchester. The only exception was a Salford innkeeper.

In common with all large courses, Manchester came under the auspices of the Jockey Club. The Earls of Sefton and Derby were prominent as Stewards at the course, and the Earl of Sefton represented the National Hunt Committee in steeplechases. By the end of the first world war Edward Hulton Junior, the newspaper publisher, had moved in as a director and large shareholder, and a local solicitor took over as secretary on Davies' death. Joseph Ramsden, a colliery owner and an enthusiastic owner of horses, also became a director during the Edwardian years.[22]

Davies, with Lord Leigh, was also instrumental in the establishment of Haydock Park racecourse in 1888, at Newton-le-Willows, Cheshire, halfway between Manchester and Liverpool. By 1922, a local colliery proprietor and wine merchant were director and secretary respectively.[23]

The Manchester course, the bigger of the two, had been enclosed by the early 1880s. The spectators were by then seen as the major constituency to fund horse racing, because they would pay to go in to the races. In the second half of the 1880s, *Black and White*, a Manchester sporting journal, provided some colourful descriptions of the racegoers and proud accounts of all the new facilities: the weighing rooms, paddocks, stabling, jockey rooms, and the special office for the clerk of the course at New Barns. Entry was one shilling, the same as other northern enclosed courses,[24] and a race card containing details on horse and the order of races cost three pence. The bustling crowds were all proof of the 'wonderfully successful company who hold the reins'.[25] The course got bigger. The railways and buses helped to transport over 70,000 people to the opening of the new course at Castle Irwell in 1902.[26] It possessed 'step stands' to accommodate 12,000, held 29,000 in the rings (the betting and spectator enclosures) and catered for almost 30,000 in the grandstand and next to the railings of the course. Twenty turnstiles clicked the punters through at admission prices which reflected their varying levels of wealth and social esteem. Admission to Tattersall's was three times the entry price of the silver ring, and ten times that of the cheap ring. The more expensive the admission price, the better the facilities and the view.

Caroline Ramsden, daughter of Joseph Ramsden, wrote with pride in her autobiography that the Manchester course was more popular and successful than older-established meetings:

> The Lancashire Plate, a seven furlong weight-for-age race for two year old's and upwards with £11,000 added, was run at the September Meeting from 1888 to 1893 and was, at the time, the most valuable race in England. The Derby of 1888 was worth only £3,675 and the St. Leger £4,350.[27]

The Company also made much of the increasing capitalisation and modernisation of horse racing, claiming in 1902 that 'one of many instances' which proved it had marched with the times was 'the fact that this year another five hundred sovereigns has been added to the value of the Manchester Cup.[28]

Such attitudes had for some years worried those who thought that money and gambling was gaining too strong a grip of horse racing, corrupting it and destroying its parochialism. In 1862 the *Porcupine*, no admirer of betting, gave space to Hugh Shimmin's nostalgia for the early days of the Grand National:

> Leaving the open fields after the great race, and making across the course in the region of the tents and stands, all the repulsive and disreputable features of the racing ground are met with. The class of people has changed. You don't hear the truly joyous laugh, you don't meet with much heartiness. Men rush wildly about looking for 'sweep holders'. Some are eagerly in search of their debtors, others are as eagerly trying to avoid their creditors, and on many faces despondency casts a shadow.[29]

In 1868, Anthony Trollope felt that the quintessentially English characteristics of fair play in sport and moderation in betting on race horses ('unquestionably the noblest gambling in existence') were in danger of extinction if racing became 'unreasonable in its expenditure, immoral and selfish in its tendencies, or worse of all, unclean and dishonest in its traffic'.[30] Trollope was fearful lest the ownership of horses and the control of the sport become too detached from the aristocracy. He trusted the Jockey Club to guard the noble values in racing.[31] Yet fears for the future of horse racing were evident within the ruling class itself, some of whom were critical of the Jockey Club. In 1885, Lord Cadogan, a landed aficionado of what he termed 'old fashioned meetings' attacked the Jockey Club for presiding over an increasingly commercialised, hence corrupt, 'state of the turf': 'Owners of horses are no longer satisfied with the prices offered for competition at old fashioned meetings, and the stakes must therefore be increased to thousands where hundreds used to attract large fields of horses'.[32]

There was a clear split amongst horse racing elites, which has never been fully resolved, between the traditionalists and those of a more entrepreneurial outlook. Those who viewed mass gambling as a crude modern imposition into racing have sought to legitimise the sport by emphasising bloodstock breeding and the pursuit of equine perfection. This was Lord Astor's position in the 1950s, for whom betting was a necessary evil.[33] Astor, a Labour peer, wanted to get rid of bookmakers and introduce a tote monopoly, a cause which was later taken up with greater force by the chairman of the tote in the mid 1970s, Woodrow Wyatt.[34]

The traditionalists were also concerned at the effect of betting on the racing itself. Cadogan lamented that the weight-for-age races, the 'best class of racing' designed to ensure good breeding and healthy animals were increasingly less common than 'the second class of racing' – handicaps – in which the weights to be carried by each horse were 'arbitrarily appointed' by the handicapper, a course official. Some fifty years after Cadogan was writing, the trainer John McGuigan complained at the ad hoc and inconsistent handicaps applied to the same horses at different courses. Handicapping affected the considered 'form' of the horse, and was associated with the increase in betting, but the instigation of a 'third class of race', as Cadogan saw it, artificially inflated the number of races to enable more betting to take place than previously. This was the aforementioned selling-plate race, which he saw as the most deplorable symptom of the commercialisation of horse racing and its increasing dependence on mass betting.[35] Such complaints, and the spectre of enclosures and spectatorism, were behind the revision and strengthening of the Rules on Betting by Tattersall's Committee in 1886. The Jockey Club also curbed the number of two-year-old weight-for-age races in the late nineteenth century.[36]

Another problem of mass betting and commercial racing was the crowd. The big new betting crowds were a reminder of an urban working-class culture, and contributed to a longing for the old days of what had been a rustic pleasure. For traditionalists, the appearance of the mob at the races signalled not just the growing evil of betting but also the break up of a friendly parochialism which allegedly found its truest expression in the older country meetings, and has since been more strongly identified with smaller point-to-point races.[37] At big meetings especially, a problem of social control accompanied the racegoers as the trains and charabancs disgorged them in race towns. The gate, or sometimes the turnstile, allowed onto the course not just a motley crew of bookmakers and betters, but a sub-sporting underclass of tipsters, fraudsters, card sharpers, pickpockets and ruffians. Even *Black and White*, proud of the recently enclosed New Barns course, pointed out in 1887 the 'harmless necessary policemen and the usual tag-rag and bobtail' to be found at the meetings.[38]

On the course as off it, the bookmaker was in the van of this transformation. This was not surprising, as he was allowed onto the course to take cash bets. But, until the 1928 and 1934 Acts which standardised the arrangements for on-course betting, the bookmakers had to be careful where they stood, and to keep to their allotted pitches, and to keep out of the better class of rings which were reserved for the better class of bookmakers and backers. To stand in an unauthorised position was to become a 'place' to which people resorted and caused an obstruction under the terms of the 1853 Act and the 1879 Racecourse Act. Yet many magistrates were reluctant to convict due to confusion in interpreting the law.[39] Cadogan wanted all ready-money bookmakers off the courses, once and for all. 'It is', he wrote:

> an undeniable fact that ready-money betting encourages and fosters the most objectionable class of backers and layers, and lies at the root of all the widespread evils which we now have to deplore. If the reader will look at the army of betting men plying their ready-money trade inside and outside the enclosures at any race meeting, clad in coats of many colours, openly displaying the paraphernalia of their calling, and defying the regulations under which they are permitted to pollute the racecourses with their presence, he

will be able to estimate the enormous importance of the change which would be effected if the authorities would energetically endeavour to put down so crying an evil.[40]

'Outside the enclosures' meant the new bookmakers so detested, as shown in chapter 2 by Disraeli and others. In the Tattersalls' enclosure would be found the biggest bookmakers, and in the lesser rings and outside them were the smaller operators. This pattern was established by the last quarter of the nineteenth century. *Fraser's Magazine* in 1874, echoed Disraeli in dividing on-course bookmakers into patrician and plebeian camps: 'Inside the chief betting ring are to be found the Leviathans of the business; outside "Tattersall's" enclosure are to be found their parasites'.[41]

Yet it is interesting to note that the preference for the old days among turfites even extended to the new bookmakers, the major beneficiaries of ready-money betting. For Dyke Wilkinson, there had even been a better class of 'old fashioned welshers' who were 'endurable parasites' applying 'simple methods'. They had been supplanted by the new 'brutal school' of welshers who went about their business 'in whole battalions', terrorising the 'lawful authorities' inside and outside the rings.[42]

By the late nineteenth century, the defaulters, thieves, sharpers and others who came to the races for extra-betting purposes were known to the police under the criminal category of 'racecourse thieves.' For Detective Jerome Caminada, of the Manchester force, they were recruited from the travelling poor and 'the gutter children, who can be seen in the streets of all our large towns, selling newspapers, matches and other small articles'.[43] The Hackney notebooks for Charles Booth's survey of London poverty in the 1880s contain a couple of brief references to such groups. One, a labourer and hawker, was 'rather a shifty character' who exhibited coconuts at race meetings in company with gipsies. A cabinet maker, whom Booth placed in the comfortable category of class 'E', those who earned more than enough to beat the poverty trap, also went off with the gipsies to Epsom to sell coconuts.[44] For the police, travelling criminals in the crowd were difficult to detect, and photographs of racecourse criminals have been circulated from the Metropolitan Police to local forces from the later nineteenth century to the present day. In addition, the police had to cope with local gangs of sharpers and with fights between thugs hired by bookmakers to defend their pitches. Not just the 1920s but the 1950s witnessed some vicious rivalry. Also, smaller country point-to-point meetings were not immune from violence and fraud.[45]

Many tipsters at the courses were from the ranks of the poor. For the twentieth century, some flamboyant examples are recorded photographically, such as 'The Black Tipster', a 'Turf Adviser' who dressed in a tatty policeman's uniform,[46] and 'Prince Monolulu', famous between the wars for his cry of 'I gotta 'orse'.[47] Both black, they may have been excluded from more regular employment by racial discrimination. Mark Benney was probably more typical of the poorest tipsters, trying his hand at a pretence of inside knowledge at Epsom in between spells of both legal and illegal employment.[48] The most successful tipsters, it appears, were privy to 'inside information' from jockeys and trainers such as John McGuigan, a trainer whose tipster friends sold their information on fly-sheets for a few pence at racecourses.[49] Yet tipsters had a fraudulent image. Edwardian literature produced a famous tipster in Edgar Wallace's 'Educated Evans'. He was based on the real life Peter Christian Barrie ('Ringer Barrie') who began as a tipster after he was caught running 'ringers', camouflaged horses entered under false names.[50] In 1920 *Punch*'s absent-minded 'Tim Tipster of Liverpool', a novice handicapper of chances, needed to be given a shout by those who bought his tips if he proved to be a winner.[51] Not surprisingly, tipsters were vilified by anti-gambling commentators as exceptionally unprincipled germs in the disease of horse race betting.[52]

The machinations of the tipster were described by MO in 1947:

> 'It's a sure thing mate, only a bob, there's three horses, all sure things, for a bob.'
>
> A young man of twenty fishes out a shilling, passes it over and the tipster opens his race card and points to three horses marked with 'X'. He is short, ferrety, and wears a cap and a long raincoat. 'These are the horses, got your card?' The young man produces his race card. 'Here's a pencil, now mark them off.'
>
> The young man obeys, hands back the pencil, and the tipster disappears into the crowd.[53]

Tipsters probably had little influence on the formation of odds and starting prices. It is doubtful that enough tipsters achieved a consensus over possible winners which punters would collectively act upon and thus alter the odds given by bookmakers. The bookmakers in the rings, aided by a complicated system of communication known as tic-tac, were the key figures in the determination and alteration of starting price odds in ante-post betting.

Tic-tac was a semiotic language, a secretive form of what George Orwell might have termed 'tradespeak' for those 'in the know', that is, bookmakers and the clerks and tic-tac men they employed. A clerk often tic-tacced for a bookie as well. The system worked in the following way: a horse which was heavily backed by punters would have its price odds, that is the price of winnings offered in return for the stake, reduced by the bookmaker in order to minimise outlay should it win. The most heavily backed horse was the 'favourite'. An example of short odds is 'two to one', where the punter would receive two pounds for one pound staked. An example of long odds is thirty-three to one. A horse which he ignored or backed only slightly, perhaps because it was the first time the horse had run, or it was ridden by an apprentice jockey, had its odds lengthened in order to tempt punters to put their money on this unlikely winner. The bookmaker expected them to lose their money, and made a considerable profit if they won, as he did not have to pay out on the favourite. There was an onus upon the bookmaker's pocket to thus make the odds on unfancied horses as attractive as possible to the punter, so he or she had to know what other bookmakers were offering. The tic-tac was employed by the racecourse bookmaker to keep him informed of the latest betting on each horse by a complex set of signals. (The origins of tic-tac are discussed below.) The bookmakers in the rings constantly chalked their changing prices up on the boards and it was important for all bookmakers, who were competing with each other, to have quick access to the prices others were offering. The clerk took the information down on a 'twist card', so-called because the numbers were twisted round as they were written down to mislead punters who might see the information and act upon it. The clerk also recorded details of bets made and winnings paid.

From the 1870s the Exchange Telegraph Company based their transmission service on this system of relaying starting prices at the course. An Extel employee on the floor of the ring signalled the latest information to another Extel worker on the grandstand. This was then taken down and telegraphed to the London office of the Exchange Telegraph Company. This in turn was telegraphed to sub-offices in Manchester, Liverpool and Glasgow. It was then relayed to all subscribing bookmakers who rented the 'Extel' ticker tape machine.[54] The 'blower' system, introduced in the later 1920s, worked on the same principle, as shown in chapter 2.

Steven Hamer, who clerked and tic-tacced for other bookies before becoming a bookmaker himself in the 1950s, recalled that a crafty tic-tac could, in arrangement with his employer, signal false odds and set up a run of bookmakers offering false prices above, and therefore less attractive than, those which the offending bookmaker was chalking up. This was a way of rigging the market at the course. It obviously affected the starting price odds of certain horses.

The language of tic-tac resembles a gambling version of the way in which stocks and share prices were transmitted across the floor of the Stock Exchange. Steven Hamer described numbers in tic-tac largely as reversals of proper spellings or obvious word derivations. For example, one is 'uptie', two is 'owt', three is 'earth' or 'carpet', 'four is 'ruof', five is 'evif', six is 'x's' and so on.[55] Some examples of tic-tac signals clearly show that when the movements were quickly carried out the majority of punters would have experienced difficulty in understanding them. Like the twist cards the aim was to deny first-hand knowledge to the clientele. 'Evens' was indicated by the movement of two fingers of both hands up and down. This was mouthed as 'yours to mine'. Five to four was given by moving the right hand down to the left wrist ('on the wrist'). Six to four was signalled by moving the right hand to the left elbow ('half arm'), and seven to four was shown by moving the right hand to the left shoulder ('neves to rouf').[56]

The language of tic-tac owed much to the 'back-slang' of the costermongers in London and other large cities. Mayhew mentioned the game of 'Ehrt pu', ('Three Up') for 'yenap rouf' or 'exes' or a 'top of reeb,' which was common amongst the young poor in the mid-nineteenth century.[57] In 1877 the sporting correspondent of *Fraser's Magazine* observed that the 'inhabitants' of the courses 'speak a language of their own', and he pointed out that many on-course bookmakers had once been costermongers. This explained their 'occasional rudeness' and the use of 'horrid oaths'.[58] C.E.B. Russell for Edwardian Manchester observed that a number of lads who earned their living in the streets tended to frequent racecourses locally.[59] The osmosis between the language of racecourse gambling and the subcultural patois of the poor was and still is evident in the use of rhyming slang to describe the characters and components of racing and betting. Rhyming slang was a unique linguistic invention of the Cockneys of east London, and has long been more commonly used at southern racecourses than in the north and midlands. 'Pink lint' for example, rhymes with 'skint', and is used to describe a penniless punter. 'Joe Rooks' are the bookmakers' books, 'Holy Ghost' refers to the finishing post and 'nanny goat' to the tote.[60] This last example illustrates that this is an evolving and easily adaptive language, as the tote was not introduced until 1928.

The linguist Lesley Milroy, discussing the concept of a 'speech community' makes the obvious point that 'marginals' share a different language which is expressive of different values and economic strategies 'from those found in the mainstream of upwardly mobile industrial society'.[61] For social workers and racing journalists, then, this linguistic code, when spoken in sentences littered freely with blasphemies and four-letter words, must have appeared not simply foul but also difficult to penetrate and comprehend.

Although the racecourse was an obvious magnet for the casually employed who could peddle tips or try their hand at bookmaking, race meetings also provided intensive bursts of work for the more established working-class traders or innkeepers who accommodated the travellers, be they punters or the jockeys, trainers and stable lads and others prominent in the organisation of the turf. Jack Preston's widowed mother, for example, supplemented a meagre family income by working in the catering section at Castle Irwell during race meetings. After 1919 the family moved to Great Cheetham Street West, near to the racecourse, where his mother began to board members of the racing fraternity, with help from the whole family. They achieved a reputation for good lodgings and many racegoers, including some for Haydock Park who travelled to the course from Manchester by train.[62]

These informal economic links between the Preston family and the local racecourse enabled Jack to become friendly with many leading jockeys of the 1920s, such as Steve Donaghue and Keith Piggot, Lester Piggot's father. As a fellow racing enthusiast, Mick Burke in neighbouring Manchester remembered, Tod Sloan lived in one of the 'gentry houses' in St Andrews Square. Sid Manville, remembering his Brighton boyhood of the 1920s, writes of his excitement at being winked at by 'the great Steve Donaghue'.[63] As McKibbin notes, jockeys were subject to the same hero worship as footballers today.[64]

Other local traders gained work from the races, such as Emmanuel Goodman's father, who was both a tailor by trade in Manchester and a heavy gambler. Goodman implies that his father, an Ashkenazi Jew from Russia, who took to wearing a morning suit and a 'topper' on his way to the races or the synagogue, was partly anglicised by his close association with the Turf. He did tailoring for the trainers and other workers at Castle Irwell and his gambling took him to many local racecourses.[65]

For local bookmakers in or near a race town the meetings provided an opportunity to make money at the course, as well as to demonstrate their largesse amongst racegoers. At Castle Irwell local youngsters such as Maurice Levine and his pals would open the doors of the taxis in which the bookies arrived and usually receive a tip. The smaller less wealthy local bookies who did not employ a clerk could put the lads to profitable use by holding their boards to advertise the bookie and his prices. Some lads earned up to seven shillings and sixpence for an afternoon's board-holding.[66]

On-course bookmakers were, as spokesmen for their organisations have made clear, made up largely of off-course bookmakers attending race meetings. But a number of solely course bookmakers, who held regular jobs outside of betting, visited local meetings to earn extra money in the cheaper rings. It is difficult to assess the number of racecourse-only bookmakers. The best figures the writer has found were given by the National Bookmakers' Protection Association to the Willink Commission in 1950. They claimed that they numbered 521 of a total membership of 4,702, a little over 11 per cent.[67]

Bookmakers, like punters, were charged admission to the different rings to accept bets. Alfred Tyler, the Secretary of the Racecourse Bookmakers Association, (RBA) formed in 1903 to protect the interests of bookmakers at the racecourse both from the impending legislation and from the demands of racecourse companies and punters, told the 1923 Parliamentary Enquiry that Tattersall's admission fees were twenty-two shillings and sixpence, considerably higher than the three or six shillings charged by various courses for entrance to the small rings.[68] Credit betting was done in Tattersall's enclosure and the expensive rings. The smallest bets of all were taken outside the rings by the 'men who call themselves bookmakers', whom he distinguished from 'the straight-forward, honourable man'. For this reason Tyler wanted a licensing system introduced to rid the turf of undesirables.[69] There were about five hundred members of the RBA by 1923, mostly based in England and Wales. Most bookmakers kept to a few local or regional courses to keep travelling expenses down, and because they had 'connections in the particular districts where they are well known'.[70]

The RBA had been formed to voice any grievances of course bookmakers to the Tattersall's committee, the wing of the Jockey Club which dealt with betting disputes. Excessive or dishonest claims by punters, the need to differentiate between regular bookmakers and those most likely to welsh or default, fiddling by clerks and tic-tacs, excessive charges for facilities by racecourse management and the need to eliminate racecourse violence were the main reasons for the formation of the Racecourse Bookmakers Association. In 1918 the Turf Guardian Society (TGS) was formed for the same reasons. The leading light of this organisation was the wealthy London bookmaker Walter J. Randall, a friend and associate of T. H. Dey, who was also a member. Both Randall and Dey were wealthy off-course bookies concerned to identify the interests of the turf with bookmakers. The TGS was made up more of larger bookmakers than the RBA, as was the Bookmaker's Protection Association (BPA), established in 1921 to combat the growing threat of protection rackets existing in race towns both on and off the course between the local criminal subculture and bookmakers.[71]

The elitist conception of the bigger bookmakers over the smaller ones was nurtured by the BPA and bookmakers' organisations. It improved the professional image of betting and made it easier for wealthier or well established bookmakers to set up pitches at the courses. The Act of 1934 enabled this exclusion to come into operation. In collusion with the racecourse authorities the NBPA and the TGS arranged for allocations to favour the bigger bookmakers in these organisations. This was the complaint of a Middlesex racecourse bookmaker to the Willink Enquiry:

> At point-to-point meetings a practice is in operation which is a direct infringement of Section 12 [1934]. One bookmaker pays the Hunt Committee a fixed sum for the betting right and then allocates the pitches to all his followers. This causes resentment with rival bookmakers over the favoured pitches.[72]

He also claimed that fees and an unfair deposit were asked of smaller bookmakers in order to meet winnings in the event of a bookmaker's not being able to pay out any winnings due. The larger bookies could also, of course, refuse to take bets from those who wanted to hedge part of them. Hence not just strong-arm but more subtle tactics could be used in the struggle for pitches. This was a major source of tension between bookmakers, and there is little doubt that smaller bookmakers were disadvantaged in what was really a legitimated protection racket.

Yet all bookmakers, from 1928, had a common interest in their opposition to the tote.

II

In December 1926 the stewards of the Jockey Club and the National Hunt Committee, in the light of the precedent of the imposition of betting duty, made representations to the government for a scheme to get money for horse racing. The British thoroughbred, they argued, was in peril, and they stressed the 'desirability of making betting contribute more directly not only to the sport of horse racing but also to the development of horse breeding'.[73] Thus most historians of turf history, echoing the claims of the Racecourse Betting Control Board established to run the tote, have argued that the tote was introduced to secure money for the assistance of horse breeding and racing. This is mostly true but a major factor in the agitation for the tote by the Jockey Club and the NHC was that it would be a cleaner and more easily monitored form of betting than with bookmakers, free from the possibilities of welshing with a resulting more favourable image of turf betting. A member of the National Hunt Committee, for example, argued to the 1932–3 enquiry that the tote would remove the opportunities for fraud:

> The advantages of having the 'Tote' at Hunt meetings and point to points is most marked. In the old days these meetings were the happy hunting grounds of welshers and all sorts of blackguards. The simple country people were easy prey for them. Now they can bet with all safety on the 'Tote', knowing that they will be honestly treated'.[74]

In Europe, the predominance of bookmakers at the course was unique to Britain and the Republic of Ireland. In Eire the idea of the Tote as of the betting shop was introduced in advance of Britain. In France, the original home of the totalisator in the form of the *pari mutuel*, the perquisite of the tote paid 20 per cent of the value of all stakes into the sport of horse racing, a precedent emphasised by those concerned to secure greater and stronger links between betting and the economics of horse racing.[75]

The principle on which the tote operated was the pooling of the stakes of all those who betted with it. The size of the pool determined the size of the odds. The tote was established only on 'approved racecourses', that is those courses approved for a certificate of licence by the Racecourse Betting Control Board. The personnel of the board was largely aristocratic, with a couple of civil servants thrown in for good measure. It was comprised of a chairman and eleven others, of whom the chairman himself and four members of the administration were appointed by the government, and the rest by the Jockey Club and the NHC.[76]

A government which had perceived the fiscal advantages of taxing off-course credit bets was keen to derive revenue for horse racing from the source of the tote. The anomaly of prohibition of off-course ready-money betting whilst taxing the tote was not lost on anti-gambling campaigners and those writers concerned with the pure amateur status of sport.[77]

The board's first meeting was in September 1928 and one of its first decisions was that the work of operating the tote was to be under the auspices of the board and not left to individual racecourse companies. It was agreed and met with 'the consent of the Home Secretary' that 60 per cent of the boards' income was to be reinvested into improving and maintaining racecourses in proportion to the amounts staked with the totalisator at each meeting. Six per cent taxation was deducted for flat meetings, monitored by the Jockey Club, and 10 per cent for National Hunt steeplechases. The Racecourse Association, a conglomerate of racecourse companies, objected to the level of taxes, as they have ever since, arguing for more money to be spent on improving course facilities. But they welcomed the overall development of the tote and not surprisingly agreed that installation costs should be covered by the board. Also financially attractive to the course owners was the new charge for the provision of places for bookmakers to 'stand up' on their course, usually five times the normal admission price, and they were given discretionary freedom to utilise any funds accruing from additional charges made of bookmakers.[78]

At the outset the tote faced two major problems of acceptance. One was practical and the other was the opposition of the bookmakers. The apparatus of the tote went through an experimental phase at first as various levels of technology were tried and found wanting. The machines varied from the hand-cranked variety to the more effective electrically operated types patented by inventors and companies. The machines issued tickets which were dispensed at windows from the tote building. The first tote buildings were established at Newmarket and Carlisle in July 1929. By 1931 they were installed on 108 racecourses for use at 561 race meetings. This amounted to 8,340 tote windows nationally. During the trial and error phase the electric 'Amplion', 'Julius' and 'Lightning' machines were all subject to criticisms of slowness, and subsequently modified. Yet all but the most rudimentary horse races and dog tracks possessed electric totalisators by 1939. Due to the size of the crowd and the lack of space, courses such as Liverpool, Manchester, Lingfield, Epsom and Kempton Park began with 'partial schemes' from the early 1930s. The tote here was housed in cheap temporary buildings, usually in inauspicious positions. In the north west, Haydock Park was the first course to introduce full totalisator facilities. It took £28,000 at the autumn meetings of 1929, comprised of stakes with an average value of £1.10 shillings.[79] However, by 1934 Aintree, Castle Irwell and Haydock Park had all replaced the hand-cranked systems with electric totalisators. Liverpool's course now possessed 134 windows in two new buildings in the members' enclosure and at Tattersall's. The Manchester course was more democratic, with thirteen windows in the members' enclosure building, thirty four in Tattersall's, 100 in the silver ring and seventy in the cheap ring, numbering 217 in all. Haydock Park had three buildings. Thirty-nine windows served Tatt's and the members' enclosures, thirty covered the silver ring, and ninety four served the cheap ring (163 in total).[80]

Another problem facing the board and racecourse executives was bookmaker opposition. The board argued that 'vested interests' were trying to foster a prejudice against the tote, and it certainly met with some verbal and practical opposition from bookmakers over the first few years of its life. In the long run bookmakers at horse races had little to fear from the tote. Despite an early confidence on the part of the RBCB the Tote has been a disappointment. As Rothschild noted in 1978, in the period 1928–61, before the Racecourse Betting Control Board was replaced by the Horserace Betting Levy Board, the tote contributed an average of £270,000 a year to horse breeding, racecourse improvements and veterinary science. This was not as much 'as its supporters had hoped'.[81] At the races, the more varied and competitive terms bookmakers could offer to punters and the lively and colourful presence of bookies within the 'traditional' culture of British racecourse betting cushioned bookies from the tote threat.

The tote also tried to tap off-course betting. This was accomplished through the company of Tote Investors' Limited, a private agency taking credit bets. The tote odds and prices were transmitted between the course and tote offices via the 'blower', under an agreement with the London and Provincial Sporting Agency. This took one quarter of the total pool of credit bets by 1937.[82]

The tote lost out on the stakes of off-course working-class punters, who were not to be denied a flutter on this new gadgetry. The late 1920s and early 1930s saw a proliferation of the 'increasing evil' of tote clubs in the towns and cities. The Bishop of Manchester, Dr Guy Warman, informed the House of Lords in 1932 that the unemployed were the biggest attenders and were at the most risk. The little tote machines found in these clubs were made by companies such as the Essex Auto Manufacturing Company, who also made slot machines.[83] Drinking, and a little flutter in a warm club were an obvious attraction, but all of the arguments of the anti-gamblers were directed at the clubs:

> Membership of these clubs was nominal. Election was of the flimsiest, in most cases the subscription was one shilling a year . . . Through these clubs you get an increase in gambling, an increase in poverty in many a home, an increase of misery, an increase of the shiftlessness and restlessness which is doing harm in demoralising and degenerating our people.[84]

* Tote clubs were largely killed off by the 1934 Betting and Lotteries Act, which made them illegal, and facilitated working-class access to totes by legalising them at dog tracks.

Later, the legitimate off-course totalisator business suffered war damage. After September, 1939, racing was stopped for a while, and the tote offered only a limited service on a restricted racing calendar from October of that year. Most importantly, tote offices off-course were
* closed down.[85] The war years thus gave back almost all of the trade to the bookmakers, so not surprisingly they resented the reintroduction of the tote following the demilitarisation of many major racecourses used
* as military bases during the war. As a founder of the Turf Protection Society (TPS) wrote in 1946:

> Make no mistake, the R. B. C. B. can be the means of eliminating the course bookmaker, and the re-establishment of Tote Investors' Offices all over the country could be the start of a campaign to sound the death knell of the Starting Price Offices, which throughout the war operated quietly and efficiently. The existence of modern, up-to-date Totalisator buildings on all racecourses, and Tote offices in all principal cities and towns, is a daily increasing threat to every bookmaker.[86]

But it was all this up-to-dateness and the implied standardisation which put many punters off the tote. Totalisator betting was conducted in units of two shillings. Tickets for bets were purchased for two shillings or for a greater number of units. The statistician A. P. L. Gordon argued that placing stakes with the bookmaker was more flexible than totalisator betting, so 'a greater number of backers would be impressed with the superiority of bookmakers'.[87] The tote, which averaged out the odds automatically with bets placed, paid out a great deal more than bookmakers on outsiders if the pool was big, but was less attractive for those who were seeking a price range which only the nominal and competitive allocation of odds could produce. This was evident in the following episode given by Mass Observation in 1947:

> One woman, aged 40, artisan class, rocks a baby in one arm and gazes intently at the race card held in her free hand. Her husband looks over her shoulder and points with a pencil, saying 'Hot Pot that's the 'orse'. The woman replies

'No, I fancy Lombard, that's what the feller on the bus said, 'Lombard' he said. The man argues, 'I tell you, Hot Pot is favourite.' The woman mutters as the man continues 'I'll put a couple of bob on Hot Pot.' 'Put it in the Tote', the woman argues. 'No the bookies give a better price.' 'Let's see', and the two of them turn and walk towards the bookies' ring where they stand for one minute watching and listening as the odds are called.[88]

In 1978, a survey of gambling literature argued that 'totalisator betting is a less attractive form of betting' and was seen as a complementary alternative rather than a threat to bookmaker betting.[89] As the call for a tote monopoly gained ground from racing interests, most notably horse owners and those who viewed bookmakers as leeches on the sport,[90] this participatory and colourful appeal of the bookmakers was used against the idea for more totalisator betting. Bob Mellish, for example, the Labour MP for Bermondsey in the 1950s, made much of this in the parliamentary debates over the proposals for ready-money betting after legalisation. He was a 'Cockney' and 'deep down [he] loved a gamble'. He also loved:

> the fun, the odds being shouted, the excitement of running from one bookmaker to another to see if better odds can be obtained, then going down to see whether one can beat the Tote at the same game. It is the colour of the scene. I do not like the suggestion that there should be drab, cold-blooded figures which no-one can work out.[91]

Mellish and Mass Observation were describing the excitement of the bet for the punters who were at the races more for a day out in the countryside than for a sustained series of studied and earnest bets. For the majority of racegoers a flutter added to the fun rather than being the main reason for being there. The sporting side of the wager was also more geared to beat the bookie than the tote here: 'a popular victory is said to be "bad for bookmakers"'.[92]

But also present at the racecourse were the professional punters who made betting their principal form of income. They risked their money as carefully as they could, keeping to favourites rather than outsiders, which unfortunately was the tote's best bet. The American sociologist Robert Herman, and also professional punters themselves, have described this outlook: the study of past form in the racing paper to weigh up the relative merits of the horses and their riders, a disinclination to contemplate large risky bets on unfancied horses, the braving of all weathers and a persistent optimism in bad periods of repeated financial losses.[93] As Gordon argued, 'the backer who bets habitually in large sums of money is seldom a supporter of outside chances'.[94] The Tote thus lost out on many bets from both day trippers and more dedicated punters.

But the majority of racegoers were there for the 'fun of the fair', to watch the social displays of wealth and status in the clothes and deportment of those who frequented the more expensive enclosures.[95] People had packed picnic lunches and took buses or trains in friendly groups. The racing was important to the day out but the ancillary attractions of the refreshment tents, the primitive roulette wheels and the usual trapping of the 'Find the Lady' shark and other gambling paraphernalia all added to the ambience of the occasion. The calling and shouting of the racecourse bookmakers and the signalling of the tic-tacs was seen as a natural part of a day at the races, whereas once they had been seen as the harbingers of its doom. Like betting itself, bookmakers have lived symbiotically with racing, profiting as much from the sense of tradition which glorifies it as from the betting. Yet the origins of this sense of tradition were, at least in the historical imagination of turf writers, pre-commercial and pre-bookmaking.

III

The association of horse race betting with the simple rustic pleasures of its parent sports of hunting and field racing has endured well into the twentieth century. This is most clearly in evidence in the racing literature which has accompanied and fed the kudos of the sport. John Freeman Fairfax Blakeborough, with over seventy titles to his name, was one of the most prolific contributors to this romantic cult of horse racing. In *Country Life and Sport* (1926) for example, he blamed the degeneration of the sport not only on mass betting but also on the creeping spread of an ugly urban landscape with its attendant class system into his Yorkshire 'Arcady' of country houses and horses. His nostalgic view of horse racing was coloured with fears for the rural landowner:

> Let us chat with the farmer about his stock, and the squire about the sad evolution which has cast a cloud over rural England, and which is quickly banishing the old class of landowners, let us revisit old racecourses and cockpits, and see how our forebears found their pleasures in the past whilst speculating to the future for the country house class and the things which have always gone to make the joy and tradition, the music, life and poetry of rural England.[96]

His lament for the 'ancient racecourses' and his derision of new 'meretricious' country dwellings for the *'soi disant'* squirearchy' spoke of a mild form of cultural despair as described by Fritz Stern for the German *mittelstand* as it faced modernity.[97] This was a sense of economic insecurity and social dislocation resulting from a perceived despoliation of an earthy, honest and rustic pre-industrial culture where the roots of status and of local self-determination had been stronger. Horse racing was viewed as a genteel and yeoman sport which belonged to a feudal past and which was an important locus of 'tradition', yet which fitted uneasily into an urban culture. This is in contrast to the USA, where race tracks form part of a commercialised menu of outdoor sporting occasions held in the larger towns and cities.[98]

Blakeborough's work crystallises the retrospective pervading much horse race journalism and literature. Superficially, it seems to shift this way and that, between a gung-ho enthusiasm for racing, a maudlin anecdotalism when describing turf events and characters and an unquestioning historicism. And historicism, as Patrick Wright has argued, is the plundering of the putative past for romanticised experiences and expressions to brighten up and also to denigrate the present by superficial comparison.[99] Certainly, horse racing is an important component of what Wright calls the 'cultural presence of the past' in English society.

Yet Blakeborough's writings, and the emotions which informed them, go deeper than the veneer of affection for the past which characterises historicist perspectives, architectural or otherwise. He attacked and feared 'commercial considerations', the basis of the growth of a capitalist economy and social relations, comparing them to 'an old system inspired by heart and sympathy'.[100] He thus believed that rustic pursuits were like an anchor to the past, keeping humanity back from the eventual possibility of a bloodless, dehumanised Brave New World. It could be objected that he contradicted himself: that nowhere did he acknowledge that the modernisation which he detested owed much to the vanguard role of a landed class. Moreover, in other works he expressed admiration for the entrepreneurialism, the innovation and economic efficiency of racecourse managements in modernising the sport. The Manchester Executive he described as 'a pioneer in the dynamic changes which have taken place in connection with the national sport during the century'.[101] The introduction of gate money, the increase in prize monies, the staging of selling-plate races, the use of the tote and the fact that Manchester was one of the first companies to install the photo finish camera (in 1948) are all, of course, based upon commercial considerations and the demands of the betting market. It was this which pushed smaller meetings to the margins. Yet in Blakeborough's perspective we can see the essence of conservative culturalism: the need to modernise without deferring to an accelerated and ahistorical view of progress. Such a perspective acknowledges economic imperatives yet seeks to contain their most corrosive effects.

When this perspective of past glories has been harnessed to patriotism, it has been a potent force sustaining the romantic image of horse racing. Not suprisingly, the spokesmen for this sporting culture were from the world of the fancy, the bookmakers who traced a lineage from the legs of old and those involved with the sporting press. The bookmaker Thomas Henry Dey saw betting as the expression of the English, not British, spirit of risk and adventurism. In his heavily patriotic discussion of 'The Sporting Instinct as Applied to Betting' he argued that Englishmen were the 'sole proprietors' of the sporting and risk instinct. This only belonged to foreigners by 'requisition'. England was the 'Valhallah', the true stadium of the 'sporting instinct' which was in the blood of every Englishman. Dey was prepared to concede its presence 'in the blood of Irishman, Scotsmen or Welshmen, [but] as a matter of historical fact it is perhaps less marked in the latter three races.' The backer was, then, 'every inch a man who sports the Sporting Instinct': it was his birthright.[102]

Perhaps in a wider and less direct sense, art has contributed to the cult of horse racing. The view of horse racing as a colourful, traditional event is evident in pictures and paintings of the big races in the Victorian years by Millais, Doré and Hall, and most notably Frith's *Derby Day*. In the twentieth century, Charlie Johnson Paynes' dramatic *The Worst View in Europe* of the 1901 Grand National and Sir Alfred Munnings' paintings of Derby Day and Ascot between the wars are perhaps best known.[103] Popular art too, especially watercolour paintings, has long captured a strong affection for racing, especially the older, rustic horse races, and for the parent fox hunts over the cream of the countryside in the England of R. S. Surtees and Nimrod, famous hunting writers in the first half of the nineteenth century. Many country pubs and antique shops possess such representations of the past on their walls. There is a sense in these pictures of what has been called 'the glamour of backwardness',[104] whilst others have seen it perhaps as the continuing green heart of feudal England dovetailed with the modern world. In such paintings the course and the countryside is active and ambient while class relations are static and cosy. They are pictures of a world untouched by cities and factories.

They are also portraits of a world devoid of faddists and spoilsports. The Grand National is particularly relevant here. Ever since the 1840s, when Captain Becher scrambled himself and his horse to safety under the trample of the horses as they negotiated a particularly dangerous water jump, the 'equine epic of the Mersey' has been viewed as an arena of 'derring do' which English sporting enthusiasts hold dear. As with Blakeborough, this has led them to celebrate the dangers of horse racing. Mirabel Topham, proud of her family's management of the Grand National for over a century, linked the bravado needed to get round the course with national character: 'if one needed a subject for a tapestry depicting British characteristics of indomitable courage and dogged determination, this time honoured 'chase might well be considered'.[105] Many horses and a few jockeys have been killed by the infamous Aintree jumps. In reply to criticism of the Grand National for this, Ernest Edwards, the tipster-gossip 'Bee', spoke out in 1939 against those who would reduce the fences to a safer size:

> The Grand National has often been the subject of a screed by the stunting press [and] as far back as 1903 people were writing to the papers complaining of the cruelty of the Grand National, to which the late Mr. Gladstone, clerk of the course, made suitable reply, 'Cut the Aintree fences and you cut the arteries of the race.'[106]

The tension between humanitarians and Grand National enthusiasts was still evident in 1957, (as it is today)[107] although the language had altered. The RSPCA felt aggrieved at being accused of 'bleating' about horse deaths by an irate local race fan.[108]

It is clear that the excitement of the action and the betting, in which outsiders had a greater chance than in most steeplechases, outweighed any criticisms of the sport for its protagonists. For Bee, the Grand National could and should never be changed as it was 'Grand' and 'National', the timeless qualities of pageantry. More recently a sociologist of horse racing who credits himself with 'impeccable proletarian credentials' has argued strongly that the spectacle and ambience of the races has proved 'sufficient to enable a suspension of social criticism and to sustain engagement with the sport'.[109]

Finally, it remains to emphasise that the elite who have governed horse racing through the Jockey Club and the NHC have not demurred from the promotion of racing as a bastion of the English way of life and a source of national esteem. Why should they? It has helped to legitimise betting, without which the sport might have perished.

Spokesmen for the Jockey Club have repeatedly emphasised the importance of horse breeding to the national sport and admitted that betting helped to finance it. Viscount Allendale told the Willink Commission that 'nothing like the number' who attended at the time would do so if racecourse betting was abolished. The Willink Commission had no intention of doing such a thing, and agreed with their sporting lordships that the horse racing industry made a prestigious contribution to the export industry.[110] The horse-owning but anti-gambling Labour peer, Viscount Astor, reluctantly saw betting as a necessary evil to a great national sport. The two sides were in this sense united by the practical benefits of betting. The Tote, then can be viewed figuratively as a financial buttress to what Patrick Wright might term the 'national-popular'[111] cathedral of horse racing, a betting-based collection box. As defenders of the tote have argued, it was also more virtuous than bookmakers, free from corruption, gang warfare and naked self interest.[112] The only problem was its refusal to produce enough money to put back into the sport. The tote turned in a mere £28.5 million in 1959 compared with an estimated £336.5 million rung-up by bookmakers.[113] Attention thus shifted back to a new levy on the bookmakers, who had just been granted legal off-course ready-money facilities. The parliamentary enquiry into the desirability of a horse race levy, the Peppiatt Commission, which reported in 1960, agreed with the general view that horse racing and thoroughbred breeding were central to our sporting heritage, that the tote had provided disappointing returns, and felt that bookmakers should pay more to support the sport. The Peppiat Committee took evidence from over twenty witnesses. Breeders, racehorse owners, trainers and racecourse owners, most of whom strongly felt that horse racing could do with a boost in funds, although the NBPA did not oppose this view.[114] They would have supported anything which they felt might undermine the tote, which in fact made a diminishing contribution during the 1960s whilst the amount from the levy grew. The tote, which from 1961 changed from the Racecourse Betting Control Board to the Horserace Totalisator Board, raised £0.928 million in 1962–3 compared with the levy's £0.9 million. The following year, however, the levy secured £1.28 million whilst the tote only improved its act to £0.993 million before dropping off, increasingly sharply, from 1964–5.[115] As the Rothschild Report of 1978 argued, the tote was all along afflicted with poor equipment which was labour intensive and expensive to run, and also from an existential crisis: did it exist simply to fund horse racing or to provide an alternative form of betting to bookmakers?[116] It was this conundrum which Woodrow Wyatt sought to resolve in the 1970s.[117]

The Horserace Betting Levy Board came into being in September 1961. It was administered by the Home Office and comprised eight members, of whom the chairman and two others were appointed by the Home Secretary, three were appointed by the Jockey Club, and the remaining two were the chairman of the tote and a bookmakers' representative.[118] The levy, which was on a sliding scale determined by bookmaker's ability to pay, was first introduced for the financial year April 1962–3. As Christopher R. Hill shows, much of the money raised went to improving the prize money of prestige races and on increasing minimum values. This owed much to the model of the Irish levy.[119]

IV

From the mid nineteenth century view that commercialisation and mass betting undermined the traditional parochial nature and honourable conduct of racing, betting became the financial mainstay of the sport. A little flutter also developed as the symbolic act around which a new sense of tradition has developed – the sporting right to bet. The bookmaking profession was seen to feed off horse racing, yet it also became part of the time-honoured carnival of a day at the races. The totalisator, a modern device, did not fit snugly into this culture.

Another old-established sport, also heavily associated with betting, was greyhound racing. But here the tote was more succesful: it lent itself more to the track than to the turf.

Notes

1 John McDonald in R. D. Herman (ed), *Gambling*, 1967, pp. 53–66.
2 Wray Vamplew, *The Turf*, 1976; *Pay Up and Play the Game*, 1988; 'Horse Racing' in Tony Mason (ed.), *Sport in Britain*, Cambridge, 1989.
3 Held at the Local History Library, Manchester.
4 This information was based upon the *Constitution and Origin of Tattersall's Committee*, kindly supplied to the writer by the Secretary of Tattersall's Committee, Reading.
5 Vamplew, *The Turf*, p. 90.
6 John Hislop, *Far from a Gentleman*, 1960, p. 227.
7 *SC 1844*, Report, pp. vii–viii.
8 Heaton Park programme, *op. cit.*; J. T. Slugg, *Reminiscences of Manchester Fifty Years Ago*, Shannon, Ireland, 1971, pp. 309–10 (first published 1881).
9 T. H. Breen, 'Horses and Gentlemen: The Cultural Significance of Gambling Among the Gentry of Virginia', *William and Mary Quarterly*, Vol. 34, 1977, *passim*.

10 Michael Filby, 'The Sociology of Horse Racing', unpublished Ph.D. Thesis, University of Warwick, 1984, pp. 26–36.
11 Vamplew, 1976, pp. 178–85; Steven Hamer, *op. cit.*
12 John Walton, *Lancashire: A Social History, 1558–1939*, 1987, pp. 91–2, 247–8.
13 E. C. Midwinter, *Old Liverpool* pp. 40–52, 1971. *Victoria County History of Lancashire*, Vol. 2, 1966, 'Steeplechasing', Arthur Willoughby-Osborne, p. 480.
14 *Times*, 26 March 1839, 28 March, 1839; Peter King, *The Grand National: Anybody's Race*, 1983.
15 Walton, *op. cit.*, p. 116.
16 This discussion is based upon *Lancashire Life*, March 1956; *Liverpolitan*, March 1933; *Liverpool Review*, 30 March 1889 and 26 March 1892; ; *World Sports*, April, 1971; King, *op. cit.*, and Hugh Shimmin, *Liverpool Life: Its Pleasures, Practices and Pastimes*, 1856, pp. 20–35.
17 Vamplew, 1976, p. 44.
18 Vamplew, *ibid.*, pp. 35–7.
19 Vamplew, 1976, p. 41; Souvenir of the Grand Opening of Castle Irwell, Manchester Racecourse Co., 1902. Held at Manchester Local History Library.
20 David Hoadley Munroe, *The Grand National 1839–1931*, 1931, p. 45.
21 Caroline Ramsden, *Farewell Manchester*, 1965, pp. 12–13, upon which much of this history of the Manchester course is based. The company file of Manchester Racecourse Co. at Companies House only dates from 1902. Company no. 74933, held at Companies House.
22 *Ibid.*
23 Company File, Haydock Park Racecourse Company. Held at Companies House, company no. 56182.
24 M. Huggins, 'Horse Racing on Teesside in the Nineteenth Century: Change and Continuity', *Northern History*, Vol. 22, 1987, p. 108.
25 *Black and White*, 23 September, 1887; see also 10 June 1887, 27 May, 1887.
26 *Manchester Evening Chronicle*, 29 March 1902.
27 Ramsden, *op. cit.*, p. 20.
28 *Manchester Racecourse Souvenir, 1902*, p. 21.
29 *Porcupine*, 15 March 1862.
30 Anthony Trollope, *British Sports and Pastimes*, 1868, p. 7
31 Trollope, *ibid.*, pp. 20–1, 48–55.
32 Lord Cadogan, 'The State of the Turf', *Fortnightly Review*, Vol 37, 1885; Guy Chapman, *Culture and Survival*, 1940, p. 113.
33 *HL Debs*, 27 June 1956, cols 97–105.
34 *RC 1976–78*, Report 1978, HMSO, Cmd 7200, Vol. 1, para. 8.27, pp. 68–9. Christopher R. Hill, *Horse Power: The Politics of the Turf*, Manchester, 1988, p. 22.
35 Cadogan, *op. cit.*; John McGuigan, *A Trainer's Memories* (ed. J. F. F. Blakeborough), 1946, pp. 101–2.
36 Tattersall's Committee, *Rules on Betting*, 1988; Vamplew, 1989, p. 234.
37 *Punch*, 17 May, 1961.
38 *Black and White*, 10 June 1887.
39 *Justice of the Peace*, 13 June 1874, 8 July 1899.
40 Cadogan, *op. cit.*, p. 11.
41 *Fraser's Magazine*, *op. cit.*, p. 75.
42 Dyke Wilkinson, *Rough Roads*, 1912, p. 260.

43 Jerome Caminada, *25 Years of Detective Life (in Victorian Manchester)*, Vol. 2, 1983, p. 7 (first published 1895).

44 Charles Booth Collection, LSE: *Poverty* notebook B45, Windsor Road, Hackney, pp. 155–6.

45 The Manchester Police Museum contains photographs of travelling thieves and racecourse criminals for the Edwardian years and the 1920s, and the West Riding Police Archive at County Hall, Wakefield contains the same for the later 1950s. On crowd control see the Aintree materials in the Eric St Johnstone papers held at the archive of European Centre for Study of the History of Policing at the Open University, Milton Keynes. On violence at a point-to-points in the 1930s R. H. Totterdell, *Country Copper*, 1956, pp. 114–18. On trouble between bookmaker-gangs in the 1950s see *HL Debs*, 27 June 1956.

46 George Chandler, *Victorian and Edwardian Liverpool and the North West from old Photographs, 1972*, plate 114.

47 Ras Prince Monolulu, *I Gotta Horse*, 1950.

48 Mark Benney, *Low Company*, 1981, pp. 107–8 (first published 1936).

49 McGuigan, *op. cit.*, pp. 157–8.

50 Dick Francis and John Welcome (eds), *Great Racing Stories*, 1989, pp. x–xi.

51 *Punch*, 30 June 1920.

52 J. Runciman, 'The Ethics of the Turf', *Contemporary Review*, Vol. 15, 1899, pp. 603–21.

53 MO, *Mass Gambling*, 1947, p. 175.

54 This discussion is based on R. A. Wooley, *The Comprehensive Guide to Betting and Bookmaking*, Sheffield, 1976; J. M. Scott, *Extel 100, A Centenary History of the Electric Telegraph Company*, 1972, and Hamer, *op. cit.*

55 Hamer, *op. cit.*

56 *Ibid.*; Wooley, *op. cit.*, pp. 126–33; *Picture Post*, 12 November 1949.

57 Henry Mayhew, *London Labour and the London Poor*, Vol. 1, 1861, pp. 13 and 17.

58 *Fraser's Magazine*, Vol 16, 1877, p. 80.

59 C. E. B. Russell, *Manchester Boys*, p. 14, Manchester 1985 (first published 1905).

60 Wooley, *op. cit.*, p. 127.

61 Leslie Milroy, *Language and Social Networks*, 1986, p. 76.

62 Jack Preston, *Memoirs of a Salford Lad*, Manchester, 1985, p. 2.

63 Mick Burke, *Ancoats Lad*, Manchester 1985, p. 24; Sid Manville, *Everything Seems Smaller*, Brighton 1989, p. 67.

64 McKibbin, 1979, pp. 174–5.

65 Jewish Museum, Manchester: Emmanuel Goodman, Side 2, Tape 102, p. 21 of transcript.

66 Maurice Levine, *From Cheetham to Cordova*, Manchester, 1985, p. 9.

67 *RC 1949–51*, Appendix of NBPA evidence, p. 116.

68 *SC 1923*, Minutes, qu. 4190, p. 145.

69 *Ibid.*, qu. 4175, p. 244, qu. 4223, p. 247, qu. 4228, p. 247, 4280, p. 251.

70 *Ibid.*, qu. 4190, p. 245.

71 Graham Greene, *Brighton Rock*; Testimony of Randall to the *SC 1923*, Minutes, qu. 3327–333, pp. 194–5.

72 *RC 1949–51*, Minutes, paras 2–3, p. 149.

73 *Racecourse Betting Control Board, First Annual Report and Accounts, 1929*, PP, 1929–30 (217) VII, p. 5.

A bit of a flutter

74 *RC 1932–33*, Memo by N. H. C., para. 8, p. 105.
75 *HL Debs*, 27 June 1956, cols. 99–100.
76 *RBCB Report, op. cit.*, p. 7.
77 G. S. Sandiland, *Atalanta, or the Future of Sport*, 1928, p. 96.
78 *RC 1932–33*, Memo of Racecourse Association, paras 7–10, pp. 240–1.
79 *RBCB Report, op. cit.*, p. 5.
80 *RBCB Report 1934–5*, Appendix 3, p. 34.
81 *RC 1976–8*, Report, Vol. 1, p. 62.
82 Annual Reports of the RBCB for 1935–6 and 1936–7, para. 21, p. 17 and para. 17, p. 10, respectively.
83 *RC 1932–33*, Minutes, qu. 6202–6238, p. 409.
84 *Manchester Guardian*, 8 December 1932.
85 *Racecourse Betting Control Board, Annual Report, 1939–40* (199), Vol. 5, paras 5–6, p. 5.
86 *Penciller*, Vol. 1, No. 1, 1946, p. 1.
87 A. P. L. Gordon, *The Statistics of Totalisator Betting, op. cit.*, p. 33.
88 MO, *Mass Gambling*, 1947, p. 175.
89 D. B. Cornish, *Gambling: A Review of the Literature*, 1978, pp. 238–9.
90 Lord Astor, *HL Debs*, 27 June 1956, cols 98–102.
91 *HC Debs*, 17 November 1959, cols 1045 and 1050.
92 Gordon, *op. cit.*, p. 33.
93 R. D. Herman, *Gamblers and Gambling*, Lexington 1976, pp. 42–58; Al Burnett, *Knave of Clubs*, 1963, pp. 201, 209.
94 Gordon, *op. cit.*, p. 34.
95 MO 1948, pp. 172 *et seq.*
96 J. F. F. Blakeborough, *Country Life and Sport*, 1926, p. 7.
97 Fritz Stern, *The Politics of Cultural Despair*, 1973.
98 R. D. Herman, *op. cit.*, pp. 42–58.
99 Patrick Wright, *On Living in an Old Country*, 1987, pp. 3, 14–27.
100 Blakeborough, *op. cit.*, p. 31.
101 J. F. F. Blakeborough, *A Short History of Manchester Racecourse*, Manchester 1958, pp. 7–8.
102 T. H. Dey, *Betting in Excelsis*, 1908, p. 23.
103 This discussion is based on John Hislop, *The Turf*, 1948, *passim*; Alan Ross, *The Turf*, 1982, p. 25, and John Welcome and Rupert Collens, *Snaffles on Racing and Point to Point Racing*, 1988, *passim*.
104 Tom Nairn, *The Enchanted Glass*, 1988, pp. 213–14.
105 Mirabel Topham, *Liverpool and Merseyside Illustrated*, March 1961.
106 Ernest Edwards, 'Bee', *Vernon' House Journal*, March 1939.
107 The 1991 Seagram Grand National got off to a late start because of protests by animal rights activists.
108 *Liverpool Evening Express*, 27 March 1957.
109 Filby, *op. cit.*, p. iii.
110 *RC 1949–51*, Minutes, qu. 889 p. 61. Report, para. 337, p. 102.
111 Wright, *op. cit.*, p. 172.
112 *HL Debs*, 27 June 1956, cols 100–1.
113 *HC Debs*, 23 May, 1960, col. 39.
114 *Report of the Departmental Committee on a Levy on Horse Races* (Peppiatt Report), April 1960, Cmd 1003, para. 19, p. 7.
115 *RC 1976–78*, Report, Vol. 1, para. 9.19, p. 79.
116 *Ibid.*, paras 8.10–11, p. 64.

117 *Ibid.*, para. 8.22, pp. 68–9.
118 *Ibid.*, para. 9.15, p. 77; Hill, *op. cit.*, pp. 22–38.
119 Hill, *ibid.*, p. 80.

Chapter 6

From coursing and flapping to the electric hare: dog racing in England to 1960

From its origins in coursing and flapping in the nineteenth century, to the introduction of the big electric stadia from 1926, cruelty, corruption and commercialism have been seen to run rampant through dog racing. Moreover, unlike the gay crowds at horse racecourses, dog track spectators have been seen negatively as 'going to the dogs'.[1] This chapter explores the relationship of dog racing to mass betting, and discusses the ups and downs in the history and reputation of the sport.

I

The history of dog racing from the 1830s until the later Victorian years is really the history of coursing. In the north west, big coursing meetings were attended by rich and poor alike although arranged by the local landed gentry. They took place at Aintree, Blackpool, Downsholland, Haydock Park, Hoskayne, Kirkby, Lytham St Annes, Simonswood and Southport. These were also sites for other animal sports and horse racing.[2] Yet the greatest coursing meeting of all was, and still is, the Waterloo Cup, established by the Earl of Sefton at Altcar near Liverpool in 1836. The event was so called because the draw for the positions of the dogs took place at the Waterloo Hotel in Liverpool. The Earl of Sefton later became President of the National Coursing Club (NCC) established in 1858, which met annually at Liverpool.[3] In 1882, the NCC founded the Greyhound Stud Book, in order to register all coursing dogs and their owners.

The biggest owners were landed gentlemen and businessmen. For example, the Altcar Club and the smaller Ridgeway Club of Lytham were patronised by the Earls of Derby and Sefton. The Blundells of Ince, who as noted in the previous chapter were colliery owners and a sporting family of the Catholic gentry, held the South Lancashire Cup meeting on their land.[4] Local mill owners, merchants, magistrates and even the Town Clerk of Bolton were members of hare coursing clubs. In the last two decades of the nineteenth century Leonard Pilkington, of the glass and chemicals family in Widnes, was entering twenty-six greyhounds in the *Stud Book*.[5]

Lancashire was the major arena for the sport of coursing. Trainers, owners, slippers (those who released the dogs to pursue the quarry) and course officials at the smaller meetings were based locally, but were drawn from far and wide for the biggest event, the Waterloo Cup, held in late winter. Over thirty clubs from England, Ireland, Scotland and Wales were affiliated to the NCC by 1900, and all sent representatives to its annual meeting.[6]

The following account of the Waterloo Cup meeting in 1911 is taken from the journal of the Humanitarian League, comprised of the reforming middle classes and not a few members of the aristocracy who wished to modernise and, as they saw it, civilise landed culture. Thus the league was strongly opposed to coursing.

> A shout from the crowd, growing every moment more excited as the short drama is about to begin, proclaims the fact that the hare is in the battle ground, and is about to meet his Waterloo. And higher still, and louder than all, the raucous cry of the bookmaker, 'Take 7 to 2' 'Take 2 to 1' rises shrill in the air. All this time a couple of greyhounds are held tight by a slipper in a box, open on two sides, in the middle of the field. As soon as the hare is beaten past the slippers' box the greyhounds tug and strain at the leash, almost dragging the slipper with them. When the hare has had about fifty yards start the hounds are released and off they dash together.[7]

Concern for the death of the hare was one thing, but in a sense it was unfair to denigrate coursing by association with bookmaking rather than with gambling *per se*. In the early 1880s the coursing establishment blamed bookmakers, thieves, welshers and blackguards for the 'objectionable feature of betting' which had 'developed itself to such an extent as to become a thorough nuisance'. In 1882, the Earl of Sefton decreed that no flags, stools 'or any of the usual paraphernalia of the betting man' were to be allowed on his land, and the police saw to it that his wishes were carried out.[8] As with horse racing, some felt that a little friendly wagering was de rigeur, but that corruption followed in the train of bookmakers, and ruined true sport. Thus in 1893, when the NCC formulated its 'Constitution and By-Laws and Code of Rules', rules thirty-nine to forty-two dealt with defaulting, discreditable conduct, 'the financial interest' of judges and slippers in results, and decreed that all bets were to stand unless the dogs were drawn.[9]

Whereas big hare coursing meetings had a genteel association, rabbit coursing was more distinctly working class. Here also, the Humanitarian League was disgusted at the sacrifice of animals for the sake of 'spurious sport'. Not just blood-crazed whippets but also bookmakers profiting from cruelty and corruption had their eyes on the stricken rabbit. The league claimed that in addition to the tortures suffered by the animal if it was caught, the so-called referee would poke out a rabbits' eye in order to blind it and 'cause it to run toward the side of the dog which the bookmaker wishes to win'.[10] There was a clear link in approach and ideology between the Humanitarian League, the RSPCA and the NAGL. In 1916 the NAGL *Bulletin* claimed that a ten-day rabbit coursing meeting near Liverpool had involved 128 dogs and claimed over 700 rabbits, 'not for the purpose of testing the dogs, but for betting and gambling'.[11]

Yet by this time rabbit coursing was nowhere near as common amongst the poor as greyhound racing after an artificial bait. The need to replace a hare or rabbit with something more accessible in urban conditions, as well as a response to humanitarian criticism, encouraged the use of imitation rodents. By the late nineteenth century, the rules of large whippet meetings in Oldham, St Helens and elsewhere 'expressly forbad the use of live bait to encourage the dogs'. The RSPCA commended working-class whippet racing as a model sport in the face of genteel hare coursing with greyhounds.[12] The use of artificial quarry signified a separation of class pastimes summed up by the phrase 'whippets for workers, greyhounds for gentry'.[13] These were flapping races, a name originally applied to rural horse races in the countryside in the early nineteenth century, but rarely used since.[14] According to greyhound racing lore, the sporting press and the *Times* index, the first big race involving false quarry took place in at the Welsh Harp sporting ground, Hendon, just north of London, in 1876.[15]

The hare itself is nothing but the skin of a real one carefully stuffed, and it stands on a carriage somewhat resembling that which gives motion to the rocking horse. Its motion is effected by means of an open tube, over which it runs, and in which is laid a rope or wire of the length required for the distance to be run. At the far end is a winch of special construction and great power, worked by hand, and, by turning this, two men give the hare any speed required. In the front of this machine is a screen of furze, into which the hunted hare runs, and disappears, much to the discomfiture of the hounds, who evidently are much puzzled as to what has become of their expected prey. The object of the invention is to provide artificial means for greyhound racing (not coursing), and it is likely to do towards that object what the 'rink' has done for skating, or the 'gyratory pigeon' for the amateur of Hurlingham.[16]

The reference to the pigeon shoot at the Hurlingham Club suggests that the idea of artificial pigeons inspired a similar development in dog racing. The Welsh Harp ground was run by a sporting businessman-come-gentleman called Warner, and the mechanical hare was invented by a Mr Geary, a pigeon shooter. Up to that time the Welsh harp was often used for pigeon shooting, both of the live and gyratory variety. However, the mechanical hare was patented not in Britain but in the USA, and regular track racing with one began in Oklahoma in 1921.[17]

Social surveys and anti-gambling literature show that whippet racing without live bait was apparently well established by the later nineteenth century. As Charles Booth's survey of London found, Bow Running Ground, Hackney Marshes, and the marshes next to Woolwich Arsenal were prominent meeting places for whippet racing amongst 'the sporting set' by the 1890s. Most races were small informal affairs, organised between local dog fanciers, publicans and bookmakers for sport and betting. There is no mention of hares or rabbits.[18]

The poor and unemployed in all parts of urban Britain kept dogs as a hobby and as a medium for sociable betting. Charles Booth came across characters such as Mr Martin, a 'dog fancier and dog doctor' living with his wife and three children in two rooms at no. 31 Parker Street, Finsbury, London, during the 1880s. Martin cut a rather selfish figure in the eyes of Booth, who placed him amongst 'the semi criminal class, people who don't get an honest living': 'Sometimes keeps a dog or two here but probably has a place elsewhere – belongs to the betting class and hardly makes his living by this trade – dresses well, neglects his wife and family who seem very poor'.[19] Similar complaints about neglect were levelled at miners who kept dogs. In 1907 J. M. Hogge saw from the window of a train passing through a mining town a 'carefully clothed' whippet, 'trotting at his masters feet into a cottage, the annual rent of which could be covered by the sale of the dog'.[20]

To raise a lean fast dog was a potentially expensive hobby. Most dogs were kept in a makeshift kennel in the back yard. Placing dogs in kennels owned by farmers and wealthier trainers and breeders was probably the preserve of the wealthiest artisans and the genteel owners of dogs.[21] The dogs had to be fed on a high protein food, such as sheep's heads or pig's trotters, perhaps donated by the local butcher or stolen as well as bought cheaply, which were boiled in an old vat or gas boiler in the back yard.

Raw eggs and prime cuts of meat were typical of the foods fed to the whippet during training.[22] It was a humorous observation amongst the locals, rather than a complaint, that 'the dogs were often better fed than the owners'.[23] Waites has emphasised the rationality and skill required in feeding and breeding for speed, and the basic veterinary skills needed by owners.[24]

The dog and the race offered the owner a chance to make a little money from betting, either with friends or with a bookmaker. Often, the chance to make money was secured with a fiddle. This was usually achieved by 'stopping' the dog. As a miner from Ashton, Lancashire, put it:

> You housed the dogs in the back yard, and that was a bit rough, but I won a few races and got myself a few quid. I started buying them cheap and selling them dear. There were no prizes, you won with your own dog – it was all the money you put on it. You stop your dog for three or four weeks until its lost a few times and all the public think its no good. Then you race it at six to one or eight to one and it comes in. How do you stop it back? I'm not giving you that – a bit too dear.[25]

But these secrets have been revealed by others, especially those with an eye for a fiddle. Again, the appearance of the bookmaker implied malpractice. Bert W., for example, remembered the dog races on a Sunday morning at Seaforth, near Liverpool, during the 1930s and 1940s:

> The owners of 'em were often tampered by bookies, or asked by bookies to feed sausages to them and things like that to stop them up so that they wouldn't win. And consequently the bookie won because the punters were having their money on the favourite dog. *Qu: They'd been nobbled?* That's right yes. Consequently the bookie would give the owner enough money to get his beer anyway, and he wasn't worried whether the dog won or lost and he'd back on what he thought was the second dog maybe.[26]

Certainly the dishonest thread in whippet racing was carried over into the commercialised greyhound racing tracks from 1926. This is discussed further, below.

As contemporary anti-gambling literature, working-class autobiographies and oral testimonies show, dog rearing and racing was especially common amongst mining communities. As with pigeon racing, the training of the animals, the informal competitiveness, and the pooling of the stakes for the prize money depended upon a shared enthusiasm for sporting and betting. Miners were central to the continuation of smaller flapping meetings, where these elements of dog racing were strongest.[27] Mick Burke, of Ancoats in Manchester remembered:

The colliers at Bradford Pit were great fellows for whippet racing and used to go on the fields up Ten Acres Lane. They would throw some kind of ball, slip the dog, and time how long it took the dog to catch the quarry. A good slipper would throw the dog about twenty yards – that was the art of the game.[28]

Not just balls, but the flapping of an old rag about 200 yards from where the slipper held the dogs, and more elaborate arrangements developed as the live quarry declined. Steven Hamer remembered that during the 1930s and 1940s a bicycle with the tyre of the back wheel removed was jacked up off the ground. Attached to this was a long rope with artificial bait at the end:

> They used a cord you see . . . and the bloke on the bike would peddle away like 'ell with the wheel going round pulling this piece of fluffy wool. It could be a cushion, could be anything. Greyhounds would chase it, dogs give chase, and you can imagine as it came round all the dogs like. Now of course they have the electric running rail. I'm talking about the old flaps, what we called the flaps.[29]

By the 1950s cars were put to this use.[30]

Flapping tracks were lower class. They were the link between coursing and the introduction of the floodlit electric circuit. Held on moorlands, town fields and wastelands, they were a fundamental part of the evolution of dog racing in Britain and its adaption to urbanisation.

The end of the first world war initiated a boom in the popularity of whippet racing. Social observers felt that the sense of release unleashed by the armistice, and the edge to life which the war had brought, increased the demand for excitement which gambling helped to satisfy.[31] Expenditure on all forms of gambling was fuelled by war savings. Moreover, a general fall in working hours from an average of fifty-five to forty-eight per week between 1914 and the early 1920s allowed more free time to many workers. Real wages increased by 20 per cent for those in full-time industrial employment over these years.[32]

In 1921, the American sociologist Whiting Williams in his study of the British working class, also saw greyhound racing as a form of post-war escapism for people cooped up in poor urban areas. It was part of what he called a 'destructive trio' of bad housing, booze and bookmakers. He gave a lively description of a flapping race near a crowded town, with the bookmakers shouting the odds, the thronging crowd of punters, the starter's whistle, the release of the dogs by the slipper after a shout or a bang, their rush towards the waving towel, and the bookies paying out winnings with 'impassive faces' from their money satchels.[33]

The sporting press was full of whippet racing after the war. From the early 1920s the *Sporting Chronicle* was sponsoring its own whippet races. During 1925, the *Chronicle* claimed, 'the number of whippets put to straight racing' and public interest in the sport had been 'so great' that it had been forced to pass on much of the sponsorship and organisation to the conglomerate company Allied Newspapers.[34]

This did not go unnoticed by people with sporting connections and with money to invest. Thus Major L. Lynne Dixson, Brigadier-General A. C. Critchley, a businessman in the cement industry, C. A. Munn, an American businessman friend of Critchley's, and Robert Grant Junior, an American and a director of Barclay's Bank, got together to form the Greyhound Racing Association (Manchester) Limited, registered as a company in October 1925.[35] According to Critchley, Munn showed him photographs of the electric stadium in Oklahoma, and Critchley quickly realised this could be 'the poor man's racecourse'. The idea was an American-style night out at the dogs, so the company established a new large stadium outside Belle Vue Gardens in Manchester, on the site of a flapping track.[36] The first meeting attracted 1,700 people, who gathered to watch the greyhounds chasing a McKee Scott hare round its running rail. The attraction was simple: unlike horse racing, which took place at often faraway meetings in the countryside during the afternoons, when most people were at work, the new sport offered on-course betting in the evenings, after work. The new, brightly lit arena was only a short walk or bus ride away, and entry fees were cheap, starting at one shilling and sixpence. Attendances were soon rocketing, so the facilities were extended and improved to cater for 25,000, a figure achieved by the spring of 1927.[37] As Downes et al have argued, the short intensive thrill of five or more thirty-second races at nearby tracks was an exciting diversion for many working class people.[38]

As well as spectators, the new stadia were magnets to local bookmakers. As one had explained to Whiting Williams: 'We can't lose. The figures will get 'em, bound to, if they keep at it long enough . . . And I've got a boy who 'as more of a 'ead for figures than I 'ave. 'E'll be a wonder at this business'.[39] In Manchester and Salford, bookmakers such as W. Ainsworth, Gus Demmy, Ted Kenny, and J. Ord all took bets at the tracks, and probably visited other local tracks, as did Jack Hamer of Bolton.[40] In the early 1930s they formed the Manchester Greyhound Bookmaker Protection Association, an adjunct of the NBPA. As we will see below, their major aim was to oppose track managements over the introduction of the tote.

There were clear links between the new stadium managements and the coursing establishment. Lynne Dixson was a coursing trainer and judge, and trainers and officials from coursing clubs were invited to become employees of the company.[41] Moreover, Lord Stanley's 'Emerald Brooch' came third in the second race at the opening meeting at Belle Vue.[42] Metaphorically, this reflected the changing positions amongst elite owners of dogs. From 1927, the names of new company-based owners of dogs such as Mrs L. Lynne Dixson came into the *Stud Book*. She entered over 200 hounds on behalf of the company in 1927, compared, for example, to a mere thirty owned by the Earl of Lonsdale. From then on, company names are given as the largest owners in the *Stud Book*, overshadowing landed names.[43]

In 1927 the conglomerate Greyhound Racing Association Trust, Ltd (GRA) was set up, with a share issue totalling £990,442. This helped to finance further tracks at White City and Harringay in London at Hall Green in Birmingham and at Marine Gardens and Powderhall in Edinburgh. Along with the Manchester Executive, it comprised retired businessmen and three gentlemen. The offices of the Trust were in Pall Mall, London, and its directors included Critchley, Lieutenant-Colonel Moore-Brabazon and Munn.[44]

In December 1927 the National Greyhound Racing Society (NGRS) was formed, to represent the commercial interests of its member tracks. At the start of the new year of 1928, Munn, Critchley and others formed the National Greyhound Racing Club (NGRC), which saw itself as the equivalent of the Jockey Club for the NGRS tracks. Dixson became the Racing Director and Critchley allotted himself the position of judge. He and his father drew up the rules of the society for racing, judging and betting, which still stand.[45] Other tracks began to affiliate to the NGRS, for example the much beloved Walthamstow in east London, started in 1932 by the bookmaker William Chandler.[46]

The instigation of the NGRS tracks stimulated other companies to follow their example, largely made up of bookmakers, licensees and businessmen. Those at Raikes Park, Bolton and White City in Liverpool were typical of these. In Bolton, for example, the bookmaker Robert Sinclair owned a major stake in the capital investment, and a number of bookmakers and local business men provided money for the new venture.[47] In Liverpool, the White City and Breck Park tracks were also local affairs, established by Merseyside businessmen and dog owners.[48]

In 1932 companies such as the Bolton Greyhound Racing Society, the Breck Park Stadium, Liverpool, and Stanley Park Greyhound Racing Company merged with others, mostly from the north west, to form part of the British Greyhound Tracks Control Society, Ltd, (BGTCS). The BGTCS held tracks at Blackpool, Bolton, Bradford, Brixton (London), Gosforth (Newcastle), Hackney Wick (London), Hazel Grove, (Stockport), Leeds, Rochdale, at Stanley Park and White City in Liverpool and Willenhall, Staffordshire.[49] By the time the Royal Commission on Lotteries and Betting had reported in 1933, over 220 dog tracks were operating in Britain, almost all of them in or near a town or city. Seventy-seven of these were licensed by the NGRS, seventy-three of these were in England and Wales.[50] At NGRS tracks alone, attendances rose from over five and a half million in 1927 to almost eighteen million by 1931. London accounted for over eight and a half million of these attendances during the early 1930s, Manchester took 1,708,430 in 1931, and Glasgow 2,037,350. Yet the NGRS figure was only half of the total thirty-eight million attendances by 1936.

By the 1940s the NGRS had divided its tracks into four groups. *Class A* consisted of fifteen tracks in the metropolitan area with average attendances of 3,500 to 18,000 for evening meetings. This represented the increasing move of the big classic races to London meetings during and after the 1930s.[51] *Class B* comprised three provincial tracks with average attendances of over 5,000 per meeting. *Class C* was the twenty-nine provincial tracks with attendances between 2,000 and 5,000, and *Class D*, thirty provincial tracks whose evening attendances averaged below 2,000. The largest concentrations of provincial tracks were at Glasgow (five), Newcastle (four), Birmingham, Liverpool and Manchester (three each), and Bristol, Norwich and Sheffield (two each). Most of the rest of the NGRS tracks were in the larger towns and middle-sized cities such as Cardiff, Coventry, Derby, Leeds and Leicester.[52] BGTCS tracks were established more in the north and midlands. In many cities both the BGTCS and the NGRS had tracks. Manchester and Salford together possessed three tracks by 1930, at Belle Vue and White City, owned by the NGRS, and the Albion Ground, Salford, a BGTCS stadium. In Liverpool, however, there were no NGRS tracks.

Apart from the growth in the number of tracks and their attendances, another indicator of the popularity of greyhound racing was the flurry of greyhound racing papers which came out as the big tracks were being established. As with the rise of the Edwardian tipster press, most of these were short lived gambits: for example, the *Greyhound Racer*, *Greyhound Racing* and *Greyhound Sports*, all published in London, and none of which lasted more than six months in 1927. Manchesters' *Greyhound News and Chronicle* managed seven editions in that year. Many greyhound sheets never made it past the registration edition. This might be taken to mean that punters did not find the dogs as newsworthy as horses, yet there was room for a good greyhound racing broadsheet. Such was the longest lasting paper, the *Greyhound Express*, begun in June 1932, and incorporated with the *Sporting Express and Greyhound Express* forty years later in 1962. A middle distance runner was the *Greyhound Outlook and Sports Pictures*, which lasted from 1930 to 1939, before the paper salvage effort, aided by the restrictions on greyhound racing, put a stop to it.[53] Electric greyhound racing was heavily restricted during the war to specified Saturdays although from 1942 it was also allowed on bank holidays.[54]

In 1947 the PGTCO was formed, to which the BGTCS and other tracks affiliated. It co-ordinated the 119 tracks outside the NGRS. These were by then known as independent tracks. The largest of them charged two shillings and three pence for entry in the late 1940s, middling tracks charged one shilling and six pence, and the smallest tracks, presumably to cover costs, asked for two shillings and six pence to three shillings.[55]

There was, then, a general three-tier structure in dog racing. At the top were the NGRS tracks. In the middle were the independent tracks monitored by the PGTCO. Beneath these were a large number of smaller more informal meetings, the truest continuation of the flapping tradition, often organised by the smaller bookmakers for betting between the owners and interested locals. From the 1934 Betting and Lotteries Act, the result of the deliberations of the committee, a bookmaker or any promoter simply had to advise the police of their intention to hold an event, of which eight per licensing year were allowed on any one spot. These were mockingly referred to as 'eight day meetings' because, as with bowls, the intentions of the legislation were easily avoided. Thus the PGTCO told parliament how the promoters of the smaller meetings simply moved their pitches around to different corners of the same field, in order to defeat the restrictions of the legislation. The PGTCO also argued that the flapping tracks were rudimentary and bad for the animals, the rough ground damaging their paws, for example.[56]

Spokesmen for the NGRS and the PGTCO were trying to deflect concern about greyhound racing away from the big stadia, because it was not the smaller flapping meetings, but the large tracks with which parliament was most concerned. Moreover, the big new stadia had since their inception stimulated wider worries about betting on greyhound racing. After the establishment of the Raikes Park track in 1927, 'Old Boltonian', the moral voice of the *Bolton Evening News* denied that greyhound racing was a sport, was fearful of its effects upon the young, lamented the aesthetic emptiness of the punters, and was critical of the disregard for the work ethic which all gambling implied:

> The popularity of the electric greyhound coursing raises in thoughtful minds the question of gambling and its effects on the public, especially the rising generation. For there can be no doubt that the whole business is chiefly a matter of gambling. As those who attend horse races have no interest in the animals, no eye for the power and prowess of the steeds or the beauty of their motion, but are only concerned about the money they may win or lose, so those who 'go to the dogs' don't care a fig about the greyhounds or their lithe elegance . . . The lure of the gambler is the hope of getting 'summat fer nowt' as we say in Lancashire. [57]

E. B. Perkins was equally sure that greyhound racing was not a sport. He argued that none of the companies had attempted to run the dogs without betting 'as they were challenged to do ' by anti-gamblers. [58]

The inextricable link with betting does not, however, mean that dog racing failed to meet the arbitrary sporting criteria of the anti-gamblers. Horse racing would fail on this count, too. Owners and trainers were certainly sportsmen and women, but the spectators also built up a genuine affection for succesful hounds which transcended their alleged status as mere instruments of betting. They appreciated their sleekness and athleticism. One such revered creature was Mick the Miller, a famous winner in late 1920s and the early 1930s, who starred in the 1934 film *The Wild Boy* alongside Flanagan and Allen, and was later stuffed, pickled and put in the Natural Science Museum at Kensington. The dog Rimmell's Black made a screen appearance in the 1947 film *The Turners of Prospect Road* in which a taxi driver's family dog wins a big race. [59] Anti-gambling criticism did not allow for the dimension of the fancy, nor any feeling for the animals beyond mere instruments of betting.

Who were the spectators at the tracks? The best information on this is post-war. Mass Observation provided a detailed analysis of the audience at the dog track after in the 1940s, and this was given indirect support by Rowntree's survey of English leisure habits a few years later. The audience ranged from groups of young people of both sexes, enjoying the evening out and a few bets, to families, groups of young married women out for a flutter, and the more regular and habitual punters, both working and middle class. It was this latter group of dog track regulars that observers focused upon most of all. MO felt that the dog track was the arena 'most likely to lead to excess', and described Roy G., an ex-RAF officer who betted heavily and was 'perfectly miserable' if he had no money to go to a race meeting.[60]

The sociologist Ferdynand Zweig found that one in five of his sample of 200 cases went to dog race meetings in the late 1940s.[61] Zweig divided his sample up into five types. First there was the 'professional type' – 'people who do nothing but gamble on racecourses'. For them, gambling was work. They made a thorough study of track conditions, for example, the type of hare, the shape of the track, the sharpness of bends, the condition of the running surface, the positions of the runners in the traps, and so on, and they related this to the past form of the dogs. They bet only within fixed limits based upon their schemes, knowing when to stop and 'taking their winnings as the workman takes his wages'. According to Zweig, they were mainly lonely bachelors, often ex-servicemen, who tended to shun responsibility associated with more regular employment and with family life. Zweig estimated they made up about a quarter of all racegoers.[62] Next were the semi-professionals who attended tracks four or five times a week but kept their regular employment. Many were fairly well off, from lower-middle and upper-working-class occupations such as small shopkeepers, small businessmen and market traders. They tended to lose more frequently, and heavier sums, than the professional types. Third came the sporting type, who treated the tracks as a hobby, attending a few times a week for a gamble on each race. Zweig roughly estimated them at a third of all racegoers. Then there were the 'unhappy types', a numerous crowd of desperate gamblers to be found at the tracks in all weathers, shouting loudest during the races. These were the poorest, the lumpen, often physically or emotionally crippled. Like Booth some sixty years earlier, Zweig saw this group as those most likely to neglect their family's well-being for the sake of their 'wistful illusions', then cursing their bad luck and railing against injustice, but always nursing a vain hope that one big win would break their life's misfortune. Finally, there were the casual racegoers in groups of families or friends who attended occasionally, for a flutter and a night out. Critchley claimed that the appearance of housewives and families on the stands 'confirmed the respectability of the sport'.[63] Women were most likely to be found in this group, although Zweig felt that most women who betted on the dogs preferred to do it with the street bookmaker. Only the professionals, felt Zweig, made any profit. The real losers were the unhappy types, who lacked any notion of restraint.[64]

It was however Zweig's fifth group that caused most alarm amongst the local authorities. The appearance of families at the course was a sinister omen for magistrates concerned at the effects of betting on the young. C. M. Chapman was concerned that greyhound racing encouraged 'gambling amongst men, women and children especially among the humbler class': 'Anyone may enter the ground for greyhound racing, and many thousands of youths under twenty one, and even children, flock there to taste for the first time the fruits of gambling'.[65] A number of people who were lads at the time remembered the appeal of the greyhound stadium despite the fact that persons under school leaving age were not allowed into the tracks, and under the 1934 Act, nobody under eighteen years of age was allowed to bet with bookmakers.[66] William L., as a young teenager in Hulme in the late 1930s, went to one of Manchester's tracks almost every night of opening:

> I used to get in for nothing because you'd ask somebody to take you in, the guys [as] if you were their son or whatever. When you got in the other side under the turnstile you said thank you and I went my merry way. You could have a little bet for a shilling, play the Tote or . . . *Qu: Even at this very young age?* Yeah, I mean you might get the odd bookie give you the looks, 'give me that money' or 'who you with?' or 'you kidding?', but they'd take the bet.[67]

William got money for betting from doing odd jobs, or selling back jam jars. A typical weekend for one Jewish eighteen-year old featured the billiard hall and then the Salford Albion track on a Friday night. Saturday evening was much the same but was followed often by an all-night cards session. Sunday was a cards or coin gaming day.[68] Like the role of pool halls and policy rackets in the bachelor culture of young American men, the dog track was part of a pattern of gambling transmitted from generation to generation which was especially tied in with the transient independence of the young single male.[69]

The view of the dog tracks as a dangerous temptation to the young, to the naive or unhappy, and as a shabby arena for heavy betting raised the hackles of greyhound track owners. In the face of criticisms of greyhound racing, track promoters played down the betting and made some rather grand claims for dog racing. To the parliamentary enquiry of 1932–33 the NGRS stated that: 'national thrift had increased in districts where greyhound racing was specially established. So far from having any demoralising effects [it has] reduced betting in the streets and workshops, and no social ill effects can be traceable to it'. It was further claimed that greyhound racing had diminished reliance on pawnbrokers, decreased drunkenness and cultivated good behaviour in crowds.[70] Sir David Owen, the questioner, said he had 'listened with very great interest to the elegant advocacy of greyhound racing' and was 'beginning to think it was going to be a great factor in the social amelioration of the people'. He concluded, in line with the thrust of anti-gambling campaigners, that the statements of the NGRS were 'propaganda and partisan', an advocation of business interests only. Owen was also unimpressed at the claim of the National Greyhound Racing Club to be the equivalent of the Jockey Club in dog racing because he saw it as too financially involved to be unbiased in arbitration.[71]

The greyhound companies had left themselves open to charges of crass commercialism by their illegal introduction of the totalisator at the tracks from 1928. This had been only intended by parliament to raise money for horse racing, seen as a needy and prestigious national sport, but dog track owners introduced the tote at their tracks to compete with on-track bookmakers and to secure extra revenue for the sport by deducting money from the pool. As with horse racing, the totalisator machine itself was a rudimentary affair to begin with, being usually a hand-worked mechanism issuing tickets – receipts – to the value of the bets staked. At the bigger tracks buildings were erected to dispense the tickets from windows. Almost all the tracks in Lancashire had totalisators by 1932.[72]

A number of cases brought against the greyhound companies by anti-gambling campaigners and local licensing authorities proved inconclusive, but ironically the case brought by the Leeds bookmaker Irving Shuttleworth against Leeds Greyhound Racing Company was successful, and outlawed the use of totes at dog tracks in 1932 and found against the company under the terms of the 1928 Act.[73] The companies made a great deal of fuss, warned of mass bankruptcies without the totalisator takings, and most ignored the ruling. This provoked police warnings, for example against the White City track in Liverpool.[74] The White City track and others belonging to the BGTCS also banned bookmakers from this time. According to the businessman James Shand, the manager of the Liverpool track and a leading spokesman of the BGTCS, this was done 'to keep the neighbourhood good'.[75]

However, a high court action not long after the Shuttleworth case reversed the decision – grist to the mill of the greyhound racing companies. More significantly the Betting and Lotteries Act of the following year attempted to erase the inconsistencies of the law by allowing the totalisator to operate on all non-athletic tracks for 104 days in a licensing year.[76] The aim was to allow dog racing twice a week, but the tracks arranged with each other to avoid overlapping, that is, to race only on specified days of the week, so that for example in Manchester, the

Salford Albion would open on a Tuesday and Friday, the Belle Vue ground on a Saturday and a Wednesday, and the White City on a Monday and Thursday. This was possible because different licensing authorities granted applications to different tracks. Manchester Watch Committee granted Belle Vue's application, and Lancashire County Council approved that of White City. Furthermore, many tracks wanted to race three times a week in the summer, when the weather and the evenings were warmer and brighter, and only once a week during the inclement winter. As the *Manchester Evening News* concluded in May 1935, despite the intentions of government to limit dog race betting to 104 days a year, 'it is possible that Manchester and Salford enthusiasts may still be able to "go to the dogs" six days a week after the new regulations come into force on July 1'.[77] In other words, the greyhound companies accused flapping tracks of getting round the legislation, yet took their own measures to do the same.

It is not surprising that the governmental view of the totalisator at dog tracks continued to be unfavourable. Thus in 1947, Hugh Dalton, the Labour Chancellor of the Exchequer, took a belated revenge on behalf of government in his decision to increase the levy from 6 per cent to 10 per cent for the proprietors of dog race totalisators. During his budget proposals he told the House of Commons that he did

> not propose to levy a duty of this kind on the horse totes [which] operate on quite a different basis. They are owned by the Racecourse Betting Control Board and are not run as the dog totes are, for private profit – a very important distinction. The amount, about ten per cent, which they already deduct from the sums staked, is devoted, after of expenses, to the improvement of horse breeding; and I am advised by my right hon. Friend the Minister for Agriculture that horses are good exports.[78]

Greyhounds were also exported, mostly to Ireland and Australia,[79] yet this went largely unremarked upon by government.

The totalisator continued as a bone of contention between the greyhound track owners and government. Spokesmen for the greyhound associations argued to the Willink enquiry that money which passed through the tote did not fall into the pockets of management but subsidised the poorer owners and trainers, and contributed to the upkeep of kennels and to the payment of veterinary fees. Thus most money bets circulated to the ongoing benefit of dog racing. Not surprisingly, The PGTCO shared the view of the NGRS on this, who pointed out to the Willink Commission that bets on the tote at dog tracks had dropped off sharply since the increase of the tax. They denigrated the 'injustice of placing this penal taxation on the greyhound totalisator and allowing the horse racing totalisator to go untaxed'.[80]

Resentment at this financial discrimination and the view of the greyhound authorities as a second-class jockey club to a second-class sport was most clearly manifested during the course of enquiries of the Willink Commission in 1949–50. Lord Brabazon of Tara, a member of the GRA, interrupted questions put to other members of the group by the chairman of the enquiry Henry Willink. Brabazon was 'distressed' by Willink's suggestion that in introducing the totalisator at dog tracks before the passage of the 1934 Act the companies associated with the NGRS had been operating 'outside the intentions of Parliament'. Yet Willink was right when he argued that the government had originally intended totes for horse-racing only.[81]

The NGRS had the biggest interest in the tote. Most estimates on betting for their tracks give the tote a clear lead over bookmakers. The Board of Customs and Excise reckoned that stakes with track bookmakers were between 60 to 70 per cent of those with the totalisator. The social survey of betting estimated that one half of those attending tracks bet with the totalisator only, one-quarter with bookmakers only, one-quarter with both. A major reason for this, it felt, was most bookmakers would only accept bets to win or each way, whereas the totalisator also offered forecast bets, where the backers tried to name the first and second dogs in a race, and paid out on both.[82] Perhaps it was also due to the incorruptibility of the tote, which could not enter into illicit arrangements with owners or bookmakers.

Yet the totalisator situation was different on most of the smaller, independent PGTCO tracks.[83] On the whole, there was more betting between owners and friends. Here there was a 'preference for bookmakers':

If the owner puts a substantial bet on the totalisator he discloses this fact and tends to lower the odds against himself. This class of better prefers to bet with the bookmaker who gives a fixed price. The marked tendency is for the betters to wait until the last possible moment before making their bet. These factors and the comparatively small crowds attending P. G. T. C. O racecourses tend to reduce the totalisator turnover.[84]

On balance, the Royal Commission guessed the level of bookmaker betting on dogs to be about 80 per cent, or four-fifths, of totalisator betting, as many of the smaller PGTCO tracks had only rudimentary totes, or none at all.[85]

Totalisator takings reflect the post-war boom and slump in greyhound racing. With the release of war restrictions on dog racing, greyhound totalisators took £200 million in 1946, yet this dropped to £72 million by 1950 and further to £62 million by 1960. Attendances fell from 6,329,834 at the large tracks in 1946 to 3,820,413 by 1950.[86] From a post-war peak, then, things were suddenly on a downward turn for dog racing, and this was reflected in internal divisions within the world of the canine fancy.

III

Of all the social groups involved in greyhound racing after 1926 perhaps least is known of the constituency of owners and trainers and their relationship to the track companies. Dogs were either privately trained or track trained. Some owners paid to have their dogs trained at the tracks. Others, usually of lesser means, trained their own.[87] The dogs were bought from large breeders with kennels, or bred locally within the informal network of dog keepers. In general, the smallest owner-trainers and breeders (many dog fanciers were all three) have remained associated with the smallest informal meetings and 'flapping tracks', which was by then used as a generic label for all tracks outside the jurisdiction of the NGRS or the PGTCO Estimates of the number of owners racing their dogs at both NGRS and independent PGTCO tracks for 1949 showed there to be more dogs and owners and independent tracks. At the latter, about 13,000 owners raced between 18,000 and 19,000 dogs, compared to the NGRC estimates of between 12,000 and 15,000 dogs at its tracks.[88] These estimates did not include coursing, the smallest flapping dogs, and pet greyhounds.

The parliamentary enquiries with regard to dog racing contain sadly little detail on owners and breeders and their status within the industry. Yet one greyhound racing company spokesman described not his own courses but the smaller unlicensed tracks as: 'one man businesses which meet the local sporting need of owner-trainers (miners for example) and the attendance at these courses may be anything from 150 to 1,000'.[89] As noted, the smaller flaps were more closely-knit occasions than larger more heavily capitalised affairs, and most betting was with local bookmakers rather than the tote, therefore less money could accrue directly to the track promoters through this mechanism. The PGTCO knew that 'the smaller racecourses cannot afford, and are not indeed expected, to give sufficient prize money to recompense the owner'.[90]

The dog owners at the NGRS tracks were wealthier followers of the fancy. The sporting press, especially the greyhound racing papers from the 1940s, with the *Greyhound Stud Book*, where many track companies and lesser owners began to register their dogs from 1927, and also popular histories of greyhound racing, all show clearly that company directors, many wealthier bookmakers and businessmen from all areas of commerce, and a still considerable number of genteel owners, many with a career in the army behind them, ran their hounds at the biggest tracks.[91] Instead of raising the dogs in a back yard these wealthier owners invested in kennels and paid professional breeders to nurture the animals. The big companies bought the cream of the Irish and English Stud. 'Mick the Miller' was raised by a Catholic priest and a kennel owner in Killough, County Offally, before his purchase by a London bookmaker in 1929.[92] Following a similar strategy to the Jockey Club to secure greater finance and respectability for the sport, leading NGRS officials argued that British greyhounds were the world's finest, but their lineage would be mutilated by higher taxes on profit and the subsequent limitations on reinvestment.[93]

The *Greyhound Owner*, and the *Greyhound Breeder and Exporter*, both formed in 1946, were the mouthpieces of the smaller owner-trainers and breeders who raced both on NGRS tracks and also the independent tracks. These two papers amalgamated in 1949 to become *The Greyhound Owner and Breeder*. These were times when many greyhound enthusiasts were worried at the turn the sport was taking, and the NGRS was singled out for criticism by many smaller owners. In 1946 the *Greyhound Owner* spoke of its disquiet at 'the increase in the number of company-owned greyhounds'. It lamented the decline of open races in which all owners could race their dogs, and felt that the 'private owners rights to run their dogs now seems to be the fundamental issue'. Unfortunately, a couple of attempts since 1935 to establish national associations of owners as a more powerful force within the sport had failed.[94] Four years later the *Greyhound Owner and Breeder* called for a revision of the rule which enabled any registered NGRS owners who raced at independent tracks to be warned off, and for a national registry for all dogs, which would make for more 'open races'.[95] It was the lack of such a registry which, paradoxically, enabled the NGRC to claim that it was merely trying to keep undesirables out of its tracks in order to prevent fiddling.[96]

The ownership of winners of the classic races at NGRS tracks seems to support the impression that private owner-trainers fared badly against company dogs. At the Scurry Gold Cup, run at Clapton from 1928, there were only three privately trained winners before 1960. Almost all the winners were trained at the large London tracks. There were only three privately trained winners in the Oaks, at Harringay, between 1927 and 1960. In the Laurels, run at Wimbledon, not one privately trained dog won before 1962. Private dogs fared slightly better in the English Greyhound Derby at London's White City, where seven dogs attributed to private owners came in first between 1927 and 1960. Most big races were sponsored by the greyhound companies, bookmakers, and newspapers.[97]

Many of the smallest private owner-trainers who wrote to the *Greyhound Owner and Breeder* were clearly disillusioned with NGRS stadia. They preferred flapping tracks, and resented that corruption at the big stadia (discussed below) stained the sport at the bottom: 'Dog racing does not have to take place in big palatial stadiums. What people like me want is the small track where an inexpensive dog can be run without whispers and guessing about identity'.[98] Another small owner – 'two dogs at most at any one time' – felt it was 'high time the flapping owner was raised in status a bit and not treated with suspicion everywhere he goes'.[99]

A major cause of these complaints was the closely knit business connections and oligarchic structure of greyhound racing, the self-regulatory nature of the sport from above. 'Bywayman' the opinion columnist of the *Greyhound Breeder* and, from 1949, of the *Greyhound Owner and Breeder*, articulated a general feeling of resentment on behalf of those owners who were excluded from the management and the profits of the sport. He blamed excessive capitalisation and authoritarian practices for giving an image of an 'insiders sport' which was not truly competitive. Critchley, Dixson and others, he wrote 'had a powerful influence' on greyhound racing 'mainly, I am sorry to say, in its direction as a big-money producing racket':

> Their ideas and efficiency worked wonders on the rapid installation of excellent stadiums and running tracks. But at the same time they had too much influence in the handling of the sport. It would have been better had they leased their tracks to groups of sportsmen, owners and trainers etc, who would have preserved the elements of true competition, national competition.[100]

As late as 1978, the Rothschild Commission noted that greyhound racing was still more tightly organised than horse racing, with greater control from the top.[101] In horse racing, owners and breeders have helped to control the sport through access to the Jockey Club, whilst the NGRC has remained almost exclusively composed of company directors and officials. Thus to parliamentary enquiries since 1932 the NGRC has given evidence on behalf of all concerned with greyhound racing, claiming to represent the racing officials, – whom they appointed – and the companies, breeders, owners and trainers.[102]

Bywayman's complaints were expressed at a difficult time for the image of greyhound racing. Dog racing had long been associated with malpractice, but a number of post-war scandals were spectacular reminders to the public of this. A famous doping scandal had occurred in 1946 when a number of dogs at a London track were fed with fish containing just enough chloretone, an alcohol-based sedative, to slow the dogs down without other physical symptoms.[103] In 1950, the famous 'Waggles' substitution scandal involved three brothers who were committed to trial at the Old Bailey for running greyhounds whelped in Ireland under false names in England.[104] In the north, miners complained bitterly of the 'big boys' from the largest tracks who were pushing themselves onto flapping tracks with 'unbeatable dogs' and destroying proper competition and betting.[105] As Zweig noted in 1948, for Yorkshire miners, in the small races stakes were 'usually small', between the three and five shillings mark, but he noted a 'widespread distrust against the unfairness of the game on some dog tracks'.[106]

The general decline in racing attendances was blamed in part on such · unfairness and corruption, and there is some contemporary evidence to · support this view. Rowntree and Lavers found one punter who felt it was 'no good' unless you were 'in the know', three thought the sport was 'too crooked', and others described dog racing as a 'swindle, 'not honest' and 'corrupt'.[107] Although it suited anti-gamblers to portray people at the tracks as bland, lonely or obsessive, they failed to account for these criticisms of the sport both from spectators and the smaller dog owners.

Three further suggestions have been posited for the post-war decline. Firstly, the NGRS blamed the introduction of a betting tax on dog race tote turnover in 1947. Secondly, the fuel crisis of that year, was also seen by the society to expedite this decline. It did short-term damage to dog racing. The regular demands on electricity which the lighting, the tote and the electric hare made from over two hundred tracks nearly every week, was considered to be more costly by the government than the needs of football and horse racing, daylight sports. Football and horse racing suffered modifications of the normal schedules but, to the chagrin of track owners, greyhound racing was shut down for six weeks in the winter of 1947–8. The sport was also limited to regular specified days until July 1949, 'with various local authority areas [joining] together to ensure racing was not held on different days in adjoining regions'.[108] This upset the co-operative arrangements mentioned (see p. 152) to defeat the eight day regulation. The return to normality of the racing calendar and the football league fixtures soon after the fuel crisis was over certainly provided more accessible opportunities for regular betting than the restrictions on dog racing. Finally, it can be argued that the sport possessed a novelty value between the wars, which was boosted from 1945 by the lifting of war restrictions and the post-war release of tension. Yet it could not compete in the longer term with other demands for the attention and the money of the working-class spender, most notably, television sets, cars, milk bars, record players and rock music, and from 1961, the licensed betting offices.[109] These alternative attractions removed many punters from Zweig's casual racegoers category, and the largest greyhound tracks have increasingly since the 1950s been visited regularly by a more limited constituency of mostly working class men, usually from skilled occupations.[110] Yet, despite its decline, dog racing still remained the second-biggest spectator sport after football in the 1950s, a point recognised by the BBC, which began to transmit some of the classic greyhound races from the mid 1950s. The commentator Harry Carpenter's career on the small screen dates from this time. He had been a writer on the *Greyhound Owner* and the *Greyhound Breeder and Exporter* in the 1940s.[111] Now, however, he is better known for his boxing commentary.

Notes

1 Ferdynand Zweig, *The British Worker*, 1952, p. 143; Charles Dimont, 'Going to the Dogs', *New Statesmen and Nation*, 30 November 1946.
2 This discussion is based on John Ashworth, *Strange Tales from Humble Life*, 1877, pp. 133–46; *The Victoria County History of Lancashire*, Vol. 2, 1966, 'Coursing', by Harold Brocklehurst, pp. 472–6; J. W. Bourne, *The Greyhound Record*, Vol. 1, 1901, p. 141; pp. 144–9. David Brown, 'Sketch of the Waterloo Cup', *Greyhound Stud Book*, 1882, pp. 33–61.
3 Roy Genders and the National Greyhound Racing Club, *The National Greyhound Racing Club Book of Greyhound Racing*, 1990, p. 273. *Greyhound Stud Book*, Vol. 1, 1882.
4 *Greyhound Stud Book*; J. F. Blakeborough, *The Turf Who's Who*, 1932, p. 45.
5 *Greyhound Stud Book*, Vol. 1, 1882, p. X. *Victoria County History*, op. cit.
6 See any edition of the *Greyhound Stud Book* for the late 1890s and 1900s.
7 Letter from John Gulland of the NAGL in *Humanitarian*, Vol. V, No. 109, March 1911.
8 *Greyhound Stud Book*, Vol. 1, 1882, p. 34.
9 See *Greyhound Stud Book*, 1927, p. 147.
10 R. H. Dude, 'Rabbit Coursing: An Appeal to Working Men' in H. S. Salt

(ed.), *The Cruelties of Civilisation, op. cit.*, Vol. 2, 1897, p. 4.

11 *Bulletin* of NAGL, November, 1916.
12 Bernard Waites, 'Popular Culture in Late Nineteenth and Early Twentieth Century Lancashire', in the Open University Popular Culture course U203 booklet, *The Historical Development of Popular Culture in Britain*, 1, 1985, p. 100.
13 Waites, *ibid.*
14 Caroline Ramsden, *Racing Without Tears*, 1952, p. 37.
15 Alan Lennox, *Greyhounds, the Sporting Breed*, 1987, p. 14.
16 *Sporting Chronicle* 12 September, 1876.
17 Genders and NGRC, *op. cit.*, p. 224.
18 Charles Booth, *Life and Labour of the People in London*, Third Series, 'Religious Influences', Vol. 1, 1902, p. 252; Vol. 5, 1902, p. 126.
19 LSE Coll., Poverty notebook B54; Parker Street, Hackney, p. 23. The Booth manuscripts for *Life and Labour of the People in London* are held at the British Library of Political and Economic Science, LSE For a discussion of economic individualism amongst the poor see Jerry White, *op. cit., passim.*
20 J. M. Hogge, *The Facts of Gambling*, 1907.
21 The dichotomy between wealthier owners who left their dogs in kennels, and the poorer owner-trainers who kept the dogs themselves becomes clearer from the establishment of the electric tracks in 1926. See below, pp. 154–7.
22 Forman *op. cit.*; Burke, *op. cit.*
23 Writer's Oral Project, J. M., letter.
24 Waites, *op. cit.*
25 Forman, *op. cit.*, pp. 193–6.
26 Bert W., *op. cit.*
27 Ferdynand Zweig, *Men in the Pits*, 1948, p. 113.
28 Mick Burke, *Ancoats Lad*, Manchester, 1985, p. 23. Charles Forman, *Industrial Town*, 1979, pp. 193–6.
29 Steven Hamer, *op. cit.*
30 *R. C.*, *1949–51*, Memo of PGTCO para. 11, p. 279.
31 John Martin, 'Gambling', in *New Survey of London Life and Labour*, Vol. 60, 1935, p. 274.
32 Arthur Marwick, *The Deluge*, 1965, pp. 304–5.
33 Whiting Williams, *Full Up and Fed-Up: The Workers' Mind in Crowded Britain*, New York, 1921, pp. 166–7.
34 *Sporting Chronicle*, 10 February 1926. See also *Sporting Chronicle*, 19 April 1926; 19 May 1926.
35 Company File for Greyhound Racing Association (Manchester) Ltd, held at Companies House, London. Company number 208979.
36 David J. Jeremy, *The Dictionary of Business Biography*, Vol. 1, pp. 827–30; Mott, *op. cit.*
37 A. C. Critchley, *Critch! The Memoirs of Brigadier-General A. C. Critchley*, 1961, pp. 131–2; Manchester GRA, Ltd, *Belle Vue Racecourse 50th Anniversary Meeting Official Racecard and Souvenir*, 1976, held at Manchester Local History Library.
38 D. M. Downes et al., *Gambling, Work and Leisure*, 1976, pp. 140–7.
39 Williams, *op. cit.*, p. 168.
40 *Licensed Bookmaker*, February 1963, p. 10; Stephen Hamer, *op. cit.*
41 *Greyhound Breeder and Exporter*, 26 September 1946.
42 Alan Lennox, *Greyhounds, the Sporting Breed*, 1987, p. 15.

43 *Greyhound Stud Book*, 1927, *et seq.*
44 *The Greyhound Racing Share Guide*, 1932, p. 17; Greyhound Racing Association Ltd, registration documents, company number 00229741.
45 Critchley, *op. cit.*, p. 141.
46 Genders and NGRC, p. 33.
47 Hamer, *op. cit.* On the Bolton track see James Power, 'Aspects of Working Class Leisure in the Depression Years: Bolton in the 1930s', unpublished MA Dissertation, University of Warwick, 1980, pp. 42–5.
48 *The Greyhound Racing Share Guide*, 1932, p. 19.
49 *RC 1932–33*, para. 1 of evidence of BGTCS Ltd, p. 354. See also *Greyhound Tracks Review*, the official journal of the BGTCS, from August 1934 to June 1935.
50 *RC 1949–51*, Minutes, qu. 92–4, pp. 24–5.
51 Genders and NGRC, *op. cit.*, pp. 31–44.
52 *RC 1949–51*, Memo. of NGRS, Appendix A, para. 6, p. 254.
53 This discussion is based on the catalogue of the Newspaper Library at Colindale, North London, and *Willing's Press Guide*.
54 F. J. Underhill, Secretary of the NGRS, *Society for the Study of Gambling Newsletter*, May, 1986, p. 6.
55 *RC 1949–51*, Memo. of PGTCO, pp. 279–81.
56 *Ibid.*, para. 11, p. 279.
57 *Bolton Evening News*, 7 January 1928, cited in Power, *op. cit.*
58 E. B. Perkins, *Gambling in English Life*, 1950, pp. 21–2.
59 *Greyhound Express and Coursing News*, 14 May 1934; *Halliwell's Film Guide*, 1986, p. 1017.
60 B. S. Rowntree and G. R. Lavers, *op. cit.*, p. 114.
61 Ferdynand Zweig, *Labour, Life and Poverty*, 1975 edn (first published 1949), p. 31.
62 *Ibid.*, pp. 32–4.
63 Critchley, *op. cit.*, p. 144.
64 Zweig *op. cit.*, pp. 34–7.
65 C. M. Chapman, *From the Bench*, 1938, p. 176.
66 *RC, 1949–51*, Minutes, qu. 6001, p. 412.
67 Writer's Oral Project: William L., born Hulme Manchester, 1923, Tape 8, Side 2.
68 Jewish Museum, Manchester: Myer (Martin) Bobker, No. J43. Tape 1, Side 2.
69 William F. Whyte, *Street Corner Society: The Social Structure of an Italian Slum*, 1981, pp. 140–2. Ned Polsky, *Hustlers, Beats and Others*, 1971, pp. 15–42.
70 *RC 1932–33*, Minutes, qu. 11 pp. 109–10.
71 *Ibid.*, qu. 1688, p. 122.
72 *Daily Herald*, 17 February 1932, in newspaper cuttings book on gambling at Manchester Police Museum.
73 *Licensed Bookmaker*, April 1963, p. 20.
74 *Daily Herald*, 19 February 1932, *op. cit.*
75 *RC 1932–33*, Minutes, qu. 5375, p. 359.
76 *RC 1949–51*, Memo. of NGRS, para. 10, p. 252.
77 *Manchester Evening News*, 15 May 1935, in Manchester Corporation Watch Committee book of Newspaper Clippings, Police Museum, Newton Street, Manchester.
78 *HC Debs*, 12 November 1947, col. 406.
79 *Greyhound Owner and Exporter*, 1946 to 1949; Genders and NGRC, *op. cit.*, p.

124.
80 *RC 1949–51*, Memo of NGRS, para. 25, p. 253.
81 *Ibid.*, Minutes, qu. 4160–1, p. 301.
82 *RC 1949–51*, Report, para. 102, pp. 28–9.
83 *Ibid.*, Memo. of PGTCO, para. 4, p. 279.
84 *Ibid.*, paras. 38–9, p. 283.
85 *Ibid.*, Report, paras 18–21, p. 155.
86 *RC 1949–51*, Report, p. 151.
87 R. Genders and NGRC, *op. cit.*, pp. 312–14. See any edition of the *Greyhound Owner, Greyhound Breeder and Exporter* between 1946–9, and the *Greyhound Owner and Breeder* since 1949.
88 *Greyhound Owner and Breeder*, 25 May 1950.
89 *RC 1949–51*, Memo of NGRS, para. 3, p. 254.
90 *Ibid.*, Memo of PGTCO, para 61, p. 285.
91 *The Greyhound Racing Stud Book*, 1950–60.
92 Genders and NGRS, *op. cit.*, p. 168.
93 *RC 1949–51*, Minutes, qu. 8, p. 259.
94 *Greyhound Owner*, 20 February 1946.
95 *Greyhound Owner and Breeder*, 27 April 1950.
96 Critchley, *op. cit.*, p. 141.
97 *Genders and NGRC*, pp. 87–102; pp. 307–8.
98 *Greyhound Owner and Breeder*, 3 May 1950.
99 *Greyhound Owner and Breeder*, 27 April 1950.
100 *Greyhound Owner and Open Race Digest*, 1950, p. 5.
101 *RC 1976–8*, Report, Vol. 1, para 10.9, p. 108.
102 *Ibid.*, para. 2, p. 259.
103 Godfrey James, *London: The Western Reaches*, 1950, pp. 203–4.
104 *Greyhound Owner and Breeder*, 3 May 1950.
105 *Greyhound Owner and Breeder*, 3 August 1950.
106 Zweig, 1948, p. 114.
107 B. S. Rowntree and R. Lavers, *English Life and Leisure*, 1951, pp. 7, 17, 30, 47, 90, 97, 99, 105.
108 Underhill, *op. cit.*, p. 6.
109 *RC 1976–8*, Report, Vol. 1, paras 10.6–7, pp. 106–7.
110 D. M. Downes et al, *op. cit.*, pp. 140–1.
111 *Listener*, 19 September 1957; *Greyhound Breeder and Exporter*, 19 December 1946; *Who's Who*, 1991, p. 302.

Chapter 7
Football coupon betting in England,
c. 1890–*c.* 1960

· Before the end of the nineteenth century, football coupon betting was
mainly a north western phenomenon, promoted by the sporting and
· coupon press and local bookmakers there.[1] By the late 1930s it was a
weekly flutter for over ten million people nationally. It had largely
superseded the pastime of informal wagering on the terraces of football
grounds. The coupons were based on a number of betting combinations,
and supplied by the large and growing pools firms, of which Littlewoods
in Liverpool was the largest, taking one half of the total stake or 'pool' of
£60 million by 1950.[2] The British football pools had become the biggest
privately-owned gambling concern in the world, and the growth of
football coupon betting was central to the rise of mass commercial
betting during the twentieth century.

   This chapter looks at the growth of the pools and why so many people
took up coupon betting on football. It will also examine the criticisms
made of football betting, and discuss the relationship of the pools to the
sport of football.

I

The establishment of regular match fixtures provided the opportunity
for fixed-odds pre-match betting, where the sizes of prizes are offered in
advance, on a grand scale. The Lancashire League, and the working-
class culture which produced it comprised the general context for
football betting. Yet this by itself does not explain why football coupon
betting was based largely in Lancashire as opposed to other heartlands
of the industrial working class. The size of a local sporting and gambling
press there was crucial, it seems. The idea of football coupon betting, as
Tony Mason argues, began with a bright spark in the local sporting
papers in the 1880s. The *Football Field* of Bolton, the *Lantern* of St Helens
and the Hulton Press's *Athletic News* of Manchester, were offering their

readers respectively fixed prizes, more commonly known as 'fixed-odds' of twenty-two shillings and sixpence, ten shillings and five pounds respectively during the 1880s.[3] These prizes reflected the varying levels of capital behind each paper. A number of small printing and publishing firms tried to sell their coupon sheets and tipping sheets on the streets. The catalogue of the newspaper library in Colindale, and the invaluable survey of the Manchester Press by Frederick Leary, lists a few of the ephemeral efforts tried out on the local public during the 1880s and 1890s. The most enduring was the *Football Programme and Weekly Calendar*, edited by the Manchester tipster 'Umpire'. It lasted from October 1889 to February 1891. The paper boasted 'Coupons on Second and Third Pages' and readers were invited to predict the winning teams of twelve matches from both the Association Football and Rugby leagues. If a draw was predicted the punter was to write 'DRAW'. Three pounds was paid for the highest number of correct predictions each week.[4] But rugby proved unsuitable from the promoters' point of view. As the *Daily Telegraph's* 'The Public and the Football Pools' argued in 1938, predicting draws on soccer matches was much more uncertain than in rugby, where draws were comparatively rarer. This complicated the business of forecasting, adding to the margin of uncertainty.[5] Perhaps the short span of the *Football Programme* was a result of many punters successfully making win-or-lose predictions on rugby.

It was the bigger publishers who were responsible for the spread of football coupon betting from the north west. Alongside the Hulton Press's *Athletic News* and *Sporting Chronicle* other big publishers wanted a piece of the action. For example, *Sporting Luck*, a paper run by a Manchester publishing and printing family, the Stoddarts, was begun in March 1890 at one penny weekly. In August, due to the success of the paper, the family transferred to London. *Sporting Luck* contained coupons for predicting the results of football matches as well as tips on horses and gossip from the sporting world. The Stoddarts also published *Football Record* at this time.

Those concerned with betting amongst the masses were soon alert to these developments. The NAGL had unsuccessfully tried to prosecute the Stoddarts in 1895 for accepting stake monies on coupon betting in defiance of the Betting Act of 1853, but they won their case against them in 1900. The Hulton Press too, were taken to court in the following year.[6] Sir W. J. Ingram, chairman of the London sporting paper *Pearson's Weekly*, also a key promoter of gambling competitions, was successfully prosecuted for a football prize game in 1900.[7] In order to steer clear of the lottery and gambling legislation, many speculators took two sorts of evasive action. Some went abroad where they could receive money by post. Other bigger promoters like the Hultons and the Stoddarts', and Horatio Bottomley of *John Bull*, as well as smaller sporting papers, began to rely more on 'skill competitions' such as Spot-the-Ball and word-games in order to escape the none-too-clear stipulations about skill in the lottery legislation.[8]

Some newspapers refused to boost sales through the immoral adver-tisement of prize competitions. For example, the *Manchester Evening News*, owned by anti-gambling Nonconformist Russell Allen, accused other proprietors of exploiting the public. 'Recently', complained a leader in March 1905 'a very insidious form of gambling has made its presence known in the North of England, and unless some means can be found for stopping this undoubted evil we are afraid the future of football will be as bad as horse racing has become'.[9]

This article blamed newspapers for 'whetting the public appetite' for easy money, but it also accused bookmakers. It reprinted a copy of a circular handed to the writer 'by a perfect stranger in a street in Wigan', which described details of this coupon 'system'. The coupons were distributed by agents of the bookmaker in the streets, around the mills and workplaces, and outside football grounds, to such an extent that bookmakers were 'doing a roaring trade ' amongst 'the artisans of the great engineering works in Openshaw and the dwellers in colliery districts like Wigan and Atherton'.

In Liverpool, the statistician Ainslie J. Robertson made a study of football coupon betting for the NAGL, and noted the prominence of local bookmakers in the distribution of fixed-odds coupons. He found that forty-two agents worked for three large bookmaking firms in Merseyside. Robertson estimated that 'perhaps 140,000 monetary deposits' – stakes – were received by the three bookmakers. Most of these were for one shilling or two shillings and sixpence. These were checked off by a 'considerable' staff. He estimated that over £8,000 was disappearing 'into the hands of these bookmakers from their clients' of which only a small percentage went the other way.[10] Robertson reckoned that by 1907 at least a quarter of a million coupons were on the market every week during the football season in Merseyside alone. Another glimpse of how the coupons were distributed is to be found in *Justice of the Peace*, the magistrates' journal. In 1909, the Liverpool police prosecuted a man for distributing handbills for a bookmaker who had offices in London and Holland. The handbills contained the odds at which the bookmakers would make bets on football at their offices, and a form for the bet. The man shelled out the handbills, of which he possessed over three hundred, to people on their way football grounds.[11] Bookmakers all over Britain copied the idea. By 1913, the *Morning Post* estimated that two million football coupons were issued every week nationally.[12]

The role of bookmakers in football betting was the transitional link · between football betting in the press and the growth of the pools firms from the 1920s. The bookmaker system was copied by other speculators · who entered coupon betting, of whom John Moores, the founder of Littlewoods, was to become the most succesful.[13] The ascendancy of Littlewoods and the role of John Moores within it is a classic 'rags to riches' story which has canonised Moores as a twentieth-century capitalist 'distinguished for talent'. At the end of the first world war, Moores was a telegraphist in Manchester with the Commercial Cable Company. No doubt the volume of racing and betting intelligence he helped to transmit, and the continuing popularity of football coupon betting in the north west after 1918 opened his eyes, and those of two of his fellow telegraphists, to the possible profits of a foray into the football betting business.

The enterprise was begun in 1922 with a combined total capital of £150 and a small office in Liverpool. Moores freely admitted that the idea for a company distributing coupons was not his, but came from a Birmingham man called Jervis, who was operating a system of pool betting based on the *pari mutuel*, from which he deducted 10 per cent commission.[14] The early organisation of Moores's venture was similar to the system of production and distribution sketched by Robertson. A printing firm was commissioned to produce 4,000 copies of their first coupon, and a leaflet distributing firm was engaged to issue them. This was one of Moores's few mistakes, as the distribution company was owned by a Methodist who hated gambling and withdrew from the contract as soon as he realised what he was doing. So the partners themselves had to give out the coupons by hand, which they did 'with the help of a few small boys' outside Manchester's football grounds.[15]

The business began very slowly, takings were less than five pounds for the first week. This suggests that most recipients of the coupons were wary of trusting their pennies to touts with no established reputation. Ten thousand coupons were given out soon afterwards at a major match in Hull, and only one was returned. The costs of printing and distribution along with office rent and expenses led to losses of £600 by the end of the 1923–4 season. The secretary was dismissed and Moores's two partners, one of whom was called Littlewood, quit.

At this point Moores mobilised the labour of his family. And he kept his regular job in the meantime, an important financial support for an aspiring entrepreneur in the gambling world. The Moores family strove hard to get the business off the ground. His wife, his sister and his brother Cecil worked for next to nothing, sending out and checking the coupons returned to the office. The value of the receipts rose to over £257 by the end of 1925 and to £2,000 by the end of the 1926–7 football season. With the increase in customers and subsequent growth in the size of the 'pool' of stake monies, the business took off. The crucial difference between pool and the fixed-odds betting offered by bookmakers is simply that in pool betting the odds cannot be known in advance, and prize monies are only determined finally once all the stakes are in. The commercial operator simply holds the bank and pools the stakes. Winners are paid out of the prize pool once the result is known.[16] Moores and other pools promoters were simply aggregators of a multitude of stakes from which they deducted a commission. This gave them a massive advantage over the local fixed-odds bookmakers whose capital paled into insignificance beside Littlewoods, Vernons (founded by Vernon Sangster) and other companies. The Bookmakers Protection Association, in their memorandum to the 1949–51 Royal Commission, lamented that fixed-odds betting on football 'was once a substantial addition to the normal betting accepted by bookmakers, but the growth of the football pools has caused a serious diminution of the football business done at fixed-odds'.[17] As a Littlewoods punter told Mass Observation in 1937: 'Well I think there's a chance of winning a good sum for a small investment. It is better than bookies' coupons.'[18]

The development of Littlewoods and other pools firms owed much to economies of location. As the Under Secretary of State argued to the Royal Commission of 1949–51, the majority of pools firms established their headquarters in Liverpool 'where, owing to unemployment in the 1930s they were able to find a cheap and plentiful supply of labour'.[19] Eighteen thousand of the total national workforce of 23,500 lived in the Liverpool area by 1950.[20] This labour supply consisted largely of women, many of whom were supplementing the family income where the husband was unemployed, or on a low income.[21] They were employed on a weekly basis for the duration of the football season as checkers; others formed part of the smaller pool of extra staff brought in at weekends to assist in processing the coupons. The Moores brothers knew that checking the coupons was boring, but that accuracy was essential. So they set out to 'eliminate the human element completely during working hours' and to make it up to the workers with canteens, sports clubs, welfare departments, theatres and pension schemes. Most of the women were checkers, also known as 'clerks'. They worked in groups of twenty under a supervisor. The supervisors were monitored by chief supervisors and an overseer kept an eye on chief supervisors. Moores felt that 'one must not put a man in direct supervision over a group of girls',[22] a principle of personnel management used in other workplaces where women were the majority of the labour force.[23] Vernons also deployed similar strategies of worker management and incorporation.[24]

Ministry of Labour statistics for the two largest firms by 1950 illustrate the proportion of female to male workers. For example, Littlewoods, with a workforce of 11,810 employed 11,004 women and 806 men and Vernons employed 614 men and 5,735 women, which was 6,349 workers in all. Men were a little over 10 per cent of the national pools workforce.[25] In the branches, men were occasionally checkers but mainly security guards, fraud inspectors and porters. The Littlewoods management was mostly male, and appointed from or by the Moores family. Outside the branches there was a minor army of Littlewoods postmen, who were employed for two days of the week delivering coupons.[26] These postmen were displaced after 1957 by the door to door 'coupon collectors'.[27]

Those who inspected defaulters arguably had the most interesting job. Most of them were usually ex CID men, employed presumably because their police background was supposed to make them more trustworthy.[28] Defaulting was the art of slipping coupons into the checking process after the soccer scores were known. This was usually attempted by a checker who slipped in a coupon after the match results. Pools companies went to great lengths to identify such coupons and ignore those who repeatedly tried it on. Unfortunately for these companies, the Act of 1845 prevented the recovery of gambling debts at law. The companies did not prosecute, but the offending employee was sacked.[29] Pools firms may also have been pleased with the moral lessons in the film *Easy Money*, written by Arnold Ridley, well-known in the 1970s for his acting role in the popular television sitcom 'Dad's Army'. Although the film extolled the virtues of a pools win, it also warned of the pitfalls of fiddling. It was described by Madge Kitchener of the British Board of Film Censors in 1947 as 'a handsome advertisement but a healthy deterrent to would-be cheaters.' (Madge Kitchener was Lord

Kitchener's niece.)[30]

The need for all pools firms to identify defaulters was one reason leading to the formation of the Pools Promoters Association (PPA) in 1934. But the major purpose of the PPA was to fight any limitations threatened by the lotteries legislation of that year, and to counter the legislation mooted by the football authorities and anti-gambling MPs in parliament. The PPA was in its own words a 'trade association', and as with bookmakers' organisations it intended to articulate the shared economic interests of the pools firms despite the competition of the market. Its biggest enemies, however, were the Football Association (FA), the national offices of the sport, based in London, and the Football League, based at Preston from 1888 to the 1950s, and then Lytham St Annes. The league was originally more concerned with administrative matters. The FA was the national official organisation of the sport.

Football officials warned of the potential threat to true competition and to the good name of the sport from football betting. John Lewis, a founder of Blackburn Rovers, a referee and an FA Councillor, warned a meeting of the FA Council in 1914 that if 'the day comes when bookmakers shall have captured the game, not a single member of that Council will remain in control of the game of football'.[31] Or in the words of Sir J. Charles Clegg, a Nonconformist and the Chairman of the FA in the 1920s, 'if betting gets hold of football, the game is done for'.[32] The problem was simple: if a player could be bought he could sell his principles of fair play. Matches could be 'arranged' to give the right results for those paying out. Money, the bane of amateurism, was the cause of corruption. Under FA rule 42 (later rule 43) passed in 1907, during the surge in football coupon betting, any club official, 'referee, linesman or player proved to have taken part in coupon football betting shall be permanently suspended from taking part in football or football management.' Clubs were also required to add a clause to their agreements with players that such an agreement would terminate upon proof that a player had taken part in coupon betting'.[33] Before 1914, the football authorities petitioned parliament for legislation to abolish football betting, but they also took internal measures. Hence the FA commissioned an enquiry into coupon betting on football in 1913, comprised of association officials, which took evidence from directors and officials of clubs and a representative of the Association Football Players Union over allegations that players were betting on the results of matches. The commission exonerated the players but concluded that 'those responsible for the issue of the coupons and their agents' were 'a serious menace to the game'.[34] The commission led to a proposed parliamentary Bill in 1913 which was postponed due to the war. It further recommended that clubs were to insert a clause in their agreements with players which necessitated the termination of any contract 'upon it being proved that a Player has taken part in Coupon Football Betting'.[35] It was clear that the players were seen to be in the most dangerous and vulnerable position in the relationship of the sport to betting. Thus the world of football management was sickened by the episode of the rigged match between Manchester United and Liverpool in 1915.[36] And in 1925, the FA tried to make an example of poor John Rutherford, the Arsenal International. An unscrupulous coupon promoter called J. A. MacWeeny claimed that the player personally vetted all coupons sent in to Turf Publishers Limited, MacWeeny's front firm. During a prolonged period of litigation, in which the FA, led strongly by Clegg, pressed for Rutherford's permanent exclusion from the game, it emerged that MacWeeny had 'deceitfully laid a trap' in which he had gained Rutherford's signature and used his name to publicise his venture. MacWeeny died during the proceedings, and the Arsenal footballer was readmitted to his club.[37]

In 1920, the football authorities lobbied parliament for another Act along the lines of the erstwhile measure of 1913. The Ready Money Football Betting Act of 1920, however, did nothing to rid football of betting. In fact, it inadvertently clarified the position with regard to credit betting which remained legal. Bookmakers and, later, pools companies, simply received the postal order or cash a week in arrears, thus ensuring that ready money did not change hands. Further assistance from the law came in 1928, with the *Sheffield Telegraph* case. This made newspaper football coupon competitions illegal under the 1920 Act, and boosted the clientele of the pools companies.[38]

Another problem for the governing bodies of football was that both league and amateur non-league clubs promoted unlicensed lotteries in order to raise funds, and received police warnings for infringements of the lottery laws. The FA Council meeting in February 1922 had been worried that 'a practice was growing of clubs and their supporters launching schemes for raising funds by sweepstakes, lotteries or other means' and warned clubs of suspension if they failed to regulate this. This stipulation was not formally relaxed until the 1950s, despite the Betting and Lotteries Act of 1934, a product of the report of the Royal Commission the previous year, which enabled charities, athletic clubs and other organisations to engage in lotteries if they registered with the local licensing authorities. Yet the FA still forbade clubs to operate a lottery.[39]

In 1935 the new president of the league, Charles H. Sutcliffe, a Methodist, initiated two further anti-pools moves. First, the league forbade clubs to put advertisements for the pools in their programmes or at their grounds,[40] but more significantly, the League, with the full support of the Football Association, tried to withhold the publication of match fixtures until two days before kick-off. Coupons could only be produced if the week's matches were known in advance. The league argued that the match fixtures were the property of the league and could not be published elsewhere without permission. This was the beginning of the 'copyright' question, otherwise known as 'the Pools War', which was not resolved until 1958.[41]

The pools companies had little trouble with the copyright issue, and managed to cobble up coupons by telephoning football clubs. The FA and the league management committee sought legal advice which confirmed that breach of copyright existed over the use of the fixtures, but in a letter to the FA, E. Holland Hughes, the secretary of the PPA argued that there was no illegal infringement. Nevertheless, the PPA offered 'an ex-gratia payment to the Football League so long as it was directed to the best interests of the sport'. As Stanley Rous argued, however, FA rules forbade the acceptance of this money.[42]

The league and the FAs moves were not only impractical, but deeply unpopular. George Orwell, carrying out the groundwork for *The Road to Wigan Pier*, noted that Hitler's re-occupation of the Rhineland was greeted with 'hardly a flutter of interest' but the decision to withhold the publication of football fixtures to defeat the pools 'flung all Yorkshire into a storm of fury'.[43] Soon after this abortive episode R. J. Russell, the Liberal MP for Eddisbury in Cheshire, with the full support of the football authorities, attempted to outlaw the pools as a lottery. His Bill was defeated in the House of Commons by a parliament mindful of the unpopularity of any such action. Russell was accused of being a 'spoil-sport' by one irate poolite who wished that Russell's name was 'on the list of those killed on the roads' at the time of the Bill's passage.[44] In 1938, an attempt by the Independent Member for Oxford University, A. P. Herbert, to ban the pools whilst allowing bookmakers to accept cash bets in a registration scheme, also failed, due to opposition from both MPs and the Home Office, who were well aware of the unpopularity of such a measure.[45]

The growth of the pools companies, however, was halted not by legislation but by war. From 1939, Littlewoods, Vernons and smaller firms combined operations under the misnomer of 'Unity Pools', encouraged by a government mindful of the economic resources Littlewoods and the biggest companies could make to war production. The smaller firms of Shermans, based in south Wales, or the London companies of Copes and Socapools opted out or were shut down, and operations were concentrated at Littlewoods and Vernons branches in Liverpool, where many of the buildings were also given over to war production. The war thus concentrated the reduced market for the pools in Merseyside. The annual profit of the total pools trade dropped from £22 million in 1938–9 to less than £5 million during the war.[46] The Post Office was unable to provide the usual extent of postal facilities, the number of Postal Orders sent dropping from £194 million in 1938–9 to £29 million in 1940–1.[47] The paper shortage sharply affected allocations to Unity Pools, who published their coupons in the newspapers instead. This led to a number of inconclusive attempts by anti gambling clergymen to stop the pools profiteering during a time of national sacrifice, until 1945 when the Reverend John Bretherton successfully established that the pools were a prize competition and infringed the Betting and Lotteries Act of 1934.[48] In the short term, the pools were allowed to continue their reduced coupon business, although, as is shown below, the concentration of the trade on Merseyside was to place the biggest firms in a highly advantageous situation after 1945.

In the meantime, criticism of the pools firms for prospering during adversity did not stop with VE day. It was, if anything, sharpened after 1945 by the problems of labour and plant shortages during the period of reconstruction. The Minister of Labour told the House of Commons that he proposed to import 4,000 displaced persons a week from Austria and Germany and to discuss the withdrawal of mainly women workers from the pools for industrial labour. The *Times* report of the parliamentary debate clearly illustrated the dislike many Labour MPs felt towards the pools as a massive gambling enterprise, and the consequent low priority they afforded to the pools as an employer:

[The Minister of Labour] proposed to discuss with the organisers of the football pools what might be done by agreement and cooperation to limit the amount of manpower employed by them and to secure for them the employment of the type of labour least suited for manufacturing industry. (Ministerial cheers). He could not forecast what the results would be (laughter). What he had in mind for the Lancashire area was that people suitable for employment industries should not be employed in the football pools.[49]

It was clear that any economic planning measures, short – or long-term, would have to negotiate the large-scale problem of labour and investment in such an organisation. These were exacerbated by the abnormal demands of the post-war economy which threw into sharp relief the difficulties of programmatic planning in a capitalist economic system. A number of Labour MPs thus sought to solve this problem by urging the nationalisation of the pools in order to redirect profits into reconstructing the economy.[50]

The idea of nationalising the pools came to nothing, probably because of the full parliamentary agenda of the Labour government up to 1950, and its political exhaustion thereafter.[51] However, in 1947 the Chancellor of the Exchequer Hugh Dalton did raise a 10 per cent tax, the Pool Betting Duty.[52] He hoped to get over £15 million per year from this source. The level of duty was doubled to 20 per cent in 1948, and raised to 30 per cent in 1949, creating revenue worth £17,218,392 in 1951, rising to £21,078,137 in 1953.[53] Littlewoods and Vernons probably spoke for all pools firms when, through the Pools Promoters Association, they pointed out to the Royal Commission on Lotteries and Betting of 1949–51, just when the labour levies were beginning to bite, the unfairness of the absence of a tax on off-course ready-money bookmaking, the unfair discrimination in favour of horse race totes, and the lower level of a 10 per cent tax on greyhound track totalisators. They contended that they also paid the usual tax on company profits.[54] It was suggested in chapter 3 that taxation represented a more instrumental attitude of government towards gambling. It was a milestone along the road to the legalisation of off-course ready-money betting on horses in 1961.

However, during the debate over the role of the pools in economic reconstruction, the internal domain of the pools industry was fracturing. In 1946, with the ending of Unity Pools, Littlewoods and Vernons declared their intention to operate independently, with the actuarial and practical advantage of the lions' share of the market concentration in Liverpool. Socapools and other smaller companies withered away, and Shermans left the PPA, and began an intensive campaign against Littlewoods' and Vernons' postal distribution. It was Shermans who introduced Australian matches to the coupons in order to maintain profits over summer when the English football season was closed. By 1949 it had increased its share as the third largest pools operator, yet it was increasingly unable to compete with the combined forces of the PPA Littlewoods and Vernons could offer their clients bigger prizes, and

Shermans was eventually taken over by Littlewoods in 1962.[55]

Littlewoods built upon this market share throughout the 1950s, thanks largely to the great success of the treble chance coupon, which had in fact originally been introduced by Strangs, the Edinburgh pools company, for the 1946–7 season.[56] Before this innovation, the 'Penny Points' coupon held sway, so-called because the coupon cost a penny, along with a host of other schemes such as 'Four Homes', 'Four Aways' and so on. Poolites had to forecast the results of football matches by putting a '1' for a home win, '2' for an away win' or 'X' for a draw, which was worth three points. Treble chance was really only about draws, or crosses. (Originally the punters were to put duck-egg 'o's but people were used to crosses so the pools companies went back to them).[57] Twenty-three or twenty-four points, that is seven or eight score draws at three points each, and perhaps a one or two no-score draws if score draws were low, spelled money. The Rothschild Commission found that there were 1,217 possible selections of eight matches out of a coupon of fifty five.[58] Thus the treble chance provided a greater number of permutations, ostensible ways of winning the big one, because the number of score draws varied from week to week, and when draws were few, it was possible for only one entry out of millions to get the right crosses by the drawn matches, and thus take the entire pool, whereas more punters shared in the prizes for penny points when predicting the results of fewer matches. The prize was less frequent, but more spectacular. The scope of the coupon made both for complicated exercises in prediction, and also meant that 'the more casual, modest punter could trust to luck for a small sum'.[59] Thus in 1946 the Penny Points peaked at £64,000, but the treble chance jackpot was £76,000. Such winnings tempted more poolites to put their money on the treble chance, thus increasing the size of the pool. In 1950 the dividend exceeded £100,000 for the first time. But following a recommendation by the Willink Commission that prizes were too large, Littlewoods and other firms voluntarily put a ceiling of £75,000 on big wins. This eventually caused a slump in the take-up of Treble Chance, and Littlewood's abolished the guideline in 1957, because people were going back over to fixed-odds coupons run by the big bookmaking firms such as William Hill and Joe Coral, which were offering bigger prizes.[60] The treble chance coupon took off again, and in the same year Nellie McGrail was presented with a cheque for £200,000 by the comedian Norman Wisdom. As Fishwick notes, the use of famous celebrities to give out the prizes reinforced both the fantasy element of the pools, and their claim to respectability.[61]

The simpler 'penny points' or 'four homes' or 'four aways' coupons were pushed right to the margins during the 1950s. It was clear that the customers wanted the chance to win very big prizes. But who were the customers? The Hulton Readership Survey of 1949–50, and the social survey of betting (1951), commissioned to publish concurrently with the Willink Enquiry, found that poolites were drawn from all social levels, but that the upper-working and lower-middle class regularly filled in more coupons per head. Stakes, not surprisingly, were higher at the top of the social scale than the bottom. For example, men earning ten pounds and over had a usual stake of four shillings and sixpence per week, whilst those earning up to three pounds a week placed a usual weekly stake of two shillings and one penny. The moderation of pools betting was evident in the average size of the stake, which the Social Survey put at two shillings and sixpence.[62] Many women did the pools, either with their husbands, on their own, or at work. In 1952 Zweig found that the interest in pools was the greatest of all forms of gambling among women, and that among women who went out to work many participated in collective arrangements for pools betting. Interest in the pools was strongest 'among single women, especially the oldest and frustrated in life' who wanted 'a dramatic change' in their circumstances. Women staked less than men. A woman earning up to three pounds a week had a usual stake of one shilling and eight pence, those on five pounds or more rarely went beyond one shilling and eleven pence per week.[63] Other findings were somewhat higher. The Hulton Readership Survey of newspaper readers for example put the average stake at three shillings and ten pence for men, and two shillings for women.[64] Zweig estimated that one in three women workers did the pools.[65] In all, women numbered about one in five of everyone sending in a coupon. In general, more people filled in a coupon than went to watch a football match, and the social spread of poolites was much wider than that of spectating.[66]

Moreover, the largely home-based activity of filling in a coupon kept the activity free of the low-life associations of the street corner bookmaker or the greyhound track. Thus to the Royal Commission of 1949–51, the Memorandum of the Roman Catholic Church argued that the Pools had become 'a national pastime' and were 'beneficial, since in many homes happy evenings are spent by the family remaining together and filling up their coupons'.[67] This was in sharp contrast to the Anglican Churches Council on Gambling whose view that pools betting was an introduction to the betting evil was seized upon by pools apologists – for example, the MP for East Harrow, A. P. Herbert, once an opponent of the pools but by then a pools adviser – as an example of dog-collared grumpiness.[68] The Catholic Church had a point. What was perhaps most significant about poolites, male or female, was that many who objected to gambling on religious and moral grounds saw the pools as a harmless little flutter, or not as gambling at all. Out of 200 people over the age of twenty surveyed by B. S. Rowntree in 1951, twenty nine people out of 113 (that is, just over 25 per cent) who professed their unwillingness to gamble on other media filled in a coupon. This was true of the working and middle class, and of men and women. For example, Mr F., a working-class man aged thirty-two, was opposed to gambling on religious grounds but did a football coupon every week because he did not regard it as gambling.

> Miss L., upper-middle-class spinster over 70: does not gamble but oddly enough she and her companion each do a football coupon but have a rule that they must not look at the football results in the Sunday newspaper until they return from matins.

> Mr. L, bus conductor, married, no children, teetotal: he never bets on horses because he would be bound to lose. On the other hand he does a football pool regularly because he does not miss a few shillings a week and it gives him a chance of making a large sum he could not get in any other way.[69]

This was the real attraction: the life-altering dream of the jackpot, impossible to achieve through a weekly wage. For John Hilton, the pools offered a solution to the problem of the 'rut' which people feel in a society where income levels and access to vaunted material comforts are widely unequal. Hilton asked his listeners to tell him why they went in for the pools, and he found that the 'desire to win a prize and get out of the rut' appeared 'again and again' in the letters sent to him.[70] Many outside of the world of the pools saw this as futile, even tragic, a metaphor for the uselessness of putting one's faith in chance to alter reality. During the 1950s the playwright Arnold Wesker wrote a sad little story of a widowed Jewish woman whose life was so drab that she grew to live for the coupon each week, to the point of falsely convincing herself she had won. Wesker highlighted the disappointment after the anticipation, the two key emotions of poolites.[71]

Both Hilton and MO emphasised the escapist impulse behind the pools dream, the promise of a life free from want and worry. This was evident in answers to the question 'Why do you bet on the pools?', asked of customers in Bolton pubs during the winter of 1938. Escape from present financial circumstances was the most common desire:

I've not always been a lucky chap but since I've betted on Littlewood's Pool I've done very well. I've 'come up' four consecutive weeks this season, and I shall win a big sum yet. I can feel it in me. Then its a nice little business for me and the wife and no more working at all hours of the day and night for me any more.[72]

Dissatisfaction with pay and working conditions was common. Nurses, when asked why they did the pools replied 'I should give up nursing' and 'I am hoping to win some day a sum which will enable me to leave this rotten job.'[73] A tailors' cutter told Rowntree in the late 1940s that the pools gave him 'just a chance of getting away from this slavery'.[74] For the unemployed a weekly flutter of a penny, sixpence or a shilling could be budgeted for, and provided the hope which, as George Orwell argued in *The Road to Wigan Pier*, helped people to adjust to the boredom and the lowering of economic horizons which came with unemployment. As one unemployed punter told MO: 'Bloody "means test" 'as put a damper on us fellows. It's so little that a fellow puts a bob on 'un doesn't miss it, and if he "comes up", he needn't tell any bugger'.[75] As Hilton noted, poolites often wrote of their weekly stakes as 'investments', and this revealed a similarity with insurance in the minds of the coupon fillers; the one pooled investments against risk, the other pooled investments based on hopes.[76]

Mass Observation argued that to be a poolite was to participate in a peer group activity as distinctive and habitual as smoking. Non-poolites, like non-smokers, were outsiders, not 'sports'.[77] Mays, in his study of Liverpool during the 1950s, found that although the pools appealed to a personal dream, they were also woven into the pattern of communal recreation for those in the poorest areas 'as casually and uncritically as a trip to Goodison or an evening in the corner pub'. Mays found that 'almost everyone without exception has a stake in one or other of the football pools'. Each secretly wanted to be the one to win, but for all the pools was a topic of conversation. They provided interest and excitement and something to look forward to.[78] Like street betting, bowling or whippet racing, the community of the activity was based upon lots of individual desires to be the winner. Thus Hoggart argued in 1957 that sociability and friendliness, as well as the thrill of the jackpot, were central to Littlewoods promotional material.[79] From the 1930s, each poolite received a weekly envelope containing two coupons, one to be given to a friend or neighbour, and, between 1936 to 1939, a copy of *Littlewood's Sports Log*. Littlewood's literature emphasised the 'Littlewoods Happy Circle' and the 'Littlewoods Loyalists'. Cecil

Moores – The Chief – wrote of lucky winners, and photographs of some of these were printed.

What of those beyond the proletarian world? John Hilton said that many who wrote to him, who already lived 'the most comfortable of lives', were proof that 'enough is never enough'.[80] It is tempting to draw a distinction between those who wanted to get out of their rut and those who just wanted more. One example of this condition appears to be Nigel Lawson, a succesful financial journalist in the 1960s, who became Chancellor of the Exchequer in 1983. Alan Watkins, an economic writer, remembers: 'When Mr. Nigel Lawson was my editor at *The Spectator* twenty years ago he used to do the pools every week. "Think of the odds, Nigel", I said. "Think of the winnings", he replied.'[81]

When people of any social class won the jackpot they usually improved their living standards by purchasing bigger houses, labour saving devices and a new car. According to Moores in 1955, most winners' houses were modest, and flashy cars rare.[82] More frequent holidays and buying of gifts for the families was common. Few gave up work for a life of unmitigated luxury or a prolonged burst of 'spend spend spend' mania. Some dabbled in investments and went into business, with varying degrees of success. As one historian of football noted, rather disparagingly in 1954, the advertising literature of the pools firms appealed to 'simple people who dream of getting a car or television set, owning their own house, buying a little business or going for a holiday abroad'.[83] There was some evidence that an acceleration into wealth immediately gave winners a sense of some of the components of a middle-class status consciousness. Politically, some ceased to vote Labour and went to the Conservatives whom they thought would better protect their wealth. Pools winners read more newspapers, both quality and popular, but, unlike non-winners, there were no readers of the *Morning Star* or *Daily Worker* in the winners' cohort. Most people gladly embraced the new comforts and securities of a pools win, but constrained this by the feeling that 'it won't change us'.[84]

Although they were sensitive to the hopes of poolites, anti-gamblers attacked the means of the coupon as a virtually impossible way to wealth. Hubert Phillips, for example (who stated his preference for bridge), told the 1949–51 Royal Commission that the odds were so long, and the influence of skill and knowledge so negligible that the pools were 'barren of intellectual or spiritual content', a useless lottery.[85] The football forecaster Harry Bone felt compelled to launch an attack on Phillips. He wrote that if everyone were put to doing something 'useful', then Phillips 'who compiles crossword puzzles for the *News Chronicle* and broadcasts in quiz programmes, might be one of the first to be axed'. Not surprisingly, he felt that the efforts made to predict results put the pools beyond the status of a mere lottery.[86]

Moreover, critics of the pools also ignored the many smaller weekly payouts made when draws were common. As Charles Madge and Tom Harrisson of MO wrote, 'these small wins are an important feature of Pools often ignored by opponents'.[87] Many people, MO reckoned about 85 per cent over three years, had won something, no matter how little it was. Such small wins maintained interest in the pools. As with betting on the horses, a regular and manageable outlay led to an occasional surfeit of cash and the nice things it could buy.

Poolites were perfectly well aware that the odds were against them, so they drew upon their personal belief systems as well as the intelligence presented to them in the sporting press. Ross McKibbin has made a convincing case for horse race betting as an intellectual exercise based on a study of the past form, the conditions, and knowledge of jockeys and sporting matters in general. Avid coupon fillers also tried to work out their own way, or 'system' of winning, and have been ostensibly helped by a number of pools 'experts' who offered their advice in leaflet or booklet form as well as from the columns of national newspapers.[88] The earliest on record appears to have been W. J. Duckworth, of 46 Church Street, Padiham, Lancashire who tried to make a fast fortune with his flysheet *The Incomparable Football Forecasting System* in 1879. A number of football coupon forecasters are given in the British Library Catalogue for the 1900s and 1920s, but when the pools took off in the 1930s the number of 'pools experts' also rose. They operated under such soubriquets as 'Flagg', 'Fortune' and 'True Form'. Self-professed experts like Eric Johnstone began his career in football pool forecasting from 1934. After the war, Bernard Ward of *Sunday Empire News* and the *Sunday Dispatch*'s Jack Boulder were prominent pools experts whilst Jack Cardwell of Old Hall Street, Liverpool, patented his 'paying permutations' and his 'spreader system' booklets, price two shillings and sixpence, for the 'pools investor of moderate means'. Arthur Hodges, who began pools forecasting for a living after he was demobbed in 1945, was still going strong in 1988. His work was syndicated out to various newspapers and journals under different noms de plume.[89]

But many poolites did not just trust to expert advice and the complicated mathematics of prediction from past results. MO noted the paraphernalia of lucky charms used to will the gamble to success: a lucky hare's foot, a wishbone from a chicken, an ivory elephant and also 'Jigu, the mystic bean of Africa' bought from the stall of a black trader in Bolton market.[90] Others simply used lucky numbers, such as the army pensioner who told MO: 'Ah've backed teams in a list wi' number seven (7, 17, 37, etc.) – away teams this season – 'un thi aw come up. Ah geet six quid odd when that worked'.[91] The Hulton readership survey of 1949–50 found that the 'special attraction' of the football pools lay in the fact that 'for a very small outlay a man can exercise his occult powers on a number of future events'.[92] In 1955 the social anthropologist Geoffrey Gorer reported that a quarter of the population believed that some numbers were lucky for them. He felt the belief in luck was strongly related to petty gambling and the football pools.[93] During the early 1970s Razzell and Smith found that the belief in lucky numbers or gadgets, expressed in what they termed 'anti form systems', was central to many strategies: 'Not only do you have to get the results right, but you have to do so when no-one else does.'[94]

The use of talismans and superstitious devices was not of course inimical to the random nature of picking eight draws from over fifty matches. Most punters knew that the odds favoured the pools firms and so deployed all manner of strategies to increase their chances and to individualise their bid. Yet the pools companies had to avoid associations of pure luck in order to escape the stipulations of the lottery laws. Hence Vernons Pools, stung by Hubert Phillips's critique to the Willink Commission, wrote to the commission stating that they knew from correspondence with clients that many kept detailed records of past match results, and sent their coupons 'as late as possible so that due consideration can be taken of last minute changes in the composition of a team'.[95] But the pools companies wanted it both ways. Littlewoods encouraged both a belief in luck and a study of past results. *Littlewoods Sports Log* was nothing more than a corporate tipping sheet, containing horoscopes, 'Teatips' based on tea-leaf divination, and articles on forehead reading and palmistry. 'Little 'ol man o' the woods', a tipster gnome, gave 'inside information' and 'Football Facts'.[96]

The culture of the pools was thus entrenched in English social life; the football officials who opposed it were fighting a losing battle.[97] Yet in the post-war years the football authorities were even weaker than they had been in the height of the anti-gambling movement. Internally, the FAs various regional bodies began to adopt different positions. At a meeting of the full council in 1946 the London FA proposed that 'since there is no evidence that Football Pools have the slightest influence on the results of matches' it was 'reasonable' to suggest that government organise the financing of sports facilities from the pools.[98] The national FA felt it 'inconsistent and illogical, in present circumstances to ask for a share of the proceeds', but it signalled a potential departure from this principle in this caveat:

> The Association has refrained from expressing what its attitude would be should the government decide to instigate some form of control of the Pools. In the meantime, its policy remains as complete opposition to all forms of betting on football.[99]

The nearest parliament came to any form of control over the pools was in 1954, when the Labour M. P. Frederick Mulley tried to force pools companies to declare the true extent of their profits. This was the first piece of legislation following the Willink Enquiry which had recommended, three years earlier, that the pools firms should publish accounts of turnover and profit.[100] In 1938 the *Daily Telegraph* had complained that the 5 per cent commission taken by the promoters was a first charge on the stake money, absolute profit before expenses and winnings were paid. Mulley felt that more of this money should find its way back to the punters. He stated that he was not anti-pools and filled in a coupon himself from time to time, but he felt that Littlewoods and other firms were in effect fiddling their clients, whom Littlewoods themselves called 'investors'. Mulley argued to the House that poolites 'be put in the same position as the shareholder of an ordinary private company'.[101]

Despite the efforts of the Liverpool MP Bessie Braddock for the Exchange constituency of the city, where Littlewoods had its main offices, to talk out the Bill by reading long tracts from a statement of the PPA, the Bill received at third reading over seventy votes in favour and less than ten against. The pools companies threatened to take themselves off to Northern Ireland where the company laws were more lenient. The economist Alex Rubner, like Mulley, later saw this as a self-accusing gesture, and argued that it was an action consistent with the 'contempt and haughtiness' with which the PPA treated requests for information from parliament. Moreover, due to the loopholes in company legislation the pools successfully resisted any controls which might lead to the disclosure of their profit beyond turnover and prizes.[102]

Legislation of a different kind boosted, or rather provided legal vindication for, the growing links between gambling and football, as for sport in general. The 1956 Small Lotteries and Gaming Act, sponsored by the

Labour MP Ernest Davies, attacked the irrelevant and anomalous state of the lottery laws. It legalised the use of small lotteries for charitable, sporting and other fund-raising purposes.[103] In the light of this Act, the FA and the league loosened the stipulation against lotteries and raffles. Supporters clubs were now free to promote such schemes, but directors, players and officials involved in the organisation of gambling or bookmaking were liable to suspension. This, of course, also meant that anybody associated with gambling would have to relinquish this connection if they were to take up any direct influence in the management of football.[104]

This general relaxation towards lotteries was part of a slow reappraisal of the FAs and the league's attitude towards gambling and the pools. The realisation of the permanence of the pools, their unwillingness to declare the true extent of their profits, and the continuing economic problems of football all conspired to force the football authorities to change their mind on copyright payments and encouraged the FA to push for a greater financial contribution from the pools. The hard economic realities of deficit, especially for the smaller clubs, helped to push the FA and the league further down the road of expediency. The instigation in 1956 of a source of state derived revenue in the 'lottery' of premium bonds was perhaps viewed also as a significant change in the government's attitude to gambling which left the FA and the league out of touch. The continuing 'copyright' question was to a large extent solved in 1958 in the case of the Football League versus Littlewoods Pools. Littlewoods paid a six figure sum to the league.[105] In 1965 the FA took its own action by stating that the pools firms were under a 'moral obligation' to pay for the use of Challenge Cup fixture lists on its coupons. A sum of £75,000 (the old jackpot maximum of the early to mid 1950s) was accepted by the Secretary of the PPA. At the end of the day, necessity had triumphed over conviction. Denis Follows, the Secretary of the FA thought the money would be put to 'good use' given the association's deficit of £40,000 the previous year.[106]

The greater accommodation between the football authorities and the pools companies was thrown into sharp relief in March 1960 when John Moores became a director of Everton Football Club. He had been a shareholder in both Liverpool FC and Everton for some years but was not allowed direct managerial influence because of his organising role – his directorships – in the pools and in the credit-bookmaking firm of H. Littlewoods. He now resigned from these and became Chairman of Everton until 1965. He also made a payment to the club of £56,000 'to enable star players to be secured'.[107]

Finally, it is revealing to compare the organisation of English pools betting with that of Sweden, where the failure of the state to outlaw and remove football betting led to the creation of a nationalised company in 1934. 'Tipping Service Inc.' was required to donate all its profits to a government agency which supported organised sports. Two members of the board were appointed by government. Revenue to the state rose from seven million kronor in 1934–5 to 180 million kronor by 1957–8. Moreover, in a similar vein to the often-mentioned view in Britain that lots of little winnings were more acceptable than one or two big ones, the Swedish pools have mainly paid out many winnings of a few hundred to a few thousand kronor. According to a Swedish historian, the advantages of this system have been scandal-free football betting, because the nationalised institution does not bribe individuals, and greater financial service to the sport of football, as to sport in general.[108]

The feeling that the pools could do more for football had supporters from different points of the political spectrum. In 1938 the *Daily Telegraph* had called for a levy of 5 per cent on stake money which would raise £2,000,000 to be spent on 'the provision of playing fields and on the promotion of sport and recreation generally' under the National Governments' physical fitness scheme.[109] Eighteen years later a similar point was made by Elaine Burton, the Labour member for Coventry, in the debate over Ernest Davies' 1956 Lotteries Bill (which legalised the use of raffles and sweepstakes for charitable, sporting and other purposes). She claimed that Swedish pools had contributed £12,000 towards the cost of sending a team to the last Winter Olympics, but that the British government still went round ' cap in hand, begging for money to send out teams to every international event that comes about'.[110]

Today, the quasi-independent 'Football Trust' has held the line since the Rothschild Report of 1978 between calls for greater finance for football from the pools, and the amount the pools companies are willing to give. This must be related to the question of whether the English poolite would want more smaller prizes instead of the chance of the big one, and the cut on prize-size that might result from a greater financial contribution to sport. The problem with the Swedish system was that it was more rational and distributive, but offered smaller prizes. The Rothschild Commission concluded in 1978 that 'the dream' of a very large prize based on the weekly stake was still seen by poolites as preferable to more prizes of an 'arbitrarily selected figure'.[111]

II

The pools phenomenon has been seen, even by sensitive observers of working-class culture and recreation, as symptomatic of a something-for-nothing ethos and as a 'universal spivvery' pervading society.[112] But the small individual sums and personal strategies employed in the weekly pursuit of the jackpot also reveal a considered and moderate attitude amongst poolites. If spivvery is characterised as opportunism harnessed to a something-for-nothing attitude, poolites can hardly be accused of it, because the majority put in more money than they get out. It can be concluded that the transcendental promise of the jackpot, offered weekly by the pools companies, and gilded by manifest inequalities of opportunity for upward mobility and vast differences in levels of personal wealth, has given football coupon betting its own irresistible, if frustrating, logic. Only the promoters and the government have been assured of a continued rake-off from the national flutter on the pools. This is in stark contrast to the returns on the hopes and stakes of the mass of poolites, and to the hard-pressed coffers of the smaller football clubs.

III

The government was, by the 1950s, making money not only from the pools, but from totalisators on horse and greyhound racing. It had also signalled its intention in 1956 to introduce legalised cash betting off the racecourse. That year also witnessed two major reforms of the state's attitude towards lotteries, namely, the aforementioned Act of Ernest Davies, and the introduction of the premium bonds. The next chapter looks at the history of sweepstakes and of the premium bonds.

Notes

1 Tony Mason, *Association Football and English Society*, 1863–1915, 1981, pp. 179–85; Ross McKibbin, *Working Class Gambling in Britain*, 1880–1939, Past and Present, No. 82, 1979, pp. 147–8.
2 *RC 1949–51*, Memo of PPA, para. 4499, p. 335.
3 Mason, *op. cit.*; see also Bernard Waites, 'Popular Culture in Late Nineteenth and Early Twentieth Century Lancashire', in Open University Course U203 'Popular Culture', *The Historical Development of Popular Culture in Britain 1*, Milton Keynes 1985, pp. 99–100.
4 Frederick Leary, *History of the Manchester Periodical Press*, Manchester, 1893, Vol. 3, p. 533.

5 *Daily Telegraph and Morning Post*, 'The Public and the Football Pools: An Inquiry', 1938, p. 5.
6 *Bolton Evening News*, 21 November 1900.
7 *Bolton Evening News*, 27 November 1900.
8 See these papers up to 1914; see also Nicholas Fishwick, *English Football and Society 1910–1950*, Manchester 1989, p. 118
9 *Manchester Evening News*, 20 March 1905.
10 Ainsley J. Robertson, 'Football Betting', *Transactions of the Liverpool Economic and Statistical Society*, 1907, p.
11 Mason, *op. cit.*, pp. 183–5.
12 *Justice of the Peace*, 3 April 1909.
12 Cited in Charles E. B. Russell, *Social Problems of the North*, 1980, p. 15 (first published 1913).
13 What follows is based upon four interviews with John and Cecil Moores in *Empire News* in October and November 1955, the publicity brochure, *Littlewoods, the Pools Firm, c.* 1980 (no page numbers), and Woodrow Wyatt, *Distinguished for Talent*, 1962, pp. 233–43.
14 *Empire News*, 16 October 1955.
15 *Littlewoods, the Pools Firm.*
16 *RC 1976–78*, Report, Vol. 1, para. 11.2, p. 127.
17 *RC 1949–51*, Memo of B. P. A., para. 51, p. 353.
18 MO archive, *Worktown*, Box 2, File F, Blair Hospital.
19 *RC 1949–51*, Memo of Under Secretary of State, para. 26, p. 3.
20 *Ibid.*, Report, p. 37.
21 Tony Lane, *Liverpool: Gateway of Empire*, 1987, pp. 95–6.
22 *Empire News*, 23 October 1955. For the experience of a woman who began as a checker in 1928 and progressed to section superviser by the end of the 1930s, Writer's Oral Project, Tape 2, Side 1, interview with Mrs Glenys W.
23 Pearl Jephcott, *Married Women Working*, 1962, on the Peek Frean's biscuit factory in Bermondsey.
24 *Vernons House Journal*.
25 *RC 1949–51*, Report, pp. 37, 167.
26 MO archive, *Worktown*, Box 1 File F, interviews with two Littlewoods postmen.
27 *Littlewoods . . . the Pools Organisation*.
28 *Empire News*, 23 October 1955.
29 *Ibid.*
30 *British Board of Film Censors Scenario Reports*, 1946–47, pp. 80–80a. I am grateful to Tony Aldgate for providing me with this reference.
31 NAGL *Bulletin*, February 1914.
32 Cited in E. B. Perkins, *op. cit.*, p. 42; Fishwick, *op. cit.*, p. 128.
33 *RC 1949–51*, Memo of the FA, para. 2, p. 430.
34 *FA Council Minutes 1913–14*, 'Report of the Commission on Coupon Betting on Football'.
35 *Ibid.*
36 Fishwick *op. cit.*, p. 128.
37 *FA Council Minutes*, 11 January 1926, pp. 1–3.
38 John Hilton, *Why I Go in for the Pools*, 1936, p. 8.
39 *FA Council Minutes*, 18 February 1957.
40 *FA Council Minutes*, 7 October 1935.
41 This discussion is based on Simon Inglis, *The Football League and the Men Who*

Made It, 1988, pp. 145–58; Charles E. Sutcliffe et al., *The Story of the Football League*, Preston, 1938, p. 41.

42 *FA Council Minutes*, 22 March 1936.
43 George Orwell, *The Road To Wigan Pier*, 1976, p. 80 (first published 1937).
44 *Liverpool Daily Post*, 24 April 1936.
45 A. P. Herbert, *Independent Member*, 1950, pp. 70–2.
46 *RC 1949–51*, Report, para. 110, p. 31.
47 *RC 1949–51*, Memo of Postmaster General, Appendix D, p. 43.
48 *RC 1949–51*, Minutes, qu. 26, p. 3.
49 *Times*, 12 March 1947.
50 *Times*, 26 July 1946.
51 Alan Sked and Chris Cook, *Postwar Britain: A Political History*, 1989, p. 87.
52 *HC Debs*, 12 November 1947, col. 407.
53 *HC Debs*, 16 December 1952, cols 179–180.
54 *RC 1949–51*, Memo of PPA, paras 47–8, p. 332.
55 For Sherman's version of post-war events see Memo to *R. C. 1949–51*, pp. 479–81.
56 This discussion of Treble Chance is based on Harry Bone, *The Truth About the Treble Chance*, 1957, pp. 7–10; Jack Cardwell, *New and Improved Spreader Pools System*, Liverpool, 1953; E. Lenox Figgis, *How to Bet to Win*, 1974, pp. 13–21.
57 Figgis, *ibid.*, p. 19.
58 *RC 1976–78*, Report, Vol. 1, para. 11.5, p. 128.
59 Fishwick, *op. cit.*, p. 120.
60 Alex Rubner, *The Economics of Gambling*, 1966, p. 134; David J. Jeremy and Christine Shaw, *Dictionary of Business Biography*, Vol. 3, 1985, pp. 240–2.
61 Fishwick, *op. cit.*, p. 121.
62 *Kemsley and Ginsberg*, p. 12.
63 *Ibid.*, p. 11.
64 Geoffrey Browne, *Patterns of British Life*, 1950, pp. 65–7 See also D. B. Cornish, *Gambling: A Review of the Literature*, HMSO, 1978, p. 27.
65 Ferdynand Zweig, *Women's Life and Labour*, 1952, pp. 145–6.
66 Fishwick, *op. cit.*, p. 122.
67 *RC 1949–51*, Memo of Roman Catholic Church in England and Wales, para. 16, p. 342.
68 A. P. Herbert, *Pools Pilot, or Why Not You?*, 1953, p. 62.
69 B. S. Rowntree and G. R. Lavers, *English Life and Leisure*, 1951, pp. 21, 37, 38.
70 Hilton, *op. cit.*, pp. 21–3.
71 Arnold Wesker, 'Pools', *Jewish Quarterly*, Vol. 6, No. 2, 1958–9, pp. 32–42.
72 MO archive, *Worktown*, Box 2, File F.
73 *Ibid.*
74 Rowntree and Lavers, *op. cit.*, p. 57.
75 MO archive, Boxes 1 and 2, File F.
76 Hilton, *op. cit.*, pp. 27, 49.
77 MO, *First Year's Work*, 1939, p. 42.
78 John Barron Mays, *Growing Up in the City*, 1964, p. 101.
79 Richard Hoggart, *The Uses of Literacy*, 1957, p. 198.
80 Hilton, *op. cit.*, p. 25.
81 *Observer*, 1 November 1987.
82 *Empire News*, 9 October 1955; Smith and Razzell, *op. cit.*, p. 189.
83 Maurice Marples, *A History of Football*, 1954, p. 220.
84 S. Smith and P. Razzell, *The Pools Winners*, 1975, pp. 165–89.

85 *RC 1949–51*, Minutes, qu. 36, pp. 546–7 *et seq.* See also Bone, *op. cit.*, p. 34.
86 *Ibid.*, p. 34; pp 80–8.
87 MO, 1939, p. 35.
88 This discussion of pools advisers is based upon the British Library Catalogue and the *Guardian*, 19 November 1988.
89 *Guardian*, 19 November 1988.
90 MO archive, *Moneysworth*, Box 48, File F. See also MO, *Britain*, 1939, p. 21.
91 MO archive, *ibid.*
92 Browne, *op. cit.*, p. 65.
93 Geoffrey Gorer, *Exploring English Character*, 1955, pp. 265–6. (The writer's father uses the birthdays and door-numbers of the close family, and one random choice, when filling in the columns of his Treble Chance coupon each week.)
94 Smith and Razzell, *op. cit.*, p. 143.
95 *RC 1949–51*, Minutes, letter from Vernons, p. 571.
96 MO, *First Years Work*, 1938, pp. 40–1.
97 Fishwick, *op. cit.*, pp. 127–8.
98 *RC 1949–51*, Memo of London FA, para. 10., p. 110.
99 *Ibid.*, paras 11–12, p. 110.
100 *HC Debs*, 29 January 1954, col. 2109.
101 *Daily Telegraph and Morning Post, op. cit.*, p. 9; *HC Debs*, 29 January 1954, col. 2112.
102 Rubner, *op. cit.*, pp. 130–1; *HC Debs, ibid.*, cols 2110–14.
103 This Act is discussed more fully in the following chapter.
104 *FA Council Minutes*, 18 February 1957.
105 Inglis, *op. cit.*, pp. 211–12.
106 *Times*, 26 January 1965.
107 John Roberts, *Everton: The Official Centenary History*, St Albans, 1978, p. 171.
108 Nechama Tec, *Gambling in Sweden*, New York, 1964, pp. 3–5.
109 *Daily Telegraph and Morning Post, op. cit.*, p. 18.
110 *HC Debs*, 17 April 1956, col. 917.
111 *RC 1976–78*, Report, Vol. 1, para. 1.13, p. 7.
112 John Cohen, 'The Ideas of Work and Play', *British Journal of Sociology*, Vol. V, 1953, p. 318.

Chapter 8

Lotteries, or sweepstakes and premium bonds

'Lotteries' can mean a wide range of gambling activities, including certain types of slot machines where skill has no bearing, pool betting, newspaper competitions, sweepstakes, and raffles. However, slot machines are more pertinent to a study of gaming, given in chapter 4, and pool betting and newspaper competitions have been considered in previous chapters. Here, the focus falls upon sweepstakes and the premium bonds, because a major theme of this book, the moderation of most betting and gambling, is especially pertinent to them, as none of the factors which make for heavy gambling are present to any significant degree in a lottery.[1] The level of personal participation, for example in card playing or roulette, the extent to which a punter believes he or she is exercising skill, or any situational influences which might determine someone to bet, for example in a betting shop, an amusement arcade or in a casino, are all absent from sweeps and premium bonds. Moreover, the lengthy time gaps between each lottery draw cannot be said to make for over-indulgence, a feature they share with the pools.

'Lotteries' is a general term for betting on a variety of pools, sweepstakes, pontoons and raffles. Chapter 2 noted the persistence of lower-class lotteries in the face of legislation from the abolition of state lotteries in 1823, and showed that the rise of prize competitions in late Victorian and Edwardian newspapers was another spectacular example of how the legislation could be negotiated. As with street betting, the manifest failure and confusion of the lottery legislation prompted important if belated reappraisals of the law by government, most notably in 1908 over newspaper competitions,[2] in 1932–3 because of the growth of the football pools, and in 1951 and 1956 when the legislation was again up for overhauling. Only the latter years, however, saw any attempt to give legal recognition to lotteries, and even then in a qualified way. This chapter traces the evolution of lottery legislation with regard to the legislation over sweepstakes, small lotteries and 'the squalid raffle' of premium bonds in 1956.

I

A sweepstake is a ticket-based form of pool betting on the results of a sporting event, usually a horse race.[3] It may have originated amongst wealthy owners and breeders of horses who got up sweepstakes amongst each other to add to the value of the racing.[4] Throughout the nineteenth and twentieth centuries, the number of raffles, sweepstakes – otherwise known as 'specs' – and other games was beyond calculation because most were illegal. What we can say with certainty however is that the abolition of state lotteries in 1823 and the earlier lottery legislation had done little to forestall them. As the editor of the *Sporting Magazine* wrote in 1847, 'our legislature never framed an act that a coach-and-six might not be driven through' and he felt that the lottery and gaming laws, 'would give free passage to a monster train of the Great Western'.[5] The legal, local, and national press and antiquarian books on gambling illustrate that public houses were the major sites of lotteries.[6] The same article in the *Sporting Magazine* described 'the Shark', the keeper of a gin palace and cheap gaming house who was one of many offering tickets of a couple of sovereigns each to hundreds of subscribers. According to reforming journalists, there were even bigger operators. James Greenwood wrote in 1869 of a little 'firm' in Deptford who regularly counted more than just their blessings. They ran a sweep to which 75,000 people subscribed. Prizes ranged from one pound to £600. Tickets were sold from a stationer's in the Strand, owned by one of the firm's 'partners', and also from public houses:

> Throughout lower London, and the shady portion of its suburbs, the window of almost every public house and beer shop was spotted with notice of the 'Specs'. There were dozens of them. There was the 'Deptford Spec,', and the 'Lambeth Spec,' and the 'Great Northern Spec' and the 'Derby Spec;' but they all meant the same thing – a lottery, conducted on principles more or less honest, the prize to be awarded according to the performances of certain racehorses.[7]

'Specs' took their name from the speculative element in these commercial ventures.[8] As Greenwood knew, the police and the magistrates could hardly keep the lid on the activity, it was so widespread. Greenwood felt that when the spec 'bubble' finally burst, it was as much to do with a growing interest in horse race betting as police action.[9]

Publicans were promoters of lotteries outside London too, and a lottery in a pub could pose similar types of problems for the police intervention as card gaming, discussed in chapter 4. As with street betting, genuine raids had to be based on a good deal of carefully gathered intelligence, which could also boost the career prospects of the policeman. Thus in Kent in 1914, a police sergeant was

> Commended by the Chief Constable for the ability shown in working up a case against George Lloyd, Licensee of the Iron Ship Beerhouse Gillingham for allowing a game of lottery on his Licensed premises & four other men for aiding and abetting the same on the 24th October 1914.[10]

Another long-standing problem for the efficacy of the legislation was that some magistrates were uncertain when to prosecute. One wrote to the 'Notes and Queries' column of *Justice of the Peace* in the 1850s describing a 'monster sweep' run by 'A. B.', a publican, with over 1,000 subscribers at one shilling apiece. 'Is A. B. or are the subscribers liable to any penalty or punishment under the lottery or any other acts?',[11] he asked.

Not only magistrates were unsure. For example, some years later, in Worcestershire, a police constable was 'admonished and cautioned' by his superiors for 'Raffling his watch at a private house in Pershore on 27 October 1883, having sold between 30 and 40 tickets at one shilling each, not knowing at the time that raffling in a private house was illegal.' Perhaps some policemen were more aware of the legality or otherwise of their actions. In 1903 a police constable from Stourbridge was severely reprimanded for 'selling tickets for a lottery thereby aiding and abetting in the commission of an offence and not reporting the fact to his superintendent'.[12]

In other words, whether they knew what they were doing or not, the police were no different from other workers in this respect. In the 1930s the *New Survey of London Life and Labour* found that in many factories and workplaces 'the sweepstake habit has for now long been established'. This, felt the investigator, was for social reasons as much as for individual gain.[13] The Chief Constables Association informed parliament in 1932 that draws at works, raffles, whist drives, Christmas clubs and minor hospital sweeps were numerous and harmless, and would invite ridicule if prosecuted.[14] Sweepstakes, as the name suggests, aggregated lots of little stakes from workers which 'at the end of two or three months add up to a very respectable winning.'[15] This was certainly the case of the Stock Exchange Sweep, established by a financier in 1902 and run by City workers. The *Times*, on 15 April 1931, carried a column on the 'Stock

Exchange Members' Mutual Subscription Fund' and its Derby Draw. First, second and third prizes stood at £15,000, £6,500 and £1,400 respectively, with one hundred runners up each winning £150.

Some sweeps were also expressions of collective self-help at times of need. For example, the lower middle-class gardeners of Watling, a new estate in north London erected in the later 1920s, paid for a new horticultural society hut from the proceeds of a Derby draw.[16] And in Trafford Street in Edwardian Salford, when Joe Toole's father was diagnosed as needing a restorative holiday to cure tuberculosis, the expenses were paid from a sweep got up between his family and neighbours. The tickets were sixpence, sold by the Toole's and their neighbours, and the prize was a cheap clock. As Toole wrote in 1935, the sweep was, 'not so big as the Irish Sweepstake, but big enough to provide the needful'.[17]

Toole was writing some five years after the introduction of the Irish Hospital's Sweepstake (IHS). The IHS was a major inter-war gambling development alongside the growth of dog tracks and the football pools. It was promoted by a wealthy Dublin bookmaker, Richard Duggan, and an ex-politician residing in the Irish capital, under the company title Irish Hospital's Sweepstake Trust Dublin, and actively supported by the Free State government. The trust was otherwise mainly composed of representatives of the twenty three hospitals who stood to gain from the sweep.[18] It was the most successful horse race lottery between the wars. At the peak of its popularity it was a regular flutter for over seven million people, that is, five million in the British Isles and the remaining two million in Eire, the USA and various Commonwealth countries. The tickets were sold by bookmakers, shops and in pubs and clubs. Held three times a year at the Plaza Cinema, Dublin, the draw was itself a tourist attraction. Pretty Irish nurses smiled and turned the drums from which a blind boy plucked the winning entries under the watchful eye of General O'Duffy, the Commissioner of Police.[19] Tickets were ten shillings apiece. The first draw was on the Manchester November Handicap in 1930, for a prize of £100,000. It was a huge success, the proceeds totalled over £658,618, from which £131,724 was deducted for distribution to Free State hospitals. Duggan was estimated to have personally taken £46,000 out of the first draw. The amount paid in commission to the ticket sellers was about £131,000, almost the same amount as was paid to the hospitals.[20] The entrants to and winners of the first draw were from all walks of life all over the English-speaking world, although mostly from Britain. Lists of winners included, most frequently, individual names and addresses, workplace syndicates, and not a few aliases such as 'Monsieur X' of 18 High Street, Georgetown, Demerara, or 'Spuds' of 17 Roehampton Lane, East London. One famous winner was the bookmaking firm of Ladbrokes in London, who had purchased a half share in a winning ticket.[21] The sweep was later extended to the Grand National, the Derby and other classic races.[22] The Metropolitan Police Commissioner, Trevor Bigham, and the Chief Cosntable of Manchester, James Maxwell, pointed to the countless numbers of illegal sweeps which were occasionally raided, but they spoke in terms of near admiration for the Irish sweepstake, 'the fairest ever'.[23]

Others were less impressed with the whole operation, and some feared for the health of the turf. A *Times* leader warned that bribery would follow in the train of the massive prizes offered by the sweep.[24] But most criticism of the IHS stemmed from resentment that money from British pockets was flowing across the Irish Sea to the Republican Exchequer. The *Times'* Dublin correspondent could not resist stating that the financial support for the Irish hospitals 'by the world's liking for a sporting chance cannot be held to accord with Arthur Griffith's proud maxim, "Ourselves Alone"'.[25] The Lotteries Group, a parliamentary lobby of MPs was set up in the early 1930s, whose main aims were to stop the money going to Ireland by liberalising the lottery legislation to allow for a similar scheme here.

For different reasons, Mary Stocks, of the Liverpool Council for Voluntary Aid, was concerned at the growing popularity of the IHS and other, smaller, sweepstakes on Merseyside during the early 1930s which she saw as part of a general increase of gambling amongst the poor. Furthermore, she argued that the claim hospitals wanted money from this source was bogus,[26] but she perhaps underestimated the problems of the hospital services in both Britain and Eire, the underfunding from government at a time of world economic depression. Stocks also ignored the sense of philanthropy and the voluntarist tradition to which the IHS appealed and which, as we have seen, underpinned many smaller sweepstakes. Lotteries were in fact viewed by hospital spokesmen as a means of shoring up the gaps of an inadequate funding programme. Thus a representative of the British Hospitals' Association proposed a central lottery fund to mobilise the goodwill and capital of the British public: 'The generosity of the British public is wonderful, and during these last difficult years they have made it quite clear that they wish for the continuation of the voluntary hospitals system'. He felt that the expensive capital projects required by many hospitals, but held back by cuts in public expenditure, could be met out of a lotteries fund.[27] The Irish sweepstake was a foreign lottery, however, promoted from abroad to solicit the stakes of British punters. The Post Office, with the support of the Labour Home Secretary J. R. Clynes, went so far as to stop packets of tickets addressed to agents for sale in this country, and over 9,000 letters bound for Dublin were opened by the Post Office, and stakes returned to senders. Such actions were Canute-like in their futility, and the Irish Hospitals Trust and their agents received only 'nominal penalties'.[28] Moreover, the Chief Constable of Manchester felt that to engage in a campaign against sellers of tickets – bookmakers, shopkeepers and publicans mostly – would be unpopular and unrealistic due to the scale of the operation which would need to be mobilised. He told parliament that people shared tickets in the form of syndicates in workplaces so that the amounts sold were no real guide to the amount of people participating.[29]

William Davison, a Conservative MP and Magistrate, was clearly impressed by the Irish example. He told the Royal Commission that he wanted to repair the anomalous and unpopular state of the lottery laws in Britain, and to introduce a fund-raising lottery here. He argued that in most continental countries the state or municipalities benefited financially from the lotteries with no hint of national demoralisation towards gambling. He also resented the fact that the £3 million paid into Irish Free State hospitals was in large part from British pockets. He felt that the law criminalised an activity of which 'a large section, if not a majority of the community approves', and felt that the totalisator which drew state taxation from a pool of stakes was a precedent anyway.[30] Davison's solution, in the form of a Bill, was an ongoing Lotteries Commission, a regulatory body set up to administer three or four big lotteries aimed at national public works schemes. He wanted local authorities too, 'in Manchester or Liverpool or wherever', to operate lotteries under these auspices. His Bill also illustrated a concern that a few massive prizes were bad, and proposed many little ones which were more fair to the generality of subscribers.[31] His 1933 Bill was passed, after a first reading, by the Conservative-dominated National Government, but was granted 'no further facilities' in the light of more pressing economic demands. Yet it was the closest the law had come to a major revision with regard to lotteries since the 1820s.

Thomas Levy, secretary of the Lotteries Group, agreed with Davison that 'a moderate live law' was better than a 'prohibitive dead one' and distinguished between the 'small unobtrusive lottery or sweepstake and the big promotion like the Irish sweepstake, dealing in millions of pounds and offering fortunes as prizes'.[32] A feature of most parliamentary debates on lotteries or pools, in the 1930s and the 1950s, was that small schemes were more acceptable than big ones.

The Irish Hospital Sweepstake was thus legislated against because it was too big, but also because it was foreign. The 1934 Betting and Lotteries Act thus made greater legal provision for small charitable and sporting club lotteries, but prohibited the advertising of a foreign lottery in Britain and the sending of lottery tickets through the post. It also made it an offence to purchase a ticket in such a lottery although, as the Royal Commission of 1949–51 argued, purchasers were not normally the subject of police intervention.[33] Sales of IHS tickets fell after 1934. Total receipts dropped from an average of £11,500,000 a year before 1934 to an average of £5,000,000 a year for 1947, 1948 and 1949, illustrating that the activities of the promoters had been 'severely restricted' by the Act.[34] Yet despite this, the Irish Minister for Health, Nöel Browne, was still able to embark on a major modernisation of the Republic's hospitals from the mid 1950s, funded in large part from the real and projected income of the sweep.[35]

II

In general, the Royal Commission of 1949–51 felt, like previous government enquiries, that whilst the lottery laws were anomalous and complicated, they managed to prevent a flood of big lotteries, so no changes were proposed.[36] This institutionalised feeling that small lotteries were alright was, after Willink, extended to small social clubs who used lotteries to raise funds and were still liable for prosecution. In 1956 the Labour MP for Enfield, Ernest Davies, mindful of the contribution lotteries and sweeps made to working-men's clubs and local Labour party branches, wanted to render small lotteries for 'charitable, sporting and other purposes' immune from prosecution. The Bill, which was passed just prior to Macmillan's 'premium bonds budget' was given cross party support, and became known in the press as 'the Clubs Competitions Bill'. The CIU and local athletics clubs were behind much of the parliamentary lobbying for this bill.[37]

During the parliamentary debates over Davies' proposal, the feeling that 'the bigger the lottery, the bigger the element of gambling, the more suspicious I become'. was not an uncommon pronouncement.[38] There were a number of amendments based upon differing viewpoints as to what constituted an acceptable level of prize monies and promoters' expenses. The latter was eventually fixed at 10 per cent, of turnover to cover expenses, the printing and issuing of tickets, and the maximum prize level was given as £750.[39]

The Act was significant on two levels. Firstly, it repudiated the working principle of the lottery legislation since 1823, which the Willink Commission had endorsed, that small lotteries which were not private or charitable lotteries did not require any special status within the lottery legislation. Davies' bill sought to enable small lotteries to raise funds free from the fear of police intervention. Its second important feature, then, was that it democratised the lottery laws, and in this it shared the basic concern of the Betting and Gaming Act of 1960. Working-mens' and other clubs soon made the most of the new facilities. For example, by December 1957 sixty-seven small lotteries in Bolton 'were registered under the Small Lotteries and Gaming Act, 1956'.[40]

But whilst this suspicion of large-scale lotteries was a major factor preventing their introduction, the government was planning to raise revenue from a very big national scheme which clearly depended for its success upon the chance of winning prizes. Premium bonds also broke with a legislative precedent of over 130 years' standing.

III

The idea of using premium bonds to raise revenue for government was first introduced, not in 1956 but in 1908, by witnesses to the Joint Select Committee on Lotteries and Indecent Advertisements. A number of bankers and businessmen argued that premium bonds were raising a great deal of money on continental bourses, and were issued by both national and city governments.[41] They argued that bonds did not involve loss, but rather were a high-security investment which encouraged thrift. They felt that the accusations of gambling and fraudulent practice were unfair, because the money invested was never at risk, and called for premium bond issues to be floated on the Stock Exchange. The committee's report ignored the question of premium bonds. However, the witnesses in favour of the bonds were merely ahead of their time.

Premium bonds got their next big chance towards the end of the first world war. The National Government, headed by the Welsh Non-conformist David Lloyd George, was searching for a means of financing the military campaign in a conflict which the government had expected to last only until Christmas 1914. The usual mechanism of taxation, augmented by the War Savings Certificates introduced in 1916, were considered an insufficient source of revenue. Hence the Select Committee on Premium Bonds was appointed to 'enquire into and to report on the desirability or otherwise of raising money for the purpose of the War by the issue of Premium Bonds'.[42] The committee reported early in 1918 after examining thirty-five witnesses comprising a number of bankers from Britain and abroad, the Chief Constables of Manchester and Leeds, official witnesses from the Treasury, Board of Trade and Chamber of Commerce, three Labour spokesmen, leading anti-gamblers and a couple of employers.

The working definition of premium bonds adopted by the Commission was that:

> Premium Bonds should mean Bonds repayable after a fixed term of years at par plus a moderate rate of compound interest, not less than the 2.5 per cent now paid on the Government Savings Bonds deposits and having the feature that a certain number should be drawn each year for payment at a premium and above the issue price, both issue and premium being paid free of tax.[43]

The major constituency to be tapped was the working-class small saver, the artisans and labourers who, it was felt, had been relatively enriched by the munitions work required for war. Based on an appraisal of the rather disappointing take-up of War Savings Certificates, which offered a level of interest and return attractive only to bigger 'investors', the committee felt that there was:

> clear proof that the weekly wage earners, especially the men, demand an investment which would appeal to them primarily in that there would be a chance of substantial increase of their capital, and that the ordinary rate of interest, amounting as it must to the small investor only to a few shillings a year, even at the rate of five per cent, is of secondary importance to them.[44]

It was felt that a means of revenue raising targeting the working-class saver could only be successful if offered the chance of a spectacular instant gratification. What was not stated in committee, although it was a logical outcome of this argument, was that the element of gambling presented a more attractive and potentially more fruitful mode of investment than saving *per se*. The prize draw, which was to have been a quarterly event, implicitly directed itself to this rationale. A number of witnesses argued that saving by itself with a moderate rate of interest was not attractive to most workers. Lord Cunliffe, who had been instrumental in the establishment and administration of the War Loans Committee, argued from his research that artisans and the labouring class, especially in Lancashire and Yorkshire, were the constituency where the potential for state-derived revenue had least been realised. Cunliffe drew a distinction between this group and the larger investor who would be less attracted by the element of chance and more by the exception of income tax and super tax on his investment.[45]

Major Frederick John Scott, of the Ministry of Munitions, was involved in the regulation of the 20,000 War Savings Associations in the munitions industry which aimed to cream off the extra earnings of munitions workers. He argued that the idea of a lottery had appealed more to workers at the Woolwich Arsenal in London than savings schemes because of the chance of a prize. But he thought that women were more content with the savings associations than men.[46] Perhaps this was because women, who were less inclined to gamble anyway, had less to invest on the bonds than their male counterparts. They earned less. The average wage at Woolwich Arsenal was five pounds per week and the 'experts' – the tool fitters – could earn twelve to fifteen pounds for a week's work. Yet throughout the rest of the metropolitan area and in the provinces the average weekly income for a female munitions worker was two pounds and fifteen shillings. In London there were between 16,000 and 18,000 women employed in munitions and this, argued Scott, 'would reduce the average'.[47]

The discussions in committee may be said to have hinged upon three major themes, each of which exacerbated the unease of some MPs, despite a majority of witnesses who were favourable to the concept of premium bonds. These were, firstly, the question of national character and its expression in the means found to raise revenue. Secondly, there was a misunderstanding of working-class habits of saving and spending, based upon an alleged spendthrift attitude, from which only labour spokesmen demurred. The third and most central bone of contention was whether or not premium bonds were a gamble and thus a state lottery or a legitimate form of saving.

In 1918 a Swiss banker with particular knowledge of foreign lottery schemes was asked by a Home Office spokesman to expand on the reasons for the varying levels of issue and participation in premium bonds between countries. He wanted to know why 'such a rotten country as Turkey' had almost the same level of bonds in circulation as Austria, 'which is one of the best'. Both countries had bonds worth over £31,100,000. Moreover, 'if Germany keeps away from them, and Turkey goes in for them, do you not think it is a rather ominous thing?' Germany was cast in a rather spendthrift light as a 'great borrower' of money. More pertinently, Germany, like Holland, Belgium, France, Italy and Switzerland, operated bonds on a municipal level whilst Austria, Turkey, Russia, Serbia and others issued government bonds. Thus provision of and access to bonds in these latter countries was more national.[48]

There was little exploration of the role of revenue derived from premium bonds as a factor in sound finance, a way of helping to balance the exchequers' budget. It may be argued that an imperial country with a treasury still dominated by orthodox economic thinking felt uneasy about a lottery scheme which it identified with its lesser continental competitors.

The question of bonds and national character surfaced in other ways. More pragmatic economic thinkers felt that premium bonds would appeal to a peculiarly British sporting culture. The banker Sir Richard Vassar Smith, for example, felt that they 'might appeal to the sporting instinct in most classes and this would cause them to take up the bonds'.[49] Vassar Smith denied that premium bonds were gambling in the form of a lottery because 'no man loses his subscription'. Yet the term 'sporting instinct' was the language of the fancy from the culture of betting and sport, and protagonists of the bonds who sought to exploit this inadvertently pointed to the real basis of the appeal of bonds to the sporting type.

The relation of premium bonds to the working-class economy and spending habits occupied much of the 1918 Select Committee's time. For example, it was argued that munitions workers especially were indulging in lavish displays of expenditure on unnecessary things. This was the tenor of the Chief Constable of Manchester's testimony. Peacock claimed his views were supported by the 'protectors of the morals of Manchester' the Watch Committee: 'Even such necessaries as food and clothing are not infrequently purchased on an extravagant scale, and the expenditure on amusements is always generous, especially so in cases of licensed houses, pictures, theatres, music halls, sports, etc'.[50] Jewellery, expensive furs and pianos were purchased in preference to War Savings Certificates at the level of fifteen shillings and six pence where take-up had been 'considerable but nothing like what there ought to be'. The committee made much of a tale, verified by Peacock, of a working man 'wearing a muffler round his neck' who purchased a piano at a cost of eighty pounds and, because it was such 'a splendid piece of furniture' bought another one for the opposite corner of the room.[51]

A problem for those who sought to re-direct this extra disposable income into state premium bonds was that extravagant spending might result from a big win in the prize draw, the very principle on which the premium bonds were to sell themselves. Lord Cunliffe, for example, did not think that lots of moderate winnings were dangerous but felt that 'great big' winnings 'might damage a whole family'.[52]

Labour witnesses to the 1918 enquiry defended the right of workers to spend their surplus income as they saw fit and, more significantly, pointed out to the Select Committee that a number of working-class savings schemes were already in operation. The parliamentary spokesman for the Co-operative Movement viewed premium bonds as subversive of to the working-class tradition of collective self-help and as 'contrary to all the principles and practice of co-operative and working-class thrift'.[53] Will Thorne, of the Gasworkers Union and a member of the Social Democratic Federation, who was 'not very much enamoured' of the premium bonds at all, argued that the working-class had little money to 'invest', and what little they had was often sucked up by the insecurities of what B. S. Rowntree and other social investigators termed the 'poverty cycle'. He claimed that the 250,000 workers he represented, whose wages ranged from thirty five shillings to fifty shillings a week, had little in the way of excess income and were often confronted with contingencies and economic demands which necessitated a quicker access to savings than the premium bonds scheme could give. Thorne thus felt that 'it would be better if the wage earning classes, where they have a few pounds to spare', put their money into the Post Office 'where it would be a saving to the country'.[54]

J. H. Thomas of the National Union of Railwaymen, pointed to the range of smaller informal savings strategies alongside the larger institutions based on working-class thrift. He saw the bonds as unnecessary: 'There are Slate Clubs, Co-Operative Societies, Employers Banking Societies, local Savings Clubs, all manner of things where a few shillings have been saved from week to week and with regard to which no temptation is required for a further inducement'.[55] Thomas also defended the working-class from accusations of reckless spending, arguing that the purchase of a piano and various luxury items was 'to their advantage' because it enabled workers to 'have a house which [would] be an attraction to them, and instead of deprecating that, I welcome it unhesitatingly'.[56]

Thorne and Thomas were also critical of the notion that the state should solicit finance for the war from the pockets of the poor with the temptation of a gamble. Thomas felt that a few gamblers might have put a few pounds into premium bonds but it would not yield enough revenue 'to carry on the war for a couple of days'. In terms which anticipated Labour criticisms of Macmillan's scheme in 1956 he argued that there was 'no half-way house between recognising a state lottery and legalising betting'.[57]

This problem of the gambling component of Premium Bonds, or whether there was such an unethical element in the scheme at all, underpinned most considerations of their moral and actuarial basis and centred upon two key points. Firstly, that one kept one's stake so it was not a proper gamble. Moreover, interest was offered on the bonds which meant that a return on investment was guaranteed. Secondly, and counter to this, was the element of chance involved in the entering of the bonds for a few prizes in the draws. As well as the fact of this, one lost the interest if the bond came up. It could be argued then that the interest was gambled. These two points were thus framed by the following consideration: were premium bonds a gamble or a form of saving or a bit of both?

Comparison with industrial insurance premiums was inevitable. Here, the worker got back the money he paid in along with a moderate level of compound interest. But the whole notion of insurance rested upon the fact that whilst the worker was saving he was also betting figuratively with the insurance company against an unknowable future and on an unknowable accident upon which the receipt of a large cash payment rested. Meanwhile the insurance companies aggregated the millions of premiums and profited by investing parts of them as loans to other companies. These were in turn justified by the anticipated fortunes of these businesses.

In 1918 the anti-gambling campaigner E.B. Perkins argued to parliament that in insurance 'there was no possibility of anybody being a loser' because every investor got their capital back along with the interest. But in premium bonds 'he either gets a prize or he loses the whole of that special part of the interest which is involved in the lottery.[58] Yet premium bonds offered either the interest or the big win, and always returned the initial investment. Perkins did not explore the issue that in insurance one had to suffer physical damage or death to get the big early payment. The premium bonds offered the chance of this with no threat of injury.

However, the committee felt that the element of chance was sufficient to render the enactment of premium bonds as a controversial break with existing legislation and to provoke an uproar from the anti-gambling lobby. The Committee was mindful of the complicated precedent of previous legislation with regard to lotteries which determined that 'no issue which involves an element of chance could be made without an Act of Parliament'.[59] They were also unsure of the practical success – the financial return – of premium bonds and doubted whether the drafting of a complex piece of legislation was worth it. The estimated revenue, based upon the earlier findings of the Committee upon War Loans for Small Investors, was put at £80–100 million. More significant than this, however, was the probable outcry which would result from anti-gambling quarters if the bonds were issued. The committee thus doubted whether the amount of new money to be obtained: 'would justify any change of a contentious character in our financial methods (and felt that) such a proposal might cause a controversy in the country which would be most undesirable'.[60] In 1956, as in 1918, the questions of national character and of saving versus gambling were central to the controversy over the issuing of premium bonds. What was different was that the strength of the anti-gambling lobby was greatly diminished. 'The church and chapel spokesmen', said the *Economist* after the budget debate in June 1956, 'are a sad shadow of their predecessors'.[61]

During the Commons debates over Harold Macmillan's budget proposal to introduce premium bonds, the Latin civilisations became the corrupt and impoverished yardstick against which a British scheme could be measured. The Liberal leader Jo Grimond felt that bonds were more suitable to Latin countries with inflationary pressures upon financial management.[62] There they served a more urgent function as a means of fiscal derivation. C. R. Hobson, the Labour member for Keighley, was more forthright. The government, he argued:

> are reducing the country to the level of a South American Republic . . . I find it difficult to express my indignation. The Government started on the slippery slope of betting when they gave us prior information that they were considering the installation of betting shops. I suppose it naturally follows that they should engage in some form of national lottery.[63]

Cyril Osborne, a Conservative Member, re-invoked the spectre of a financially incompetent Latin Europe. He implied that premium bonds would undermine the strength and rectitude of the British currency:

> the very word 'sterling' suggests stability and it (does) not seem to me right that it should be bolstered in a manner that I have always thought of as being associated with France or Italy, whose currencies are a dreadful example to us.[64]

It appears that those who disapproved of lotteries under the auspices of the state were prepared, in varying degrees, to resort to crude national caricatures of corruption and incompetence to bolster their case. Such cross-bench criticism did little to stem Macmillan's resolve to introduce the bonds. In his budget proposals he took the opposite line to his detractors in justifying them by reference to overseas examples.

It was plain, too, that the 'sporting' British public were keen on the idea of a national lottery, whether it took the form of premium bonds or any other scheme, and were not fearful of notions of national degradation. In 1950 Mass Observation had found that out of 2,071 people questioned 71 per cent were in favour of a national lottery.[65]

In his 1956 budget speech Harold Macmillan, the Conservative Chancellor of the Exchequer, had less compunction about the problems of national character and the gambling element. In an important passage introducing the premium bonds he made much of them as an investment, as 'something completely new for the saver in Great Britain.' He denied that it was a pool or a lottery as 'the subscriber cannot lose': 'The investor in the bond which I propose is saving his money. He will get it back when he wants it. But as long as he holds it saved his reward, instead of interest, is the chance of a tax-free prize'.[66]

'Chance' and 'saving' were the key words here, as Macmillan thought chance complemented rather than compromised the savings habit. In the same mode as the 1918 Select Committee he was after the extra incomes of the working class. This could be achieved by encouraging 'the practice of saving' amongst those who 'are not attracted by the reward of interest, but do respond to the incentive of fortune'. The state, he argued, had 'hitherto fought shy of using chance as an incentive to save' because of the 'unreasonable fear' of moral objections raised to this principle.

Within the House of Commons, however, Labour MPs objected that the premium bonds should have been included in the proposals to legalise betting which the government had issued in April, 1956. R. J. Mellish, the Labour MP for Bermondsey, voiced a similar fear to Will Thorne's some thirty-eight years earlier: 'Since the gambling instinct is rather prevalent, will there not be a tendency to draw money from the Post Office savings to buy the bonds in the hope of getting extra cash by way of prize money?'[67]

This was designed to undermine Macmillan's' claim that the bonds were a savings scheme. Harold Wilson, the Shadow Chancellor, could not have been more scathing of the budget and the 'squalid raffle' of premium bonds:

> We had a shambling, fumbling, largely irrelevant and at one point, degrading speech. The Chancellor told us that the Budget was proposed under the piercing eye of Mr. Gladstone. There was one passage that was quite obviously written under a portrait of Horatio Bottomley.[68]

What was absent from the protracted debate which took place over premium bonds was any real concern at the allegedly spendthrift habits of the working class. Unlike in 1918 there was little fear that, either with or without a sizeable prize in its pocket, the working class was a victim of its collective penchant for instant gratification and extravagance. The 1950s were of course a period of sustained economic growth and full employment which, unlike the more sectional opportunities offered by the first world war, provided higher wages and regular work to most sections of the working class. This general prosperity by itself cannot explain the more liberal attitude by government, but it was the foundation, against the privations of the war years of 1939–45, of a largely unarticulated change of attitude towards working-class budgets. As Arthur Marwick has argued, a greater libertarianism, a tendency to trust people with their own moral and economic affairs, was abroad in the so-called post-war consensus. This implied 'the great release from older restraints', the lifting 'of paternalistic Victorian controls' from British society.[69] The introduction of the premium bonds, rescinding the principle of the 1823 Act, the Small Lotteries Act also introduced in 1956 and the 1960 Betting and Gaming Act were all products of this liberalisation.

It could be argued, however, that the bonds, like the legalisation of betting, were a cunning conservative attempt to trick the working class into a more economistic and selfish attitude in the face of a burgeoning welfare state. Socialist ideals of egalitarian collective provision were compared with the 'I'm all right Jack' attitude made famous by the Boulting Brother's film of the same name. The *Tribune*, Labour's newspaper, saw the introduction of the premium bonds and the legalisation of ready-money betting as part of 'the Casino Society' of possessive individualism. Macmillan was caricatured as a croupier and a fairground barker, and compared to Hughie Green, the host of a contemporary television quiz show called *Double Your Money*. It was only a short stretch of the satirical imagination to the 'Tic Tac Mac' of Vicky's cartoons in the *London Evening Standard* prior to the 1960 Act.[70]

Clever and witty they may have been, but these caustic snipes did not constitute anything approaching a concerted campaign to prevent the introduction of the bonds. Perhaps the best measure of on-the-ground opposition to the bonds were the thirty-seven sub-postmasters and mistresses in England and Wales who had 'declined to handle Premium Bonds on moral grounds' in 1957.[71]

In the first few years following the introduction of the bonds, the amount of savings drawn by government probably justified Macmillan's hopes. In the year from November 1957 to November 1958 sales totalled £114 million, repayments of bonds were £2.5 million and prizes to the value of £2,060,000 were paid out. There were fifty prizes of £1,000, one hundred prizes of £500 and so on down to ten thousand prizes of £25.[72] As well as prize pay-outs, just over £1.5 million was spent in advertising and costs, leaving the government with about £108 million to invest. But Macmillan's proud prediction that the bonds would attract the savings of the new small 'investor' got off to a disappointing start when it was found that ERNIE, the acronym of the Electronic Random Number Indicating Equipment, housed at Lytham, was selecting a disproportionate number of bonds denoted with the letter 'Z', that is, bonds worth £500 each. In the House of Commons it was asked whether 'the bulk of the money put into a tax-free investment is not new savings but money which would otherwise have been put into more profitable enterprises and, secondly, that what the old Book said is still true, that "whosoever hath, to him it shall be given"'. The government was forced to agree that the rich were gaining more from the bonds but felt that 'this tendency is showing signs of falling off as more small investors get their money into the draw'.[73]

Further evidence that the bonds, in their earlier years, were purchased by the relatively better-off came in a study in 1960. From 1,936 replies to a questionnaire on premium bonds, it found that 'higher occupation groups', the white collar workers and engineers held more Bonds than the middling groups such as machine operators, supervisors, draughtsmen and clerks, and the lower, miscellaneous semi – and unskilled workers.[74] The higher groups had purchased earlier, and the more expensive bonds. Thirty-five per cent of the higher groups held twenty-one or more bonds as compared with 18 per cent of the lower groups. Significantly, about half the respondents said that 'the Bonds are a form of saving' as one of the main advantages, along with the hope of a prize. This was borne out by the fact that respondents felt that the purchase of more than ten bonds did not improve their chances of a prize. Most did not want fewer prizes of greater value, and felt that the longer the bonds were held, the less were the chances of winning, suggesting two key differences from football pools when appraising the bonds.[75] Skill, of course, played no part in premium bonds, so most felt luck was the biggest factor in coming up.[76] So whilst the bonds always gave their owner a return, they could be seen as more of a gamble than the pools on this level.

IV

The legalisation of small lotteries, the instigation of premium bonds, and the introduction of betting shops was no victory for a benign process of liberalisation on behalf of the government and the police. Rather, as David Dixon has argued, they grew out of the compromises in the state's role brought about by the taxation of gambling, of the manifest contradictions and inadequacies of the law, of police difficulties in operating the law, and of post-war affluence. The withering on the vine of the anti-gambling movement, too, in the face of all this, was critical. Furthermore, as noted in chapter 3, the developments in 1956 and 1960 did signal a recognition by government, elucidated in chapter 3, that betting was merely a part of a sensible pattern of spending and saving for most people. This was not a sudden post-war recognition. It had long been a nascent understanding, as was evident in Charles Cautley's scepticism about anti-gambling claims.[77] Yet such a view needed the right constellation of moral, economic and political forces in order to be allowed out of its closet, and institutionalised. The wider implications of this are discussed in the conclusion.

Notes

1 W. E. Eadington, 'Some Observations on Legalised Gambling', in W. E. Eadington (ed.), *Gambling and Society*, Las Vegas, 1975, pp. 54–5.
2 See pp. 36–7, 194.
3 Peter Arnold, *The Encyclopedia of Gambling*, 1978, p. 97.
4 See chapter 5, pp. 108–9.
5 *Sporting Magazine*, November 1847.
6 In general, see John Ashton, *A History of English Lotteries*, 1893; James Greenwood, *The Seven Curses of London*, 1985, pp. 242–6.
7 Greenwood, *ibid.*, p. 243.
8 Eric Partridge, *The Penguin Dictionary of Historical Slang*, 1988, p. 884.
9 Greenwood, *op. cit.*, p. 246.
10 *Record of Service, Kent County Constabulary*, Book 1, p. 94. Held at Local History Library, Maidstone.
11 *Justice of the Peace*, 23 July 1853.
12 *Recruitment Register 1877–1883*, Worcestershire Constabulary, pp. 136 and 173.

13 John Martin, 'Gambling', *New Survey of London Life and Labour*, 1935, Vol. 9, p. 275.
14 *RC 1932–33*, Memo. of Chief Constables Association of England and Wales, Appendix A, p. 447.
15 Martin, *op cit*, pp. 275–6.
16 PEP, *Planning*, No. 270, 15 August 1947, p. 67.
17 Joseph Toole, *Fighting Through Life*, 1935, pp. 30–1.
18 *Times*, 17 November 1930. This discussion of the IHS is based upon C. l'estrange Ewen, *Lotteries and Sweepstakes*, 1932; C. F. Shoolbred, *Lotteries and the Law*, 1935.
19 *Times*, 17 November 1930; Robert Graves and Alan Hodge, *The Long Weekend*, 1985, p. 383 (first published 1940).
20 *Times*, 21 November 1930.
21 *Times*, 18 November 1930, 24 November 1930.
22 Ewen, *op. cit.*, pp. 349–50.
23 *RC 1932–33*, Minutes, qu. 491, p. 41, for example.
24 *Times*, 22 November 1930.
25 *Times*, 24 November 1930.
26 Mary Stocks, 'Betting', *The Liverpool Quarterly*, No. 2, 1936, pp. 13–14.
27 *RC 1932–33*, Memo of British Hospital's Association, para. 11, p. 128.
28 *Ibid.*, Memo of Ernley Blackwell, para. 54, p. 6; *Times*, 17 November 1930; 20 November 1930.
29 *RC 1932–33*, Memo of Chief Constable of Manchester, para. 12, p. 52.
30 *Ibid.*, Memo of William Davison, paras 10–13, p. 52.
31 *Ibid.*, Minutes, qu. 5421, p. 366.
32 *Ibid.*, Memo of Lotteries Group, para. 3, p. 372.
33 *RC 1949–51*, Report, para. 135, p. 39.
34 *Ibid.*, para. 136, p. 39.
35 Noel Browne, *Against the Tide*, Dublin, 1987, pp. 107 and 115.
36 *RC 1949–51*, Report, para. 133–138, pp. 39–40; *Joint Select Committee on Lotteries and Indecent Advertisements* 1908, Report, 1908, para. 1, p. iii.
37 *HC Debs*, 13 April 1956, col. 605.
38 *HC Debs*, 13 April, 1956, col. 574.
39 *RC 1976–78*, Report, Vol. 1, para. 12.19, p. 167; para, 12.24, p. 168.
40 *Annual Report of the Chief Constable of Bolton*, 1958, p. 36.
41 *JSC, 1908 on Lotteries and Indecent Advertisements*, para. 1209, p. 95. See also Minutes, pp. 94–6, pp. 101–2.
42 *SC 1918*, Report, p. iii.
43 *Ibid.*, p. ii.
44 *Ibid.*, p. iii.
45 *Ibid.*, Minutes, qu. 240, p. 10; qu. 252, p. 11.
46 *Ibid.*, Minutes, qu. 520, p. 25; qu. 538, p. 26
47 *Ibid.*, Minutes, qu. 582–4, p. 31.
48 *Ibid.*, Minutes, qu. 967–69, p. 41.
49 *Ibid.*, Minutes, qu. 800, p. 35.
50 *Ibid.*, Minutes, qu. 2386, p. 94; qu. 2359, p. 96.
51 *Ibid.*, Minutes, qu. 2428, p. 96.
52 *Ibid.*, Minutes, qu. 279–80, p. 92.
53 *Ibid.*, Minutes, qu. 2098, p. 83.
54 *Ibid.*, Minutes, qu. 1815, p. 73.
55 *Ibid.*, Minutes, qu. 2746, p. 110.

56 *Ibid.*, Minutes, qu. 2749, p. 110.
57 *Ibid.*, Minutes, qu. 2746, p. 110.
58 *Ibid.*, Minutes, qu. 1688; qu. 1693–6, p. 69.
59 *Ibid.*, Report, p. iii.
60 *Ibid.*, para. 11, p. 5.
61 *Economist*, 23 June 1956.
62 *HC Debs*, cols 1074–5, 18 April 1956.
63 *Ibid.*, 18 April 1956, col. 1062.
64 Cited in Alex Rubner, *op. cit.*, p. 54.
65 *RC 1949–51*, Memo of MO, para. 12, p. 369.
66 *HC Debs*, 17 April, 1956, col. 879.
67 *Ibid.*, col. 935.
68 *HC Debs*, 18 April, 1956, col. 1014.
69 Arthur Marwick, *British Society Since 1945*, 1987, p. 16. See also chapter 3 above.
70 *Tribune*, 16 October 1959; *HC Debs*, 18 April 1956, col. 1082; *Evening Standard*, 5 November 1959.
71 *HC Debs*, 18 February 1958, col. 138.
72 John Cohen and Peter Cooper, 'A Study of a National Lottery: Premium Savings Bonds', *Occupational Psychology*, No. 34, Winter, 1960.
73 *HC Debs*, 11 December 1957, col 1260.
74 Cohen and Cooper, *op. cit.*, pp. 179, 180–1.
75 *Ibid.*, pp. 175–7; pp. 182–3.
76 *Ibid.*, pp. 177, 182.
77 Dixon, 1991, pp. 195, 203–4.

Chapter 9
Some concluding points

Some fools who are under no control, will always be found wandering away to ruin; but the greater part of that extensive deportment of the commonality are under some control, and the great need is that it be better organised.[1]

Thus Dickens called for the regulation of gambling rather than the 'legislative interference' of prohibition in 1852. He argued that parliament 'cared so little for the amusements of the people' that it failed to understand that restraint comes from below, not by decree. He was right. There is little evidence to support the view of the anti-gambling lobby that most working-class people behaved in a thoroughly uneconomic way when they gambled. Few would deny that excessive gaming has caused much suffering and hardship to individuals and their families, but the incidence of this problem was amplified by the anti-gambling league. During the period under consideration, most gambling was regular and moderate, comprised of small stakes determined by income and framed by a system of both non-rational gestures and form-informed considerations aimed to make the bet succesful. Poverty lent gambling an attractive, hopeful air but constrained expenditure on it, as shown in chapter 3. Better-off punters could gamble with higher stakes, a phenomenon which was generalised as the working class became relatively more prosperous during the 1950s.

Some politicians at the time, however, tended to miss the point about the nature of mass gambling. From the Left, the Labour MP Ian Mikardo, in an admittedly 'light hearted treatise', still saw gambling as 'a mug's game'. The country was full of mugs who lost continuously and kidded themselves that to study form and make calculated bets was an expression of skill: 'Skill? – it's all my eye and Miss Elizabeth Martin.'[2] From the other side of the political fence, the Conservative MP Angus Maude, who supported the reforming conclusions of the Willink Commission, nonetheless argued that the mass of gamblers were losers. '[N]othing' he wrote, 'so clearly demonstrates the sad incompetence of the average punter as a study of the professional gambler', who made money from betting.[3] Maude took the rather elitist view that the great aristocratic Georgian gamblers had now been replaced by 'millions of simple suckers – all bound to lose', just as Georgian architecture gave way to 'subtopia', semi-detached suburbia.[4] Popular gambling, then, was part of a shabby mass culture: inevitable, but impoverished because it was generalised.

This feeling that gambling was still somehow a losers' game was also evident in novels during the 1950s. For example, Arthur Seaton, the hero of Alan Sillitoe's *Saturday Night and Sunday Morning*, lived a pattern of instant gratification, of heavy boozing and not a little betting. Furthermore, gambling expressed Arthur's fatalism, his view of life beyond the here and now. After all, 'you never knew when the Yanks were going to do something daft like dropping the H Bomb on Moscow . . . And if they did you could say ta-ta to everybody, burn your football coupons and betting-slips and ring up Billy Graham. If you believe in God, which I don't, he said to himself.'[5] It is worth noting, however, that he also saved in the short term for specific items like a holiday or a motor bike.

Yet Sillitoe's first novel does provide a number of important hints about gambling and working-class culture. He has been described as an author who wrote about working-class experience from the inside, especially the experience of the 'rogue male'.[6] Moreover, Sillitoe was writing in the second half of the 1950s, when a relative affluence took the raw edge off poverty for many, even if it left many old habits and outlooks (the beliefs retrieved by Hoggart in *The Uses of Literacy*) intact. In Arthur Seaton, Sillitoe encapsulates, with a touch of irony, the individual aspirations, collective orientations and materialism of the post-war working-class young man. He had money in his pocket and time on his side. His spending was a mixture of the 'I'm all right Jack' attitude and generosity to his kith and kin. He revelled in the environment of pub and betting club, and he threw into relief the greater consumerism and the *que sera sera* attitude of urban working class. Arthur selfishly states that if he came up on the pools he would 'keep it all', burn the begging letters and settle down with fifteen cars and fifteen women. He had voted communist at the last election, too.

Arthur also possesses a spurious 'aristocratic connection'. He tells a tight-fisted market gardener called George in a pub one evening that Lord Earwig of the Jockey Club had phoned him up from Aintree that day to tip him about 'Last Echo' in the Grand National. George is both 'appeased and somewhat credulous' about this inside information and its esteemed origins. Two conclusions can be drawn from this. Firstly, that gambling and sport went together like a horse and carriage for most punters. This was true not only of horse racing, but also pigeon racing, bowling, football coupon betting and, less successfully in terms of its wider public image, greyhound racing, where the electrified, commercialised fancy could not penetrate smaller flapping meetings, and was susceptible to criticism from dog owners and punters alike. Secondly, Sillitoe hints at deference to the aristocratic influence over horse racing, and this leads on to an important conclusion about class relations and gambling and what Lemahieu, after J. B. Priestley, calls 'the common culture'.[7] The world of horse racing and betting, as we saw in chapter 5, did not lend itself to an articulated critique of the capitalist system on the part of the punters, but it certainly reflected the differences in wealth and power between classes and the increasing influence of businessmen and business strategies within a framework of aristocratic control. The traditional ambience of horse racing and its aristocratic pedigree, to use Lemahieu's term, 'conveyed legitimacy' upon betting. It thus became a frame of reference which incorporated but diffused cultural and economic differences, and allowed its followers to define themselves against faddists and killjoys. As the dissemination of and the demand for betting intelligence developed with the sporting press and the ticker-tape, the ethos of the fancy and its sporting hyperbole was absorbed into it. The commercialisation of betting became underpinned by a sense of traditin based upon the Englishman's right to a flutter. But as Hobsbawm argues, traditionalism 'must not be confused with passivity', even if it does not challenge authority.[8] It is important to note that all of this evolved during an era of prohibition and a moral campaign against betting and gambling which was at its height between 1880s and the 1930s. The Betting Acts made an ass of the law, but this did not translate beyond a conception akin to Hoggart's rendition of 'Us and Them.' People did not wage war upon the law, but they defied and ignored it.

For Lancashire between the Edwardian years and the eve of the second world war, Walton has described the working class as possessing an outlook 'which blended individualistic opportunism and collective material assistance' and where 'independence and deference, hard work and ostentatious leisure' were combined in economist and sociable attitudes.[9] Moreover, the belief systems of the punters reflected both the weight of older supersistions and a belief in luck, and the more rational and literate era of mass education. Some studied form, others went with the fancy. Many did both. Either way, it was all speculation, what the *Picture Post*, called 'the Poor Man's Stock Exchange'.[10]

Gambling can be seen as a moderate, economistic and expressive form of recreation. Furthermore, as argued in chapter 3 and elsewhere throughout this book, it was perceived and used as a form of self-help. It is thus difficult to accept the view that leisure in an industrialising society has become 'tamed and legitimate because separate from other concerns of peoples lives'.[11] It is also difficult to accept the related view that leisure has become 'pacified' by the conspiracy of commercialisation, privatisation (in the sense of preferring to stay at home) and individuation. This has been summed up in the memorable but superficial phrase 'from the carnival to the walkman'.[12] The argument goes like this: in the olden days, people enjoyed indigenous, self-made recreations. They mocked their rulers and participated heartily in a carnival of class expression. Today, the masses are merely consumers who sit at home and watch television, listen to synthesised music through earphones, or fill in a pools coupon. This is a pessimistic position which implies that the meanings attributed to forms of relaxation by their participants are at best futile distractions from a grasp of the truth of their own reality. It is further argued, then, that 'new initiatives and counter-developments' are required to reverse the passivity and alienation wrought by commercialisation.[13]

A social history of gambling does not support such negative conclusions, nor augur well for their ascribed remedy. Popular gambling has continuously exasperated the proponents of rational or alternative recreations and stimulated revision and changes in government policy. The culture of betting reflected both the unifying and discrepant forces in the class system, but not the taming of working-class recreation from above within some separated arena of abstraction. In an unequal society, most people had a good idea of the odds facing them, and of how the dice were loaded, and they spent their time and money as best they could. Their regular and moderate betting was part of a continually evolving culture in which leisure and economy were and are fundamental to people's lives.

Notes

1 Charles Dickens, 'Betting Shops', *Household Words*, No. 18, 26 June 1852, pp. 333–6; quote p. 336.
2 Ian Mikardo, *It's a Mugs Game: A Light Hearted Treatise*, Tribune pamphlet, 1951.

3 Angus Maude, 'Why is Gambling', *Encounter*, April 1957, p. 27.
4 *Ibid.*, p. 30.
5 Alan Sillitoe, *Saturday Night and Sunday Morning*, 1985 (first published 1958), pp. 27–8.
6 David Craig, 'The Roots of Sillitoe's Fiction', in Jeremy Hawthorn (ed.), *The British Working-Class Novel in the Twentieth Century*, 1984, pp. 105–6; p. 108.
7 D. L. Lemahieu, *A Culture for Democracy*, 1988, pp. 317–33.
8 E. J. Hobsbawm, 'The Invention of Tradition', in E. J. Hobsbawm (ed.), *The Invention of Tradition*, 1983, pp. 266, 307.
9 John Walton, *Lancashire: A Social History, 1558–1939*, Manchester, p. 353.
10 *Picture Post*, 12 November 1949.
11 Hugh Cunningham, *op. cit.*, p. 199.
12 Chris Rojek, *Capitalism and Leisure Theory*, 1985, pp. 19–23, 28–9.
13 *Ibid.*, p. 141; see also John Clarke and Chas Critcher, *The Devil Makes Work: Leisure in Capitalist Britain*, 1985, pp. 211–40.

Bibliography

Place of publication London – unless otherwise indicated.

Official reports (non-parliamentary)

Bolton Court of Summary Jurisdiction, Register.
Chief Constables of Bolton, Liverpool and Manchester, Annual Reports 1840–1962, held at these respective local history libraries.
Football Association: Report of the Commission of the FA on Football Coupon Betting, 1913, held at FA Headquarters, Lancaster Gate, London.

Parliamentary publications

Bill for the Suppression of Gaming Houses, 1854 (86) III.
Hansard's Parliamentary Debates.
Joint Select Committee on Lotteries and Indecent Advertisements, 1908, Report, with Minutes of Evidence (275) ix, 375.
Judicial Statistics, Annual Returns to Parliament 1895–1962.
Racecourse Betting Control Board, Annual Reports 1929–40.
Report of the Departmental Committee on a Levy on Horse Races, Cmd 1003, 1960.
Return of NCO's Court Martialled for Allowing Gambling and Cards 1889–90, PP 1892, Vol. L, 269.
Royal Commission on the Duties of the Metropolitan Police, 1908, Report, Cmd 4156, with Minutes of Evidence.
Royal Commission on Lotteries and Betting 1932–3, Final Report, Cmd 4341, with Minutes of Evidence, xiv.
Royal Commission on Betting, Lotteries and Gaming, 1949–51, Report, Cmd 8190, with Minutes of Evidence (41) viii.
Royal Commission on Gambling, 1978, Report, Cmd 7200.
Select Committee on Lotteries, 1808, Reports, with Minutes of Evidence, ii, 182, 323.
Select Committee on Gaming, 1844, Reports, with Proceedings and Minutes of Evidence (297) vi.
Select Committee on Betting, 1901, Report, with Minutes of Evidence (370) v, 347.
Select Committee on Betting, 1902, Report, with Minutes of Evidence (389) v, 441.
Select Committee on Premium Bonds, 1918, Report, with Minutes of Evidence (168) iii, 671.
Select Committee on Betting Duty, Report, with Minutes of Evidence, PP 1923 (139) v.

Contemporary manuscript collections

Booth Collection: *Poverty* Notebooks, British Library of Political and Economic Science, London School of Economics.

British Board of Film Censors, Scenario Reports.

Companies House: Company Registration Documents.

The Correspondence of Charles and Mary Booth, University of London, Senate House Library.

Football Association Council Minutes, Lancaster Gate, London.

Kent County Constabulary, Record of Service registers, held at West Kent Archives Office, Maidstone.

Leary, F., 'A History of the Manchester Periodical Press', Vol. 3, 1880–93, unpublished, held at Manchester Local History Library.

Mass Observation Archive, University of Sussex, Brighton.

Manchester Local History Library, Book Rarity Collection, Heaton Park Race Programmes, etc.

Manchester Watch Committee Minutes, held at the Police Museum, Newton Street, Manchester.

Titmuss Papers, Special Reading Room, British Library of Political and Economic Science.

Worcestershire County Constabulary, recruitment registers, held at Police Headquarters, Hindlip Hall, Worcester.

Newspapers, journals and perodicals

Bell's Life in London
Black and White (Manchester)
Bolton Evening News
Bulletin of the National Anti-Gambling League
Contemporary Review
Daily Express
Daily Mail
Daily Mirror
Daily Sketch
The Economist
Empire News (Manchester)
Evening Newspaper (Manchester)
Football Programme and Weekly Calendar of the Rugby and Association Games (Manchester)
Fortnightly Review
Fortune (New York)
Fraser's Magazine (Edinburgh)
Free Lance (Manchester)
Fur and Feather (Bradford)
Gore's (later Kelly's) Directory of Liverpool
Greyhound Breeder and Exporter
Greyhound Express
Greyhound Owner
Greyhound Owner and Breeder
Greyhound Owner and Open Race Digest
Greyhound Record

Bibliography

Greyhound Stud Book
Homing Pigeon Annual
Household Words
Humanitarian
Justice of the Peace
Labour's Northern Voice (Manchester)
Licensed Bookmaker
Listener
Littlewood's Review (Liverpool)
Littlewood's Sports Log (Liverpool)
Liverpolitan (Liverpool)
Liverpool Daily Post and Echo
Liverpool and Merseyside Illustrated (Liverpool)
Liverpool Review
Manchester Evening Chronicle
Manchester Evening News
Manchester Guardian
New Statesman
News of the World
Observer
Opportunity: Vernon's House Magazine (Liverpool)
Penciller
Picture Post
Planning
Porcupine (Liverpool)
Preston Herald
Punch
Racing Calendar
Racing Pigeon (Bradford)
Racing Shares
Slater's Directory of Manchester (Manchester)
The Spectator
Sporting Chronicle (Manchester)
Sporting Life
Sporting Luck (Manchester and London)
Sporting Magazine
Sports Review
Times
Tribune
Turf Guardian Society Yearbook
Turf Pioneer
Turf Snips
Turf Tips and Bookmakers Crack-Ups
Vernon's House Journal (Liverpool)
Willing's Press Guide
Winner
Winning Post
Who's Who
World Sports

Bibliography

Oral and autobiographical sources

Oral collections
Bolton Oral History Project, Local History Library, Bolton.
Chinn, C., Carl Chinn Collection, University of Birmingham.
Clapson, M., Writer's Oral Project, containing fourteen spoken testimonies, twelve questionnaires, and forty-nine letters. This was carried out in the spring of 1985.
Essex University Oral Archive.
Manchester Jewish Museum Tape Collection, Cheetham Hill, Manchester.
Manchester Tape Studies Collection, Manchester Polytechnic.
North West Regional Project, University of Lancaster.

Autobiographies and books based on oral testimony
Armstrong, K., *Hello, Are You Working?*, Newcastle, 1977.
Arrow, C., *Rogues and Others*, 1926.
Ashley, J., *Journey into Silence*, 1973.
Ashworth, J., *Strange Tales from Humble Life*, Manchester, 1877.
Battle, A., 'This Job's Not Like It Used to Be' (undated, unpublished manuscript, held at the European Centre for the Study of Policing, Open University, Milton Keynes).
Benney, M., *Low Company*, Horsham, 1981 (first published 1933).
Bentley, M., *Born 1896*, Manchester, 1985.
Browne, Noel, *Against the Tide*, Dublin, 1987.
Burke, M., *Ancoats Lad*, Manchester, 1985.
Burnett, A., *Knave of Clubs*, 1963.
Caminada, J., *25 Years of Detective Life: A Fascinating Account of Crime in Victorian Manchester*, Manchester, Vols 1 and 2, 1983 (first published 1895).
Chapple, F., *Sparks Fly: A Trade Union Life*, 1985.
Cole, H., *Policeman's Progress*, Bath, 1985.
Critchley, A. C., *Critch! The Memoirs of Brigadier General A. C. Critchley*, 1961.
Daley, H., *This Small Cloud* (manuscript version in possession of Clive Emsley, at the Open University, Milton Keynes).
Davenport, K., *My Preston Yesterdays*, Manchester, 1984.
Dawson, E., *Mother Made a Book*, 1962.
Dey, T. H., *Leaves from a Bookmaker's Book*, 1931.
Fish, A., *The Family Chatton: Recollections of Farnworth and Kearsley*, Manchester, 1983.
Foley, A., *A Bolton Childhood*, Manchester, 1973.
Forman, C. (ed.), *Industrial Town: Self-Portait of St Helens in the 1920s*, St Albans, 1978.
Gormley, J., *Battered Cherub*, 1982.
Granger, A., *Life's a Gamble*, Bognor Regis, 1983.
Hamer, S., 'The Steamer' (unpublished manuscript, Bolton Local History Library, c. 1980).
Heaton, R., *Salford: My Home Town*, Manchester, 1982.
Hewins, A. and Blythe, R., *The Dillen: Memories of a Man of Stratford-Upon-Avon*, Oxford, 1982.
Hindley, C., *Life and Adventures of a Cheap Jack, by One of the Fraternity*, 1876.
Hislop, J., *Far From a Gentleman*, 1960.
Horrocks, B., *Reminscences of Bolton*, Manchester, 1984.

Bibliography

Kay, J., *The Chronicles of a Harpurhey Lad*, Manchester, 1987.
Levine, M., *From Cheetham to Cordova*, Manchester, 1985.
Luckman, A. D., *Sharps, Flats Gamblers and Racehorses*, 1914.
Lyscom, E., 'London Policeman' (undated, unpublished manuscript held at the European Centre for the Study of the History of Policing, the Open University, Milton Keynes).
McGuigan, J. (ed. Blakeborough, J. F. F.) *A Trainer's Memories*, 1946
Manville, S., *Everything Seems Smaller*, Brighton, 1989.
Monk, J, 'The Memoirs of John Monk: Chief Inspector of the Metropolitan Police, 1859 to 1946' (manuscript edited by the author's son; copy in possession of Clive Emsley, Open University).
Naughton, B, *On the Pig's Back*, Oxford, 1988.
Newby, E., *Love and War in the Appenines*, 1983.
Potts, B, *The Old Pubs of Hulme, Manchester*, Manchester, 1983.
Preston, J., *Memoirs of a Salford Lad*, Manchester, 1983.
Ramsden, C., *Farewell Manchester: A History of Manchester Racecourse*, 1966.
Ras Prince Monolulu, *I Gotta Horse*, 1950.
Roberts, R., *A Ragged Schooling*, Manchester, 1976
Roberts, R., *The Classic Slum*, Harmondsworth, 1983 (first published 1971).
Samuel, R. (ed.), *East End Underworld: Chapters in the Life of Arthur Harding*, 1981.
Smethurst, T., *Reminiscences of a Bolton and Stalybridge Policeman, 1888–1922*, Manchester, 1983.
Toole, J., *Fighting Through Life*, 1935.
Totterdell, R. H., *Country Copper*, 1956.
Wilkinson, D., *A Wasted Life*, 1902.
Woodward, K., *Jipping Street*, 1983 (first published 1928).
Yates, A., *Arthur Yates, Gentleman Trainer and Rider*, 1924.

Contemporary articles, books and pamphlets

Ashton, J., *A History of Gambling in England*, 1898.
Bakke, E. W., *The Unemployed Man*, 1933.
Bear, W. E., 'Market Gambling', *Contemporary Review*, Vol. 65, 1894.
Bee, J. *Sportsman's Slang*, &c., 1825.
Bell, Lady, *At the Works*, 1985 (first published 1907).
Besant, W., *East London*, 1901.
Blakeborough, J. F. F., *Country Life and Sport*, 1926.
Blakeborough, J. F. F., *The Turf Who's Who*, 1932.
Blakeborough, J. F. F., *A Short History of the Manchester Races*, 1958.
Bone, H., *The Truth About the Treble Chance*, 1957.
Booth, C. (ed.), *Life and Labour of the People in London*, 17 volumes, 1902.
Bott, E., *Family and Social Network*, 1957.
Browne, G., *Patterns of British Life*, 1950.
Burns, J., *Brains Better than Bets or Beer*, 1902.
Cadogan, Lord, 'The State of the Turf', *Fortnightly Review*, Vol. 37, 1885.
Cardwell, J., *New and Improved Spreader Pools System*, Liverpool, 1953.
Chapman, G., *Culture and Survival*, 1940.
Churchill, H. S., *Betting and Gambling*, 1894.
Cohen, J. and Cooper, P., 'A Study of a National Lottery: Premium Savings Bonds', *Occupational Psychology*, Vol. 34, 1960.
Crooks, W., *Working Men and Gambling*, 1906.

Bibliography

Dennis, N., Henriques, F. and Slaughter, C., *Coal is Our Life*, 1956.

Dey, T. H., *Betting in Excelsis*, 1908.

Dickens, C., 'Betting Shops', in *Household Words*, No. 18, 26 June 1852.

Dickens, C., 'Bookmaking', in *All the Year Round*, Vol. 20, 1868.

Dimont, C., 'Going to the Dogs', *New Statesman and Nation*, 30 November 1946.

Egan, P., *Pierce Egan's Book of Sports, and Mirror of Life &c.*, 1832.

Ewen, C. L'estrange, *Lotteries and Sweepstakes*, 1932.

Gordon, A. P. L., 'The Statistics of Totalisator Betting', *Journal of the Royal Statistical Society*, Vol. 94, 1931.

Gorer, G., *Exploring English Character*, 1955.

Gosling, R., *Lady Albermarle's Boys*, 1961.

Green, P., *Betting and Gambling*, 1927.

Greenwood, J., *The Seven Curses of London*, Oxford, 1985 (first published 1869).

Hazlitt, W., 'The Fight', in *Selected Writings*, Harmondsworth, 1985 (first published 1821).

Herbert, A. P., *Independent Member*, 1950.

Herbert, A. P., *Pools Pilot, Or Why Not You?*, 1953.

Hilton, J., *Why I Go In For The Pools &c.*, 1936.

Hislop, J., *The Turf*, 1948.

Hoggart, R., *The Uses of Literacy*, Harmondsworth, 1968 (first published 1957).

Hogge, J. M., *Betting and Gambling*, Edinburgh, 1904.

Hogge, J. M., *The Facts of Gambling*, 1907.

Horsley, Canon J. W., *How Criminals are Made and Prevented*, 1913.

James, G., *London: The Western Reaches*, 1950.

Jephcott, P., *Married Women Working*, 1962.

Johnson, S., *A Dictionary of the English Language*, 1755.

Kemsley, W. F. F., and Ginsburg, D., *Betting in Britain*, 1951.

Liverpool Council of Voluntary Aid, *Report on Betting in Liverpool*, Liverpool, 1926.

Mannheim, H., *Social Aspects of Crime in England Between the Wars*, 1940.

Marples, M., *A History of Football*, 1954.

Martin, J., 'Gambling', *New Survey of London Life and Labour*, Vol. 9, 1935.

Mass Observation, *Britain*, Harmondsworth, 1938.

Mass Observation, *First Year's Work*, Harmonsdworth, 1939.

Mass Observation, *Mass Gambling*, 1948.

Mass Observation, *The Pub and the People*, Welwyn, 1970 (first published 1943).

Masterman, C. F. G., *The Condition of England*, 1909.

Maude, A., 'Why is Gambling', *Encounter*, April 1957.

Mayhew, H., *London Labour and the London Poor*, 4 volumes, 1861.

Mays, J.B., *Growing Up in the City: A Study of Juvenile Delinquency in an Urban Neighbourhood*, Liverpool, 1964.

Middleton, T. M., 'An Enquiry into the Use of Leisure Amongst the Working-Classes of Liverpool', unpublished MA thesis, University of Liverpool, 1931.

Mikardo, I., *It's A Mugs Game: A Light Hearted Treatise*, 1951.

Munroe, D. H., *The Grand National 1839–1939*, 1939.

Orwell, G., *The Road to Wigan Pier*, Harmondsworth, 1976 (first published in 1938).

PEP, 'Watling Revisited', *Planning*, No. 270, 15 August, 1947.

Perkins, E. B., *The Problem of Gambling*, 1919.

Perkins, E. B., *Gambling in English Life*, 1950.

Peterson, A. W., 'The Statistics of Gambling', *Journal of the Royal Statistical Society*,

Vol. 113, 1952.

Pilgrim Trust, *Men Without Work*, 1938.

Powell, J. Enoch, *Saving in a Free Society*, 1960.

Reed, B., *Eighty Thousand Adolescents: A Study of Young People in the City of Birmingham*, Birmingham, 1950.

Robertson, A. J., 'Football Betting', *Transactions of the Liverpool Economic and Statistical Society*, 1907.

Rowntree, B. S. (ed.), *Betting and Gambling: A National Evil*, 1905.

Rowntree, B. S. and Lavers, R, *English Life and Leisure*, 1951.

Runciman, J., 'The Ethics of the Turf', *Contemporary Review*, Vol. 55, 1899.

Russell, C. E. B., *Manchester Boys: Sketches of Manchester Lads at Work and Play*, Manchester, 1985 (first published 1905).

Russell, C. E. B., *Social Problems of the North*, 1980 (first published 1913).

Russell, C. E. B. and Campagnac, E. T., 'Gambling and Aids to Gambling', *Economic Review*, Vol. 15, 1900.

Salt, H. S. (ed.), *Cruelties of Civilisation: Humanitarian Essays*, 3 vols. 1895–8.

Sandilands, G. S., *Atalanta, Or the Future of Sport*, 1928.

Shimmin, H., *Liverpool Life: Its Pleasures, Practices and Pastimes*, Liverpool, 1856.

Shoolbred, C. F., *Lotteries and the Law*, 1932.

Shoolbred, C. F., *The Law of Betting and Gaming*, 1935.

Slugg, J. T., *Reminiscences of Manchester Fifty Years Ago*, Shannon, 1971 (first published 1881).

Smith, A., *The Wealth of Nations*, Harmondsworth, 1982 (first published 1776).

Stocks, M., 'Betting', *The Liverpool Quarterly*, No. 2, 1936.

Sutcliffe, C., et al., *The Story of the Football League*, Preston, 1938.

Trollope, A., *British Sports and Pastimes*, 1868.

Whyte, W. F., *Street Corner Society: the Social Structure of an Italian Slum*, 1981 (first published Chicago, 1943).

Willcock, J. D., *Report on Juvenile Delinquency*, 1949.

Williams, W., *Full Up and Fed Up*, New York, 1921.

Young, M., 'The Distribution of Income Within the Family', *British Journal of Sociology*, Vol. 3, 1952.

Young, M. and Willmott, P., *Family and Kinship in East London*, 1957.

Zweig, F., *Men in the Pits*, 1948.

Zweig, F., *Labour, Life and Poverty*, 1975 (first published 1948).

Zweig, F., *The British Worker*, Harmondsworth, 1952.

Zweig, F., *Women's Life and Labour*, 1952.

Fiction

Arlen, M., *The Green Hat*, 1924.

Disraeli, B., *Sybil*, Oxford, 1986 (first published 1845).

Dostoyevsky, F., *The Gambler*, Harmondsworth, 1982 (first published 1867).

Eliot, G., *Daniel Deronda*, Harmondsworth, 1987 (first published 1876).

Francis, D., and Welcome, J. (eds), *Great Racing Stories*, 1989.

Greene, G., *Brighton Rock*, Harmondsworth, 1938.

Greenwood, W., *Love on the Dole*, Harmondsworth, 1983 (first published 1933).

Lawrence, D. H., 'The Rocking-Horse Winner', in *Love Among the Haystacks*, Harmondsworth, 1985 (first published 1926).

Moore, G., *Esther Waters*, Oxford, 1983 (first published 1895).

Orwell, G, *Keep the Aspidistra Flying*, Harmondsworth, 1989 (first published

1936).

Sillitoe, A, *Saturday Night and Sunday Morning*, 1985 (first published 1958).

Spring, H., *Shabby Tiger*, 1934.

Wesker, A, 'Pools', *Jewish Quarterly*, Vol. 6, No. 2, 1958–9.

Wesker, A., *Chips With Everything*, 1962.

Secondary works

Allum, C., 'The Labour Process and Trade Unionism: A Study of the Rise of Unionisation in the Bookmaking Industry', unpublished Ph.D. thesis, University Of Warwick, 1980.

Altman, J., 'Gambling as a Mode of Redistributing and Accumulating Cash among Aborigines: A Case Study from Arnhem Land', in Calder, G. et al. (eds), *Gambling in Australia*, New South Wales, 1985.

Arnold, P., *The Encyclopedia of Gambling*, 1978.

Bailey, P., *Leisure and Class in Victorian England: Rational Recreation and the Contest for Control, 1830–1885*, 1978.

Beales, D. E. D., *The Political Parties of the Nineteenth Century*, 1971.

Bean, J. P., *The Sheffield Gang Wars*, Sheffield, 1981.

Bellringer, P., 'Gambling and Crime: A Prison Perspective', *Society for the Study of Gambling Newsletter*, Cardiff and Milton Keynes, No. 8, 1986.

Benson, J., *The Penny Capitalists*, Dublin, 1983.

Blakeborough, J. F. F., *Northern Turf History*, 3 vols. 1949–50.

Bloch, H. A., 'The Sociology of Gambling', *American Journal of Sociology*, Vol. 57, No. 3, 1951.

Braddock, P., *Braddock's Guide to Horse Race Selection*, 1987.

Brailsford, D., *Sport and Society: From Elizabeth to Anne*, 1969.

Breen, T. H. 'Horses and Gentlemen: The Cultural Significance of Gambling Among the Gentry of Virginia', *William and Mary Quarterly*, Vol. 34, 1977.

Brocklehurst, H., 'Coursing', *Victoria County History of Lancashire*, Vol. 2, 1966.

Brooke-Smith, M., 'The Growth and Development of Popular Entertainment in the Lancashire Cotton Towns', unpublished M.Litt. thesis, University of Lancaster, 1970.

Burnett, J., Vincent, D. Mayall, D., *The Autobiography of the Working Class*, 2 vols. Brighton, 1984, 1987.

Caillois, R., *Man, Play and Games*, 1964.

Carroll, J., *Breakout from the Crystal Palace*, 1974.

Chandler, G., *Victorian and Edwardian Liverpool and the North West from Old Photographs*, 1972.

Chenery, J. T., *The Law and Practice of Bookmaking, Betting, Gaming and Lotteries*, 1963.

Chesney, K., *The Victorian Underworld*, Harmondsworth, 1982.

Chinn, C. 'Social Aspects of Sparkbrook, Birmingham, in the Twentieth Century', unpublished Ph.D. thesis, University of Birmingham, 1986.

Chinn, C., 'Betting Shops and Race-by-Race Betting Before the Betting and Gaming Act, 1960', *Society for the Study of Gambling Newsletter*, Cardiff and Milton Keynes, No. 17, July 1990.

Churches Council on Gambling, *The Social Control of Gambling*, 1974.

Clarke, J., and Critcher, C., *The Devil Makes Work: Leisure and Capitalist Society*, 1985.

Cohen, J., 'The Ideas of Work and Play', *British Journal of Sociology*, Vol. V. 1953.

Bibliography

Constantine, S., *Unemployment in Britain Between the Wars*, 1980.

Cornish, D. B., *Gambling: A Review of the Literature*, 1978.

Cox, B., Shirley, J., and Short, M., *The Fall of Scotland Yard*, Harmondsworth, 1977.

Craig, D., 'The Roots of Sillitoe's Fiction' in Hawthorn, J. (ed.), *The British Working Class Novel in the Twentieth Century*, 1984.

Cunningham, H., *Leisure in the Industrial Revolution*, 1980.

Davies, A., 'The Police and the People: Gambling in Salford 1900–1939', *Historical Journal*, Vol. 34, No. 1, 1991.

Devereaux, E. C., 'Gambling', *International Encyclopedia of the Social Sciences*, Vol. 6, 1968.

Dingle, A. E., *The Campaign for Prohibition in Victorian England*, New Jersey, 1980.

Dixon, D., 'Class Law: The Street Betting Act of 1906', *International Journal of the Sociology of Law*, Vol. 8, 1980.

Dixon, D., 'Class Law: The Street Betting Act of 1906', in Tomlinson, A. (ed.), *Leisure and Social Control*, Brighton, 1981.

Dixon, D., *The State and Gambling: Developments in the Legal Control of Gambling in England, 1867–1923*, Hull 1981.

Dixon, D., *Illegal Gambling and Histories of Policing in England*, Hull, 1984.

Dixon, D., *From Prohibition to Regulation: Bookmaking, Anti-Gambling and the Law*, Oxford, 1991.

Dowie, J. et al., *Risk*, Open University Course, Milton Keynes, 1980: Block 2, 'The World of Monetary Risk.

Downes, D. M., Davies, B. P., David, M. E., and Stone, P., *Gambling, Work and Leisure: A Study Across Three Areas*, 1976.

Eadington, W. E. (ed.), *Gambling and Society*, Las Vegas, 1976.

Ellis, J., *Eye Deep in Hell: Life in the Trenches 1914–18*, 1976.

Field, C., 'A Sociological Profile of English Methodism, 1900–32', *Oral History*, Vol. 4, No. 1, 1976.

Figgis, E. L., *How to Bet to Win*, 1974.

Filby, M., 'The Sociology of Horse Racing', unpublished Ph.D thesis, University of Warwick, 1985.

Fisher, S., 'The Use of Fruit and Video Machines by Children in the UK: An Analysis of Existing Research', *Society for the Study of Gambling Newsletter*, Cardiff and Milton Keynes, No. 16, December, 1989.

Fishwick, N., *Association Football and English Society*, Manchester, 1989.

Genders, R. and NGRC, *The Encyclopedia of Greyhound Racing*, 1990.

Gillis, J. R., 'The Evolution of Juvenile Delinquency in England, 1890–1914', *Past and Present*, No. 67, 1975.

Goffman, E., 'Where the Action Is', in Dowie, J. and Lefrere, P. (eds), *Risk and Chance*, Milton Keynes, 1980.

Gomme, A. B., *The Traditional Games of England, Scotland and Wales*, Vols 1 and 2, New York, 1964.

Gourvish, T. R., 'The Government and the Business of Gambling: State Lotteries in Britain, 1750–1826', unpublished paper, given at the Institute of Historical Research, 23 February 1989.

Graves, R. and Hodge, A., *The Long Weekend*, 1985 (first published 1940).

Green, B., 'Uncle Was a Street Bookie', *Guardian*, 1 May 1991.

Griffiths, M., 'An Analysis of Amusement Machines: Dependency and Delinquency', *Society for the Study of Gambling Newsletter*, Cardiff and Milton Keynes, December 1989.

Bibliography

Halsey, A. H. et al., *Trends in British Society Since 1900*, 1974.

Harris, G. B., 'Street Betting in the Twentieth Century: It's Social Significance in the Working-Class Community', unpublished MA thesis, University of Lancaster, 1978.

Harrison, B., *Drink and the Victorians*, 1971.

Herman, R. D. (ed.), *Gambling*, New York, 1967.

Herman, R. D., *Gambling and Gamblers*, Lexington, 1976.

Hill, C., *Horse Power*, Manchester, 1988.

Hobsbawm, E. J., *Industry and Empire*, Harmondsworth, 1979.

Hobsbawm, E. J., and Ranger, T. (eds.), *The Invention of Tradition*, Cambridge, 1984.

Hogan, R., 'The Working Class Gamble: Frontier Class Structure and Social Control', *Research in Law, Deviance and Social Control*, Vol. 8, 1986.

Hood, C., *The Limits of Administration*, 1976.

Huggins, M., 'Horse Racing on Teesside in the Nineteenth Century: Change and Continuity', *Northern History*, Vol. 22, 1987.

Huizinga, J., *Homo Ludens: A Study of the Play Element in Culture*, 1949.

Humphries, S., *Hooligans or Rebels?*, Oxford, 1981.

Inglis, S., *The Football League and the Men Who Made It*, 1988.

Itskovitz, D. C., 'Victorian Bookmakers and Their Customers', *Victorian Studies*, Vol. 32, No. 1, 1988.

Jackson, B., *Working-Class Community*, Harmondsworth, 1972 (first published 1968).

Jeremy, D. J. and Shaw, C., *A Dictionary of Business Biography*, 5 volumes, 1985, 1986, 1987.

Johnson, P., *Spending and Saving: the Working-Class Economy in Britain 1870–1939*, Oxford, 1985.

Jones, D., *Crime, Protest, Community and Police in Nineteenth-Century Britain*, 1982.

Jones, G. S., *Languages of Class*, Cambridge, 1983.

Jones, M. W., *The Derby*, 1979.

Joyce, P., *Work, Society and Politics*, 1982.

Kaye, R. and Peskett, R., *The Ladbrokes Story*, 1969

King, P., *The Grand National: Anybody's Race*, 1983.

Kline, P., *Fact and Fantasy in Freudian Theory*, 1972.

Lane, T., *Liverpool: Gateway of Empire*, 1987.

Lemahieu, D. M., *A Culture for Democracy*, Oxford, 1988.

Lennox, A., *Greyhounds: The Sporting Breed*, 1987.

Littlewoods, *Littlewoods, The Pools Firm*, Liverpool, c. 1980.

Littlewoods, *A Major Pools Initiative in Support of Football*, Liverpool, 1986.

Longrigg, R., *The Turf*, 1975.

McCall, G. J., 'Symbiosis: The Case of Hoodoo and the Numbers Racket', *Social Problems*, Vol. 10, No. 4, 1963.

MacDonald, L., *They Called it Passchendaele*, 1983.

McKibbin, R., 'Working Class Gambling in Britain, 1880–1939', *Past and Present*, No. 82, 1979.

McKibbin, R., 'Work and Hobbies in Britain, 1880–1950', in Winter, J. (ed.), *The Working Class in Modern British History*, Cambridge, 1983.

Malcolmson, R. W., *Popular Recreations and English Society 1700–1850*, Cambridge, 1973.

Martin, B., *A Sociology of Contemporary Cultural Change*, Oxford, 1985.

Marwick, A., *British Society Since 1945*, Harmondsworth, 1987.

221

Bibliography

Marwick, A., *The Deluge*, 1965.

Mason, T., *Association Football and English Society, 1863–1915*, Brighton, 1981.

Mason, T., *Sport in Britain*, 1988.

Mason, T. (ed.), *Sport in Britain*, Cambridge, 1989.

Mason, T., 'Sporting News, 1860–1914', in Harris, M. and Lee, A. (eds), *The Press in English Society from the Seventeenth to the Nineteenth Centuries*, 1986.

Masters, B., *The Passion of John Aspinall*, 1988.

Meacham, S., *A Life Apart: The English Working Class, 1890–1914*, 1977.

Midwinter, E. C., *Old Liverpool*, 1971.

Miers, M., 'Winning Selections: Reporters' Tips for the National and the Derby', *Society for the Study of Gambling Newsletter*, No. 17, Cardiff and Milton Keynes, July 1990.

Milroy, L., *Language and Social Networks*, Oxford, 1987.

Moody, G. E., *The Facts About the Money Factories*, 1972.

Mortimer, R., *The Jockey Club*, 1958.

Mott, J., 'Miners, Weavers and Pigeon Racing', in Smith M. et al. (eds), *Leisure and Society in Britain*, 1973.

Mott J., *Popular Gambling from the Collapse of the State Lotteries to the Rise of the Football Pools*, Society for the Study of Labour History Conference, 'The Working Class and Leisure', unpublished paper, 1975.

Murfin, L., *Popular Leisure in the Lake Counties*, Manchester, 1990.

Nairn, T., *The Enchanted Glass*, 1988.

Newman, O., *Gambling, Hazard and Reward*, 1972.

Pahl, R. E., *Divisions of Labour*, Oxford, 1983.

Partridge, E., *The Penguin Dictionary of Historical Slang*, Harmondsworth, 1988.

Passerini, L., *Fascism in Popular Memory: The Cultural Experience of the Turin Working Class*, Cambridge, 1987.

Pearson, G, *Hooligan: A History of Respectable Fears*, 1983.

Perrucci, R., 'The Neighbourhood "Bookmaker": Entrepreneur and Mobility Model', in Meadows, P. and Mizruchi, R. (eds), *Urbanism, Urbanisation and Change: Comparative Perspectives*, Reading, Mass., 1969.

Peterson, A. W., 'The Statistics of Gambling', *Journal of the Royal Statistical Society*, 1952.

Pilley, P., *The Story of Bowls*, 1987.

Polsky, N., *Hustlers, Beats and Others*, Harmondsworth, 1971.

Poole, R., *Leisure in Bolton, 1750–1900*, 1982, unpublished dissertation, Bolton Local History Library.

Power, J., 'Aspects of Working Class Leisure During the Depression Years: Bolton in the 1930s', unpublished MA thesis, University of Warwick, 1980.

Ramsden, C., *Racing Without Tears*, 1952.

Regan, I. M., *The Greyhound Owner's Encyclopedia*, 1975.

Roberts, E., *A Womans' Place*, Oxford, 1984.

Roberts, J., *Everton: the Official Centenary History*, St Albans, 1978.

Roberts, K., *Contemporary Society and the Growth of Leisure*, 1978.

Roberts, K., 'Culture, Leisure, Society: the Pluralist Scenario' in Bennett, T., Martin, G. et al. (eds), *Culture, Ideology and Social Process*, Milton Keynes and London, 1985.

Rojek, C., *Capitalism and Leisure Theory*, 1985.

Ross, A., *The Turf*, 1982.

Rubner, A., *The Economics of Gambling*, 1966.

Scott, J. M., *Extel 100, A Centenary History of the Electric Telegraph Company*, 1972.

Bibliography

Seabrook, J., *City Close Up*, Harmondsworth, 1971.

Seabrook, J., *Working-Class Childhood*, 1982.

Seabrook, J., *Unemployment*, St Albans, 1983.

Sidney, Charles, *The Art of Legging*, 1976.

Sked, A. and Cook, C., *Post-War Britain: A Political History*, Harmondsworth, 1990.

Smith, S. and Razzell, P., *The Pools Winners*, 1974.

Spanier, D., *Easy Money: Inside the Gambler's Mind*, 1987.

Stevenson, J. and Cook, C., *The Slump*, 1979.

Sutherland, I., 'Playing the Doos', *New Socialist*, No. 20, October 1984.

Symons, J., *Horatio Bottomley*, 1955.

Tattersall's Committee, *Constitution and Origins of the Tattersall's Committee*, Reading, 1988.

Tattersall's Committee, *Rules on Betting*, Reading, 1988.

Tebbutt, M., *Making Ends Meet*, Oxford, 1985.

Tec, N., *Gambling in Sweden*, New Jersey, 1964.

Thomas, K., *Religion and the Decline of Magic*, Harmondsworth, 1978.

Thompson, P., *The Edwardians: The Re-Making of British Society*, 1984.

Underhill, F. J., 'Greyhound Racing, Betting and the Law', *Society for the Study of Gambling Newsletter*, Cardiff and Milton Keynes, No. 8, May 1986.

Vamplew, W., *The Turf*, 1976.

Vamplew, W., *Pay Up and Play the Game: Professional Sport in Britain 1875–1914*, Cambridge, 1988.

Vamplew, W., 'Horse Racing', in Tony Mason (ed.), *Sport in Britain*, Cambridge, 1989.

Waites, B., 'Popular Culture in Late Nineteenth and Early Twentieth Century Lancashire', in the Open University Popular Culture course U203 booklet *The Historical Development of Popular Culture in Britain*, Milton Keynes, 1985.

Walton, J., *Lancashire: A Social History 1558–1939*, Manchester, 1987.

Walvin, J., *Leisure and Society 1830–1950*, 1978.

Weinreb, B. and Hibbert, C., *The Encyclopedia of London*, 1987.

Welcome, J. and Collens, R., *Snaffles on Racing and Point-to-Point Racing*, Lambourn, 1988.

White, J., *The Worst Street in North London: Campbell Bunk, Islington, Between the Wars*, 1985.

Woodhall, R., 'The British State Lotteries', *History Today*, July 1964.

Wooley, R. A., *The Comprehensive Guide to Betting and Bookmaking*, Sheffield, 1976.

Wright, P., *On Living in an Old Country*, 1985.

Wyatt, W., *Distinguished for Talent*, 1962.

Wykes, A., *Gambling*, 1964.

Index to main text